STAR WARS

THE BOUNTY HUNTERS

"Though the Republic is thriving and the galaxy is — relatively — at peace, there remains a need for the likes of myself, and my associates. If you're tired of the smash-and-grab pirates in your system; if a former associate has fled with your property; indeed, if any being has done you wrong, don't hesitate: contact the bounty hunter's guild."

— GUILDMASTER CRADOSSK

184   D1335025

STAR WARS

THE BOUNTY HUNTERS

STORY
ANDY MANGELS, MARK SCHULTZ,
RANDY STRADLEY, TIMOTHY TRUMAN

PENCILS
JOHN NADEAU, MEL RUBI,
JAVIER SALTARES, TIMOTHY TRUMAN

INKS
JORDI ENSIGN, CHRISTOPHER IVY,
ANDREW PEPOY, TIMOTHY TRUMAN

COLORS
DIGITAL BROOME, DAN JACKSON,
DAVE MCCAIG, CARY PORTER

LETTERING
AMADOR CISNEROS, CLEM ROBINS,
MICHAEL TAYLOR

COVER ART
DAVE DORMAN

TITAN BOOKS

PUBLISHER
MIKE RICHARDSON

SERIES EDITORS
PEET JANES &
PHILIP D. AMARA

COLLECTION EDITOR
CHRIS WARNER

COLLECTION DESIGNER
DARCY HOCKETT

ART DIRECTOR
MARK COX

SPECIAL THANKS TO
ALLAN KAUSCH AND
LUCY AUTREY WILSON
AT LUCAS LICENSING.

STAR WARS®: BOUNTY HUNTERS

Published by Titan Books, a division of Titan Publishing Group LTD. ©1997, 1999, 2000 Lucasfilm Ltd. & TM. All rights reserved. Used under authorization. Text and illustrations for STAR WARS® BOUNTY HUNTERS are © 1997, 1999, 2000 Lucasfilm Ltd. All other material, unless otherwise specified, is © 2000 Dark Horse Comics, Inc. All rights reserved. No portion of this publication may be reproduced by any means without written permission from Lucasfilm Ltd. No similarity between any of the names, characters, persons and/or institutions in this publication and those of any preexisting person or institution is intended, and any similarity that may exist is purely coincidental.

This volume collects the Dark Horse comic books Star Wars: Boba Fett– Twin Engines of Destruction, Star Wars: Bounty Hunters – Aurra Sing, Star Wars: Bounty Hunters – Scoundrel's Wages, and Star Wars: Bounty Hunters – Kenix Kil.

Published by
Titan Books
144 Southwark St.
London SE1 0UP

What did you think of this book? We love to hear from our readers. Please e-mail us at readerfeedback@titanemail.com or write to Reader Feedback at the address above.

First edition: November 2000
ISBN: 1-84023-238-2

1 3 5 7 9 10 8 6 4 2
PRINTED IN CANADA

1840 232 382 3340

BOUNTY HUNTERS

AURRA SING

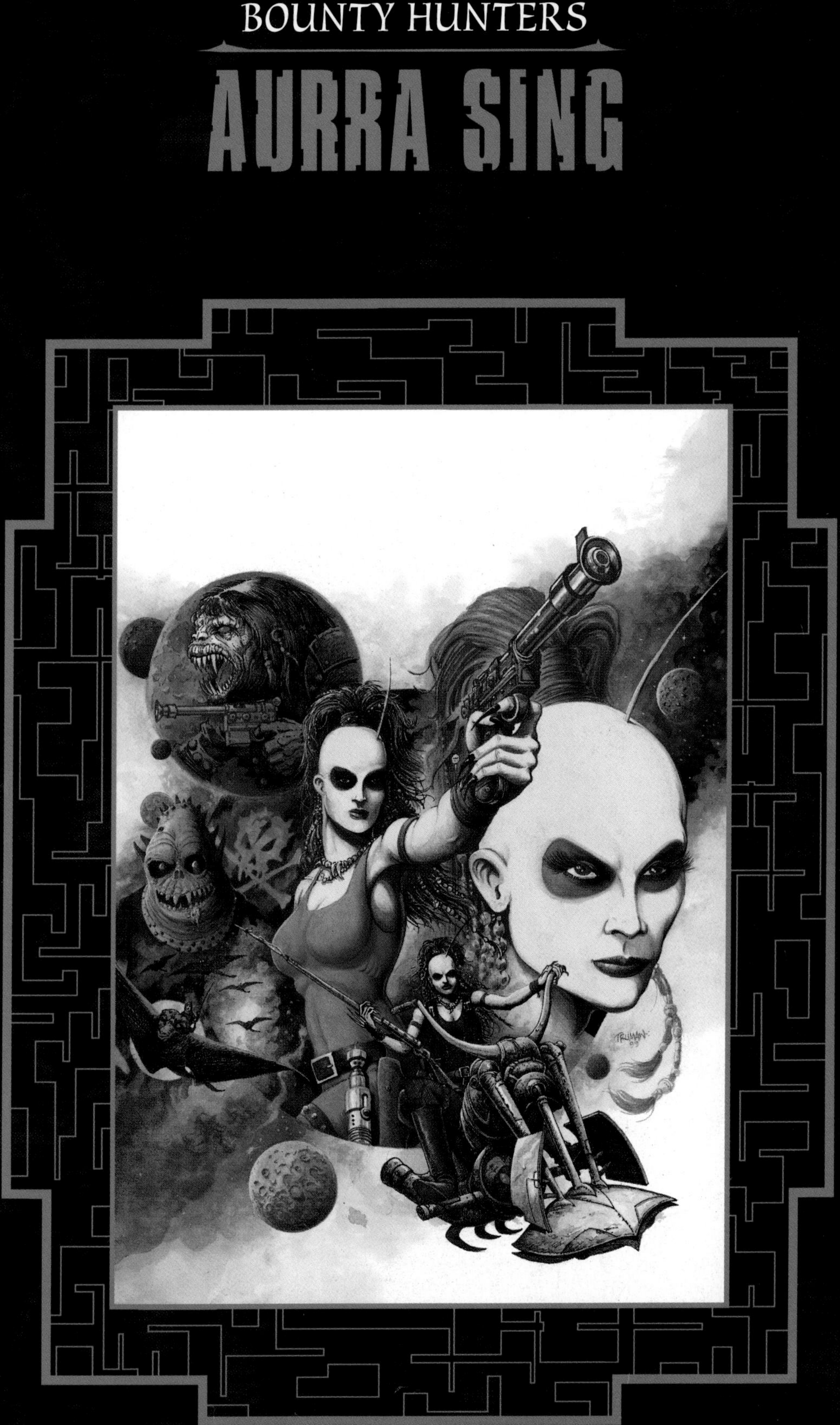

STORY AND ART
TIMOTHY TRUMAN

COLORS
DAVE McCAIG

LETTERING
MICHAEL TAYLOR

TITLE ART
TIMOTHY TRUMAN

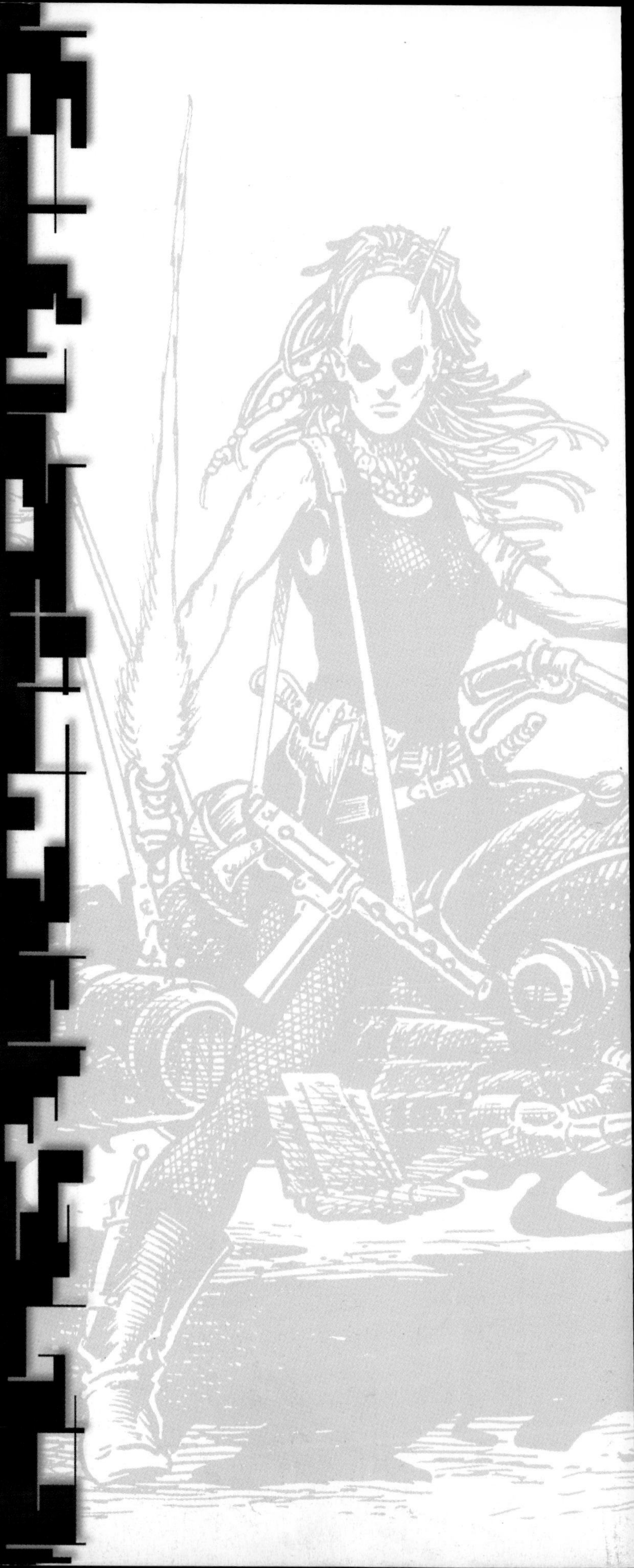

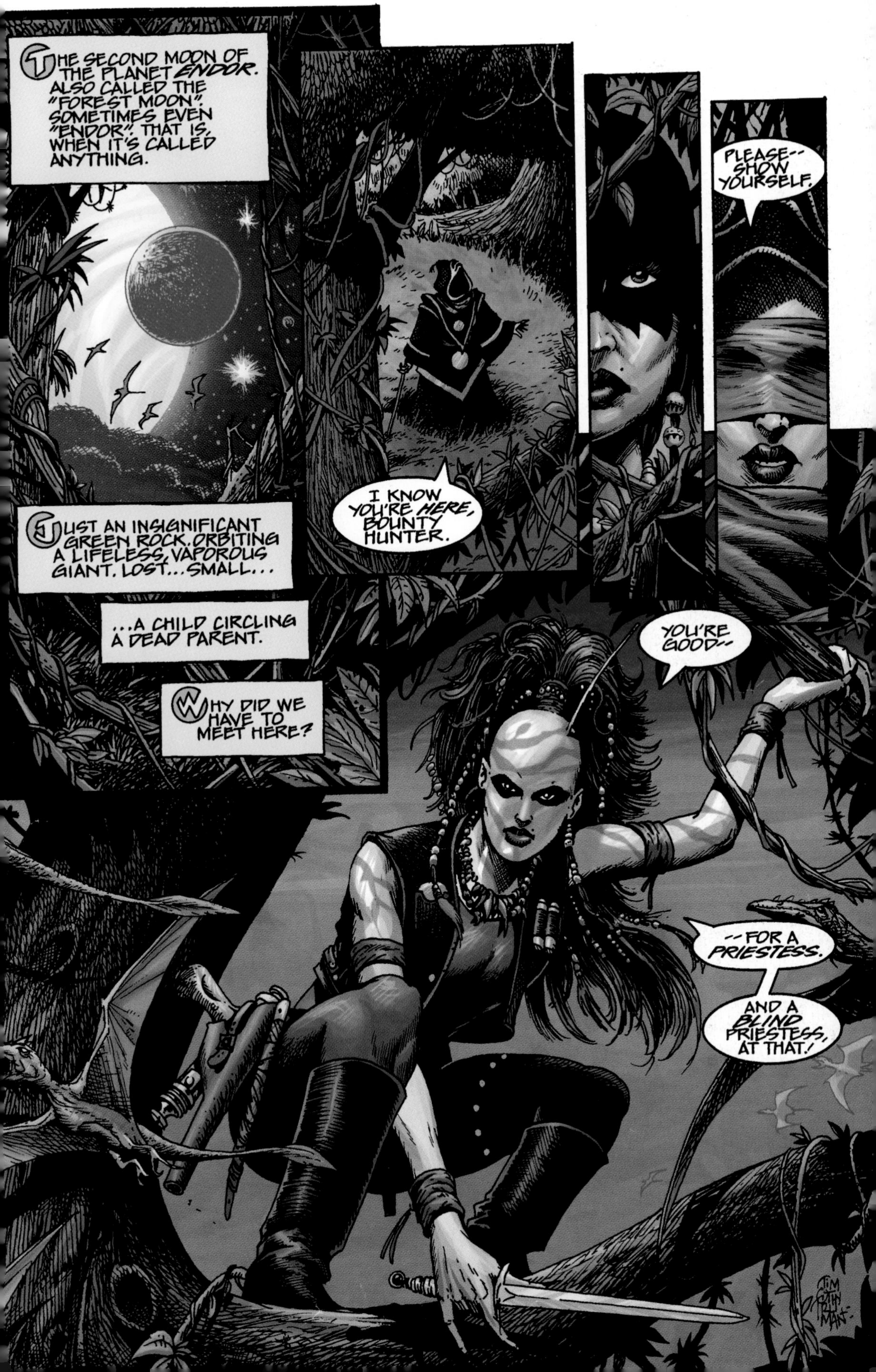
THE SECOND MOON OF THE PLANET ENDOR. ALSO CALLED THE "FOREST MOON". SOMETIMES EVEN "ENDOR". THAT IS, WHEN IT'S CALLED ANYTHING.
JUST AN INSIGNIFICANT GREEN ROCK, ORBITING A LIFELESS, VAPOROUS GIANT. LOST... SMALL...
...A CHILD CIRCLING A DEAD PARENT.
WHY DID WE HAVE TO MEET HERE?
I KNOW YOU'RE HERE, BOUNTY HUNTER.
PLEASE-- SHOW YOURSELF.
YOU'RE GOOD--
--FOR A PRIESTESS.
AND A BLIND PRIESTESS, AT THAT!
JIM GAIN RU-MAN

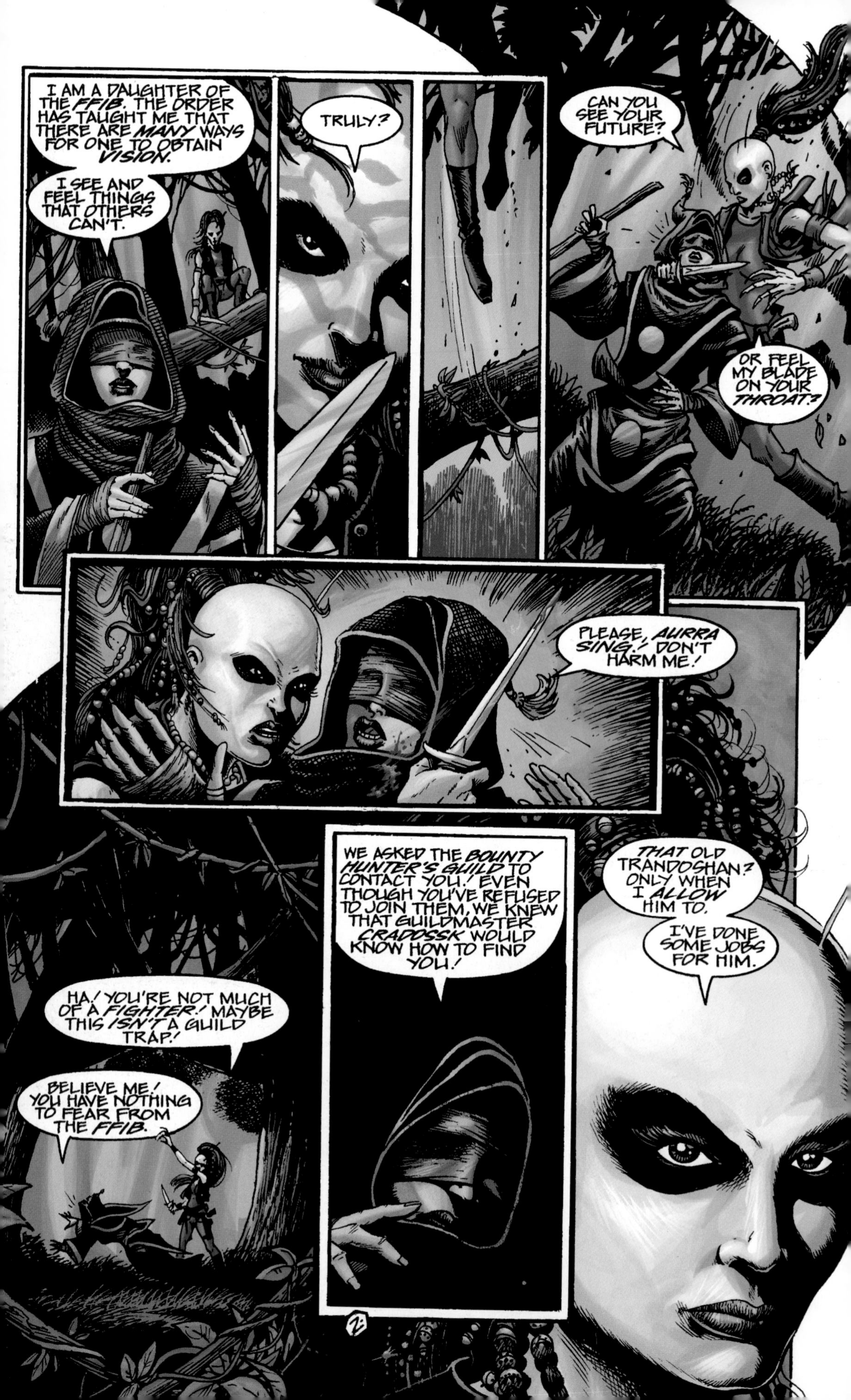

I AM A DAUGHTER OF THE FFIB. THE ORDER HAS TAUGHT ME THAT THERE ARE MANY WAYS FOR ONE TO OBTAIN VISION.
I SEE AND FEEL THINGS THAT OTHERS CAN'T.
TRULY?
CAN YOU SEE YOUR FUTURE?
OR FEEL MY BLADE ON YOUR THROAT?
PLEASE, AURRA SING! DON'T HARM ME!
HA! YOU'RE NOT MUCH OF A FIGHTER! MAYBE THIS ISN'T A GUILD TRAP!
BELIEVE ME! YOU HAVE NOTHING TO FEAR FROM THE FFIB.
WE ASKED THE BOUNTY HUNTER'S GUILD TO CONTACT YOU! EVEN THOUGH YOU'VE REFUSED TO JOIN THEM, WE KNEW THAT GUILDMASTER CRADOSSK WOULD KNOW HOW TO FIND YOU!
THAT OLD TRANDOSHAN? ONLY WHEN I ALLOW HIM TO.
I'VE DONE SOME JOBS FOR HIM.

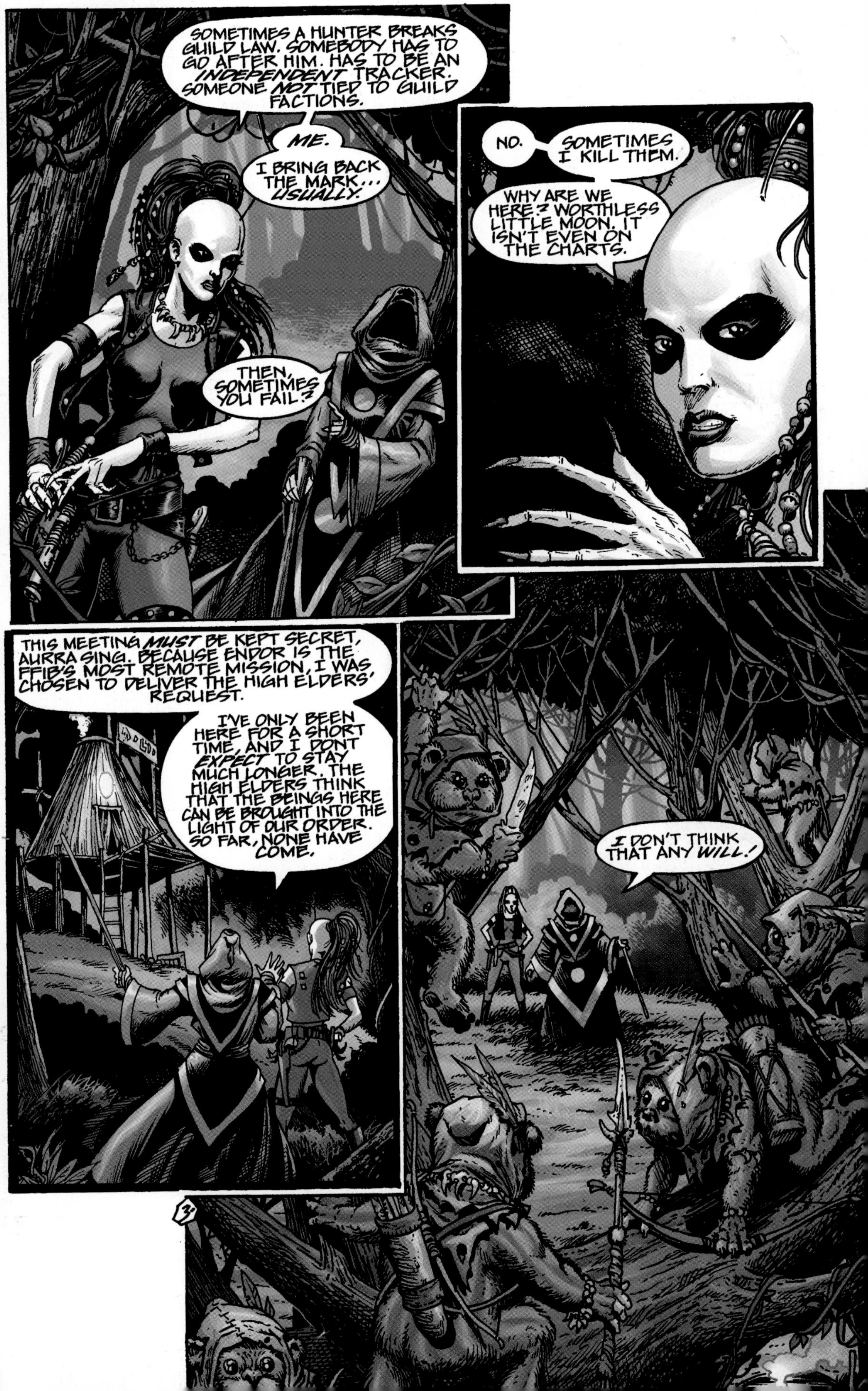
SOMETIMES A HUNTER BREAKS GUILD LAW. SOMEBODY HAS TO GO AFTER HIM. HAS TO BE AN *INDEPENDENT* TRACKER. SOMEONE *NOT* TIED TO GUILD FACTIONS.
ME.
I BRING BACK THE MARK... *USUALLY.*
THEN, SOMETIMES YOU FAIL?
NO.
SOMETIMES I KILL THEM.
WHY ARE WE HERE? WORTHLESS LITTLE MOON. IT ISN'T EVEN ON THE CHARTS.
THIS MEETING *MUST* BE KEPT SECRET, AURRA SING. BECAUSE ENDOR IS THE FFIB'S MOST REMOTE MISSION, I WAS CHOSEN TO DELIVER THE HIGH ELDERS' REQUEST.
I'VE ONLY BEEN HERE FOR A SHORT TIME, AND I DONT *EXPECT* TO STAY MUCH LONGER. THE HIGH ELDERS THINK THAT THE BEINGS HERE CAN BE BROUGHT INTO THE LIGHT OF OUR ORDER. SO FAR, NONE HAVE COME.
I DON'T THINK THAT ANY *WILL*!

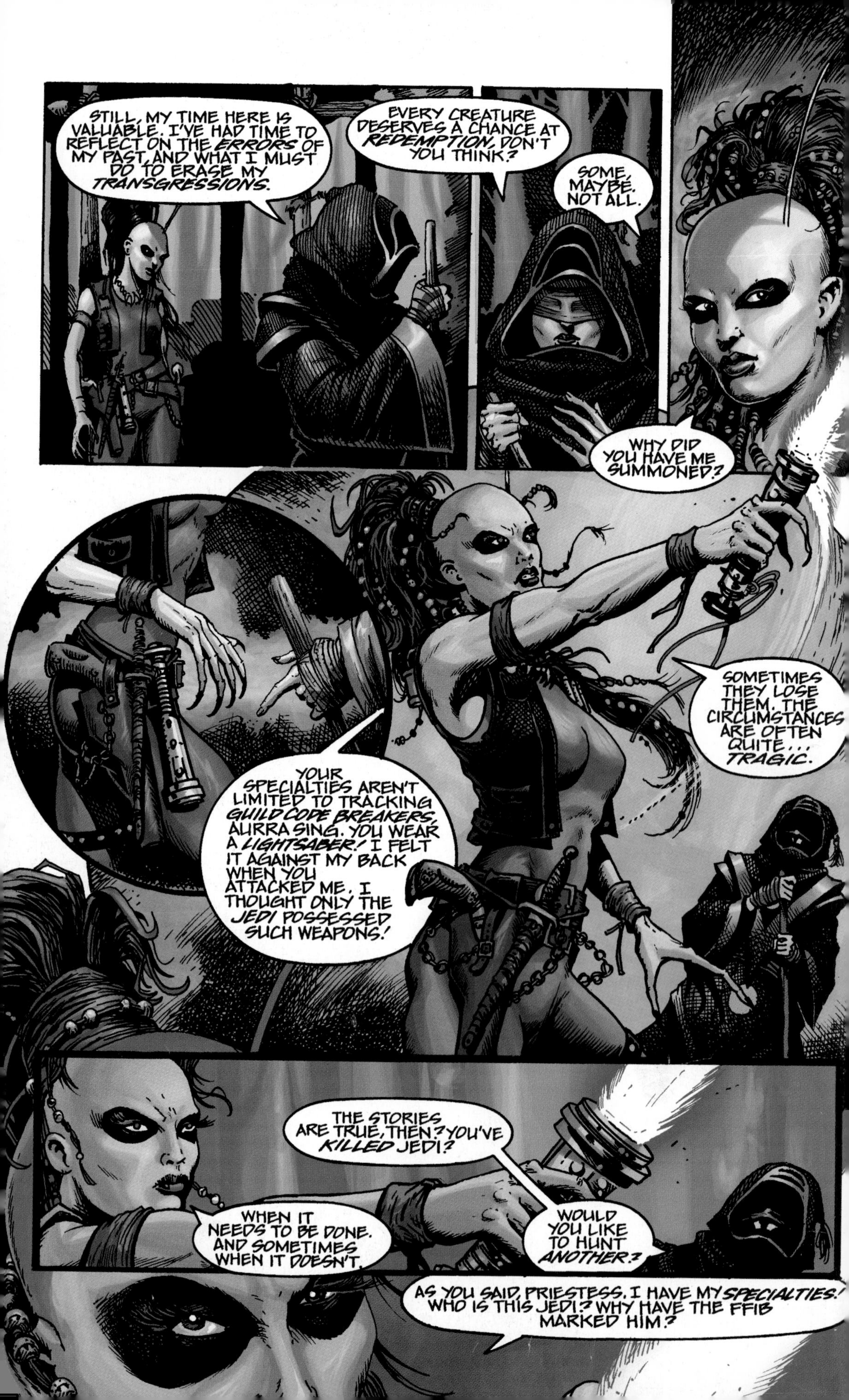
STILL, MY TIME HERE IS VALUABLE. I'VE HAD TIME TO REFLECT ON THE ERRORS OF MY PAST, AND WHAT I MUST DO TO ERASE MY TRANSGRESSIONS.
EVERY CREATURE DESERVES A CHANCE AT REDEMPTION, DON'T YOU THINK?
SOME, MAYBE. NOT ALL.
WHY DID YOU HAVE ME SUMMONED?
SOMETIMES THEY LOSE THEM. THE CIRCUMSTANCES ARE OFTEN QUITE... TRAGIC.
YOUR SPECIALTIES AREN'T LIMITED TO TRACKING GUILD CODE BREAKERS, AURRA SING. YOU WEAR A LIGHTSABER! I FELT IT AGAINST MY BACK WHEN YOU ATTACKED ME. I THOUGHT ONLY THE JEDI POSSESSED SUCH WEAPONS!
THE STORIES ARE TRUE, THEN? YOU'VE KILLED JEDI?
WHEN IT NEEDS TO BE DONE. AND SOMETIMES WHEN IT DOESN'T.
WOULD YOU LIKE TO HUNT ANOTHER?
AS YOU SAID, PRIESTESS. I HAVE MY SPECIALTIES! WHO IS THIS JEDI? WHY HAVE THE FFIB MARKED HIM?

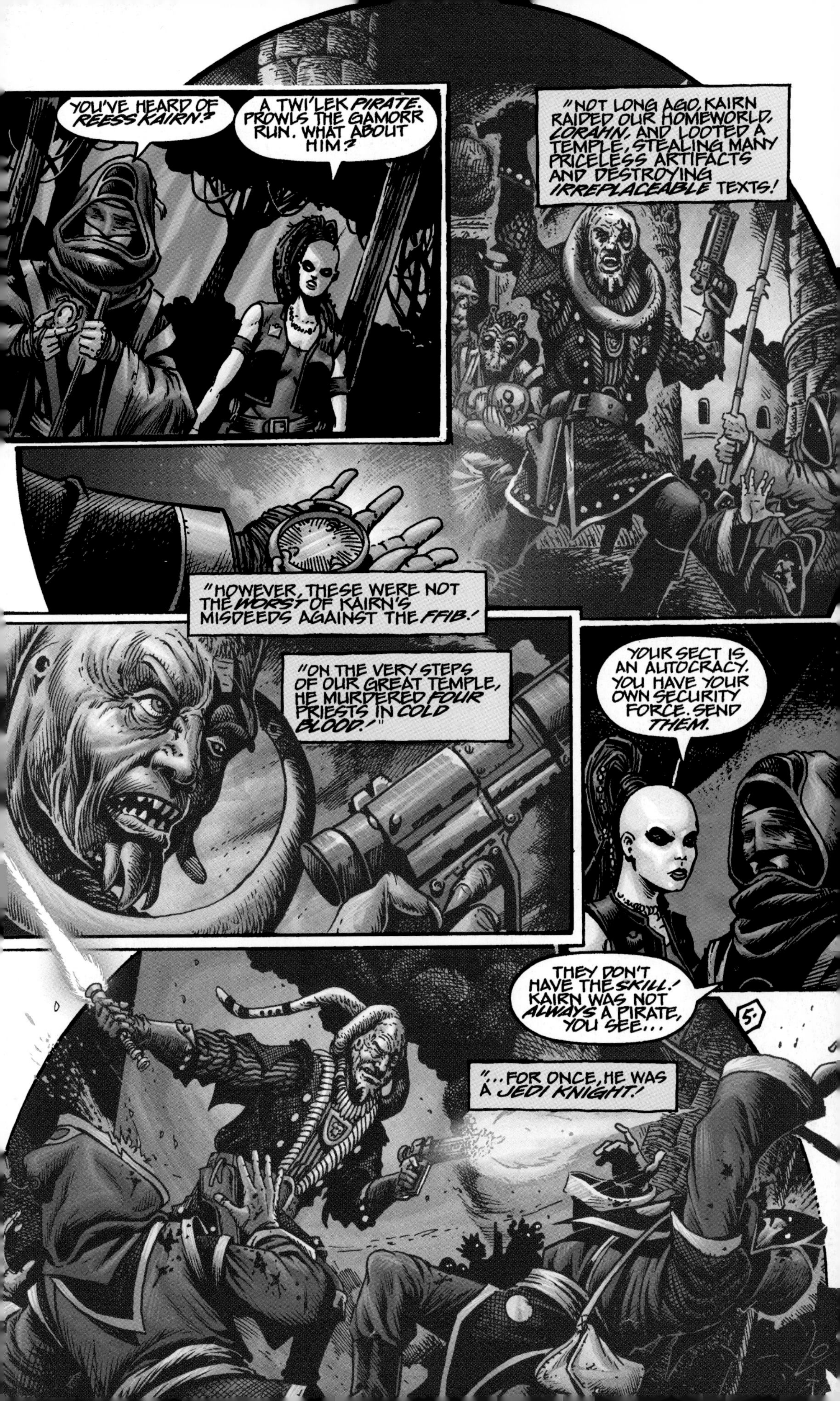
YOU'VE HEARD OF REESS KAIRN?
A TWI'LEK PIRATE. PROWLS THE GAMORR RUN. WHAT ABOUT HIM?
"NOT LONG AGO, KAIRN RAIDED OUR HOMEWORLD, LORAHN, AND LOOTED A TEMPLE, STEALING MANY PRICELESS ARTIFACTS AND DESTROYING IRREPLACEABLE TEXTS!
"HOWEVER, THESE WERE NOT THE WORST OF KAIRN'S MISDEEDS AGAINST THE FFIB!
"ON THE VERY STEPS OF OUR GREAT TEMPLE, HE MURDERED FOUR PRIESTS IN COLD BLOOD!"
YOUR SECT IS AN AUTOCRACY. YOU HAVE YOUR OWN SECURITY FORCE. SEND THEM.
THEY DON'T HAVE THE SKILL! KAIRN WAS NOT ALWAYS A PIRATE, YOU SEE...
5
"...FOR ONCE, HE WAS A JEDI KNIGHT!

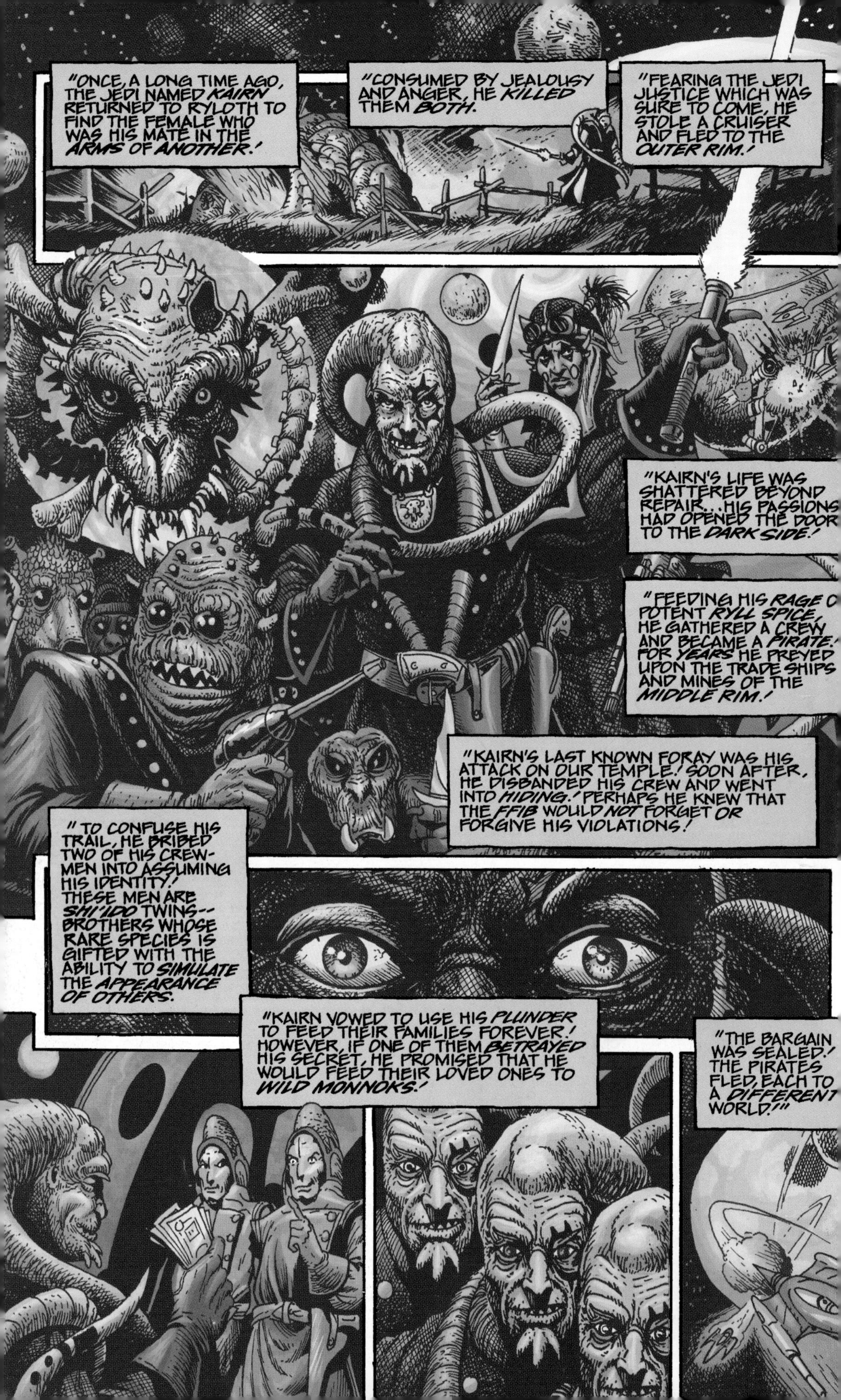
"ONCE, A LONG TIME AGO, THE JEDI NAMED KAIRN RETURNED TO RYLOTH TO FIND THE FEMALE WHO WAS HIS MATE IN THE ARMS OF ANOTHER!
"CONSUMED BY JEALOUSY AND ANGER, HE KILLED THEM BOTH.
"FEARING THE JEDI JUSTICE WHICH WAS SURE TO COME, HE STOLE A CRUISER AND FLED TO THE OUTER RIM!
"KAIRN'S LIFE WAS SHATTERED BEYOND REPAIR... HIS PASSIONS HAD OPENED THE DOOR TO THE DARK SIDE!
"FEEDING HIS RAGE O POTENT RYLL SPICE, HE GATHERED A CREW AND BECAME A PIRATE. FOR YEARS HE PREYED UPON THE TRADE SHIPS AND MINES OF THE MIDDLE RIM!
"KAIRN'S LAST KNOWN FORAY WAS HIS ATTACK ON OUR TEMPLE! SOON AFTER, HE DISBANDED HIS CREW AND WENT INTO HIDING! PERHAPS HE KNEW THAT THE FFIB WOULD NOT FORGET OR FORGIVE HIS VIOLATIONS!
"TO CONFUSE HIS TRAIL, HE BRIBED TWO OF HIS CREW-MEN INTO ASSUMING HIS IDENTITY! THESE MEN ARE SHI'IDO TWINS-- BROTHERS WHOSE RARE SPECIES IS GIFTED WITH THE ABILITY TO SIMULATE THE APPEARANCE OF OTHERS.
"KAIRN VOWED TO USE HIS PLUNDER TO FEED THEIR FAMILIES FOREVER! HOWEVER, IF ONE OF THEM BETRAYED HIS SECRET, HE PROMISED THAT HE WOULD FEED THEIR LOVED ONES TO WILD MONNOKS!
"THE BARGAIN WAS SEALED! THE PIRATES FLED, EACH TO A DIFFERENT WORLD!"

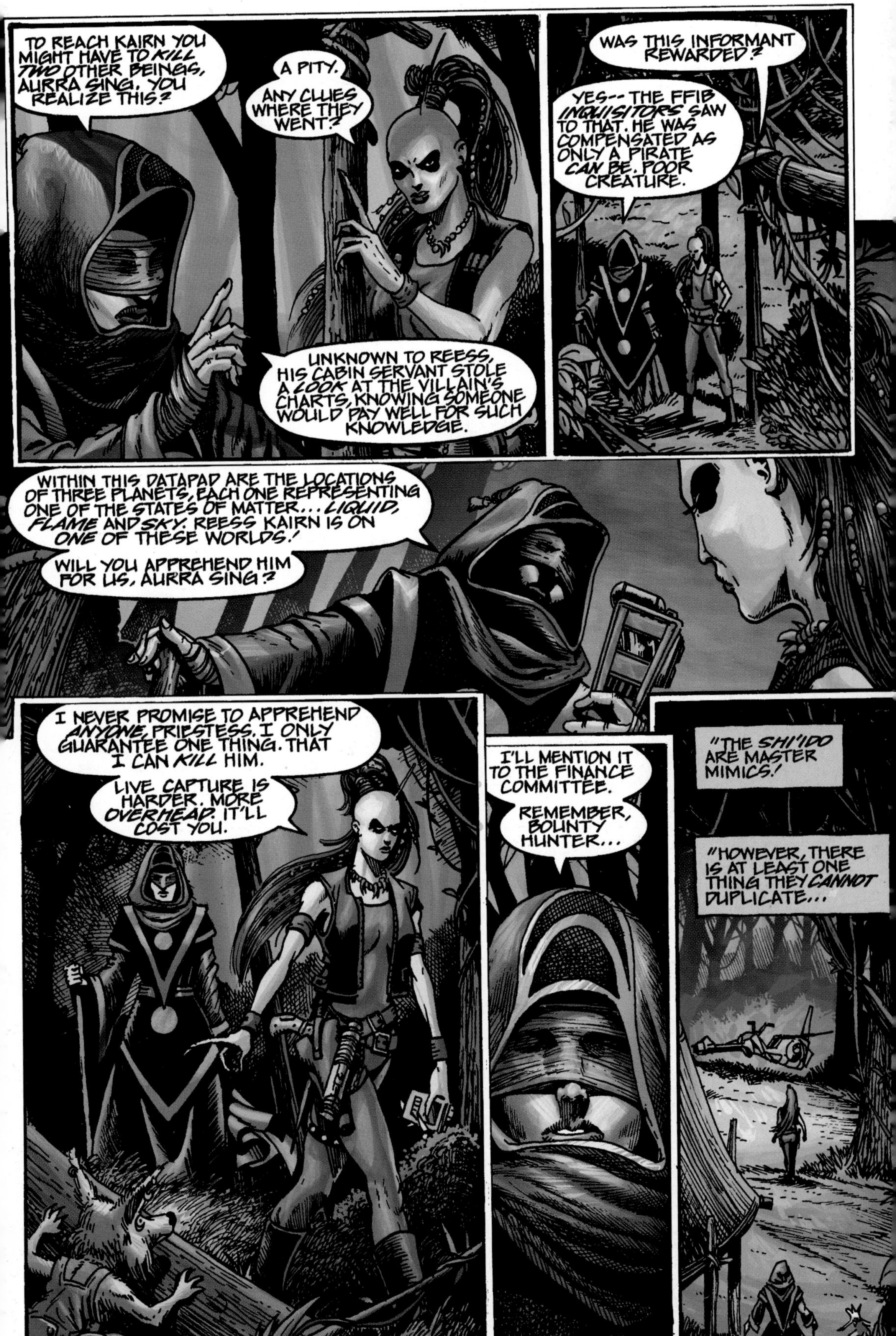
TO REACH KAIRN YOU MIGHT HAVE TO KILL TWO OTHER BEINGS, AURRA SING. YOU REALIZE THIS?
A PITY.
ANY CLUES WHERE THEY WENT?
UNKNOWN TO REESS, HIS CABIN SERVANT STOLE A LOOK AT THE VILLAIN'S CHARTS, KNOWING SOMEONE WOULD PAY WELL FOR SUCH KNOWLEDGE.
WAS THIS INFORMANT REWARDED?
YES-- THE FFIB INQUISITORS SAW TO THAT. HE WAS COMPENSATED AS ONLY A PIRATE CAN BE. POOR CREATURE.
WITHIN THIS DATAPAD ARE THE LOCATIONS OF THREE PLANETS, EACH ONE REPRESENTING ONE OF THE STATES OF MATTER... LIQUID, FLAME AND SKY. REESS KAIRN IS ON ONE OF THESE WORLDS!
WILL YOU APPREHEND HIM FOR US, AURRA SING?
I NEVER PROMISE TO APPREHEND ANYONE, PRIESTESS. I ONLY GUARANTEE ONE THING. THAT I CAN KILL HIM.
LIVE CAPTURE IS HARDER. MORE OVERHEAD. IT'LL COST YOU.
I'LL MENTION IT TO THE FINANCE COMMITTEE.
REMEMBER, BOUNTY HUNTER...
"THE SHI'IDO ARE MASTER MIMICS!
"HOWEVER, THERE IS AT LEAST ONE THING THEY CANNOT DUPLICATE...

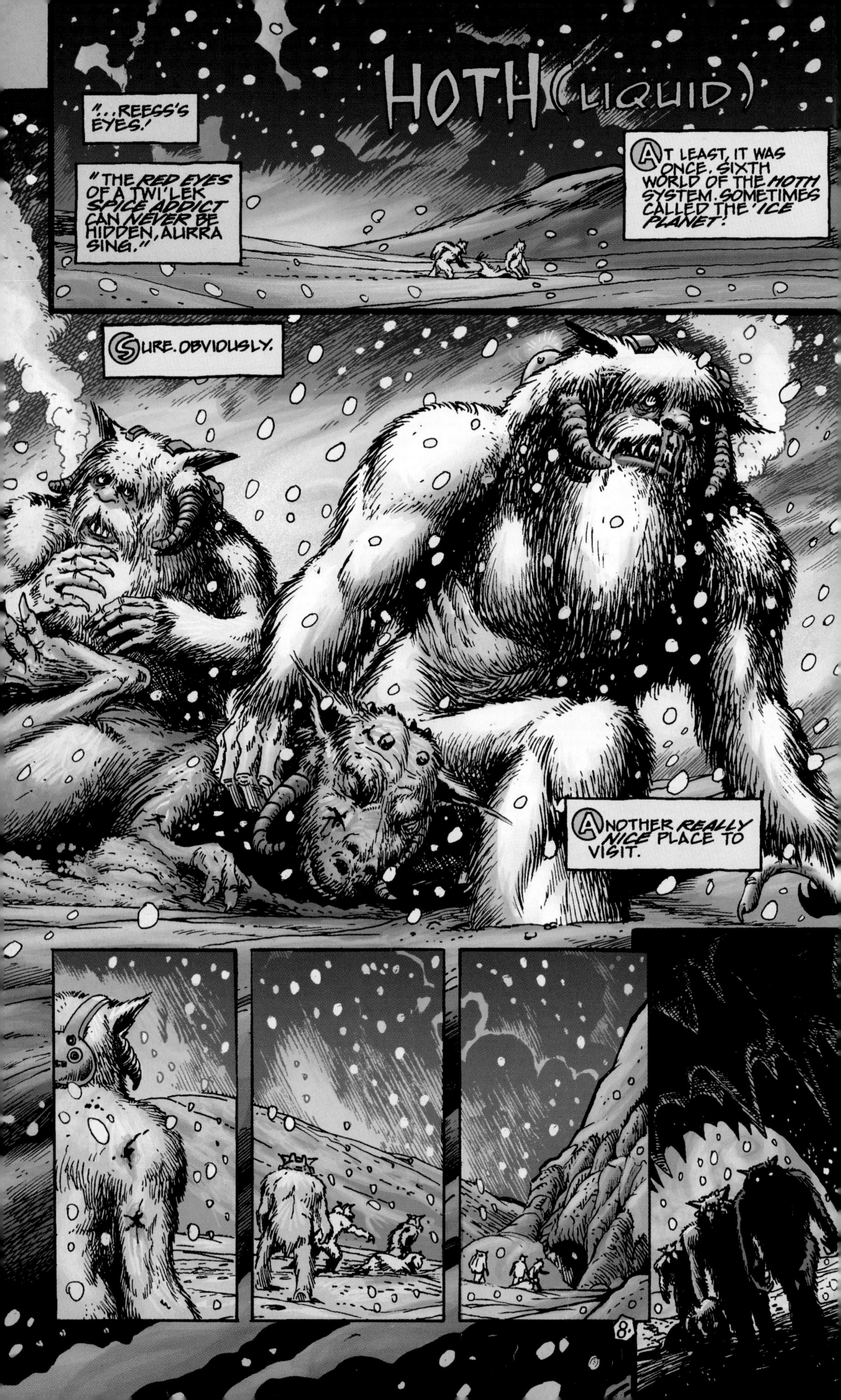
HOTH (LIQUID)
"...REESS'S EYES!
"THE RED EYES OF A TWI'LEK SPICE ADDICT CAN NEVER BE HIDDEN, AURRA SING."
AT LEAST, IT WAS ONCE. SIXTH WORLD OF THE HOTH SYSTEM. SOMETIMES CALLED THE 'ICE PLANET'.
SURE. OBVIOUSLY.
ANOTHER REALLY NICE PLACE TO VISIT.
8

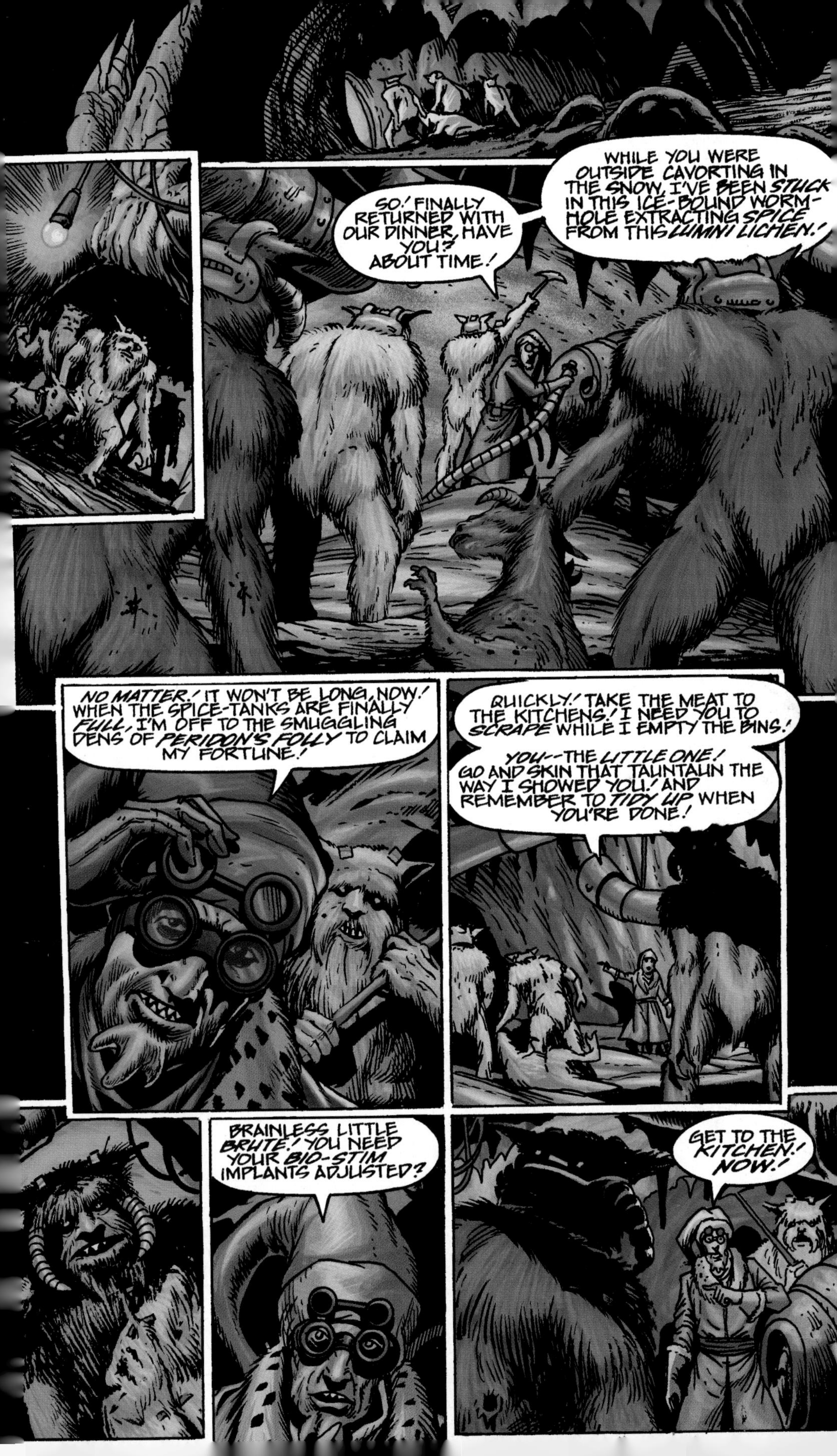
SO! FINALLY RETURNED WITH OUR DINNER, HAVE YOU? ABOUT TIME!
WHILE YOU WERE OUTSIDE CAVORTING IN THE SNOW, I'VE BEEN STUCK IN THIS ICE-BOUND WORM-HOLE EXTRACTING SPICE FROM THIS LUMNI LICHEN!
NO MATTER! IT WON'T BE LONG, NOW! WHEN THE SPICE-TANKS ARE FINALLY FULL, I'M OFF TO THE SMUGGLING DENS OF PERIDON'S FOLLY TO CLAIM MY FORTUNE!
QUICKLY! TAKE THE MEAT TO THE KITCHENS! I NEED YOU TO SCRAPE WHILE I EMPTY THE BINS!
YOU--THE LITTLE ONE! GO AND SKIN THAT TAUNTAUN THE WAY I SHOWED YOU! AND REMEMBER TO TIDY UP WHEN YOU'RE DONE!
BRAINLESS LITTLE BRUTE! YOU NEED YOUR BIO-STIM IMPLANTS ADJUSTED?
GET TO THE KITCHEN! NOW!

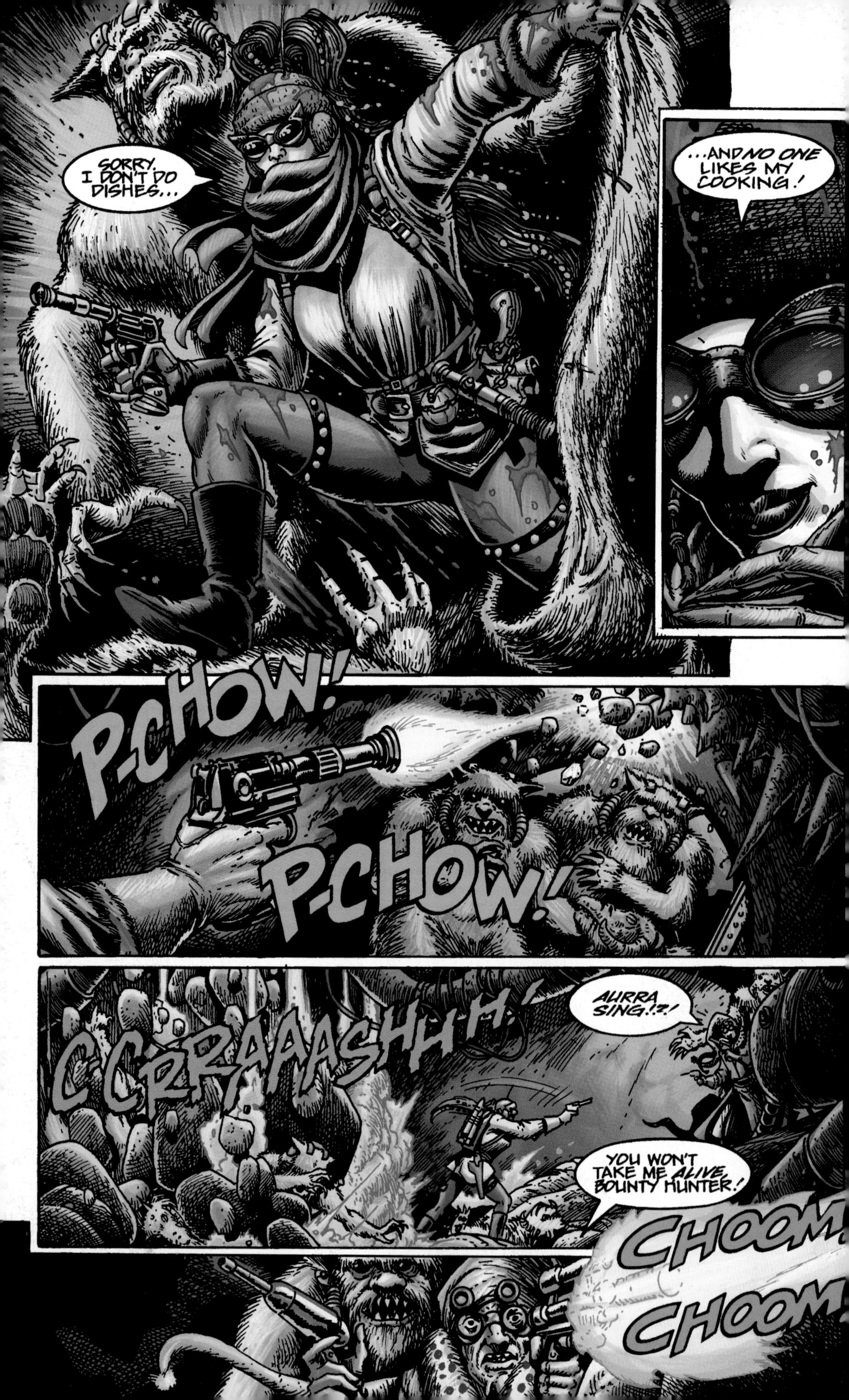
SORRY. I DON'T DO DISHES...
...AND NO ONE LIKES MY COOKING!
P-CHOW!
P-CHOW!
CCRRAAAASHHH!
AURRA SING!?!
YOU WON'T TAKE ME ALIVE, BOUNTY HUNTER!
CHOOM!
CHOOM!

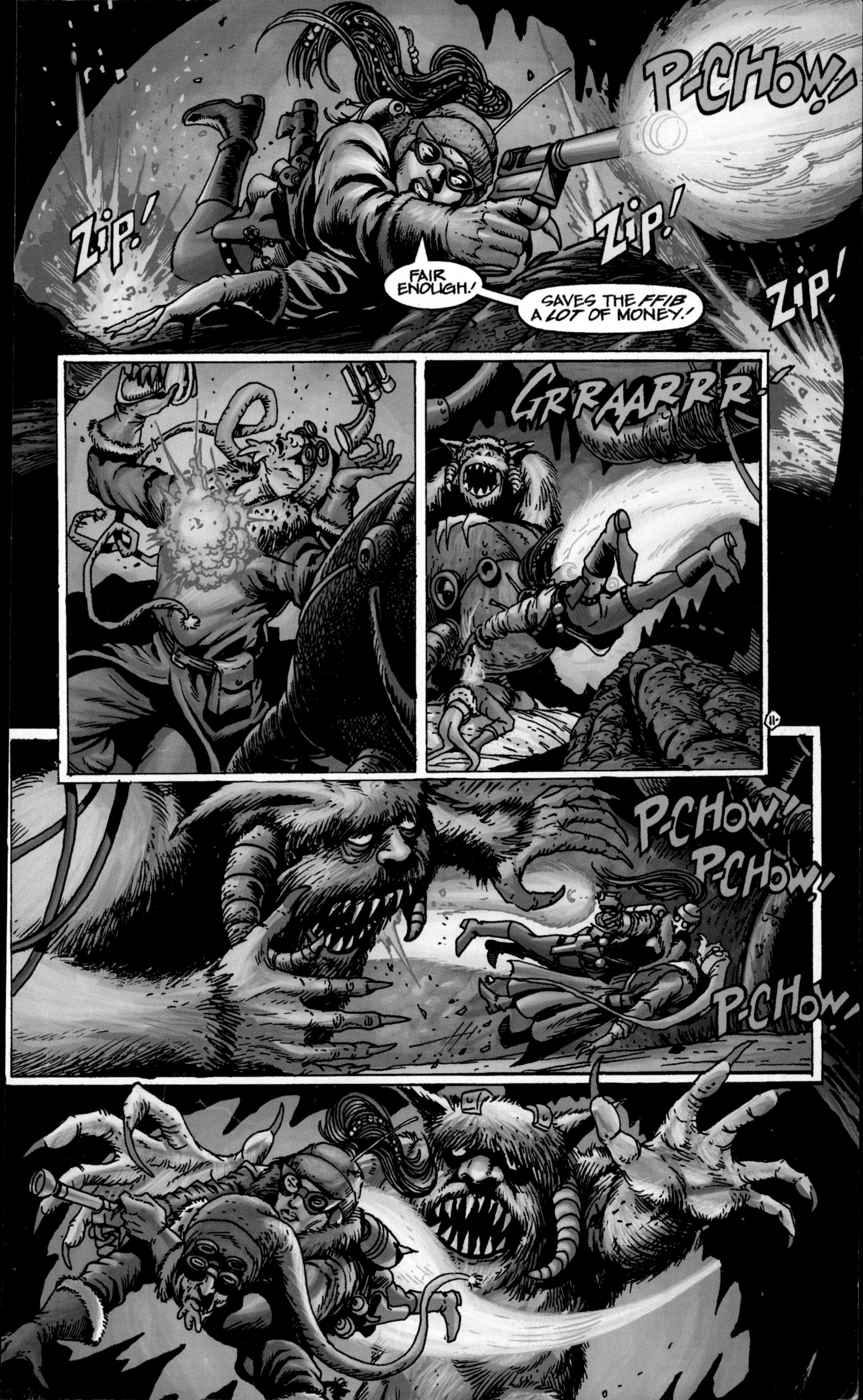
P-CHOW!
ZIP!
ZIP!
FAIR ENOUGH!
SAVES THE FFIB A LOT OF MONEY!
ZIP!
GRRAARRRR!
11
P-CHOW!
P-CHOW!
P-CHOW!

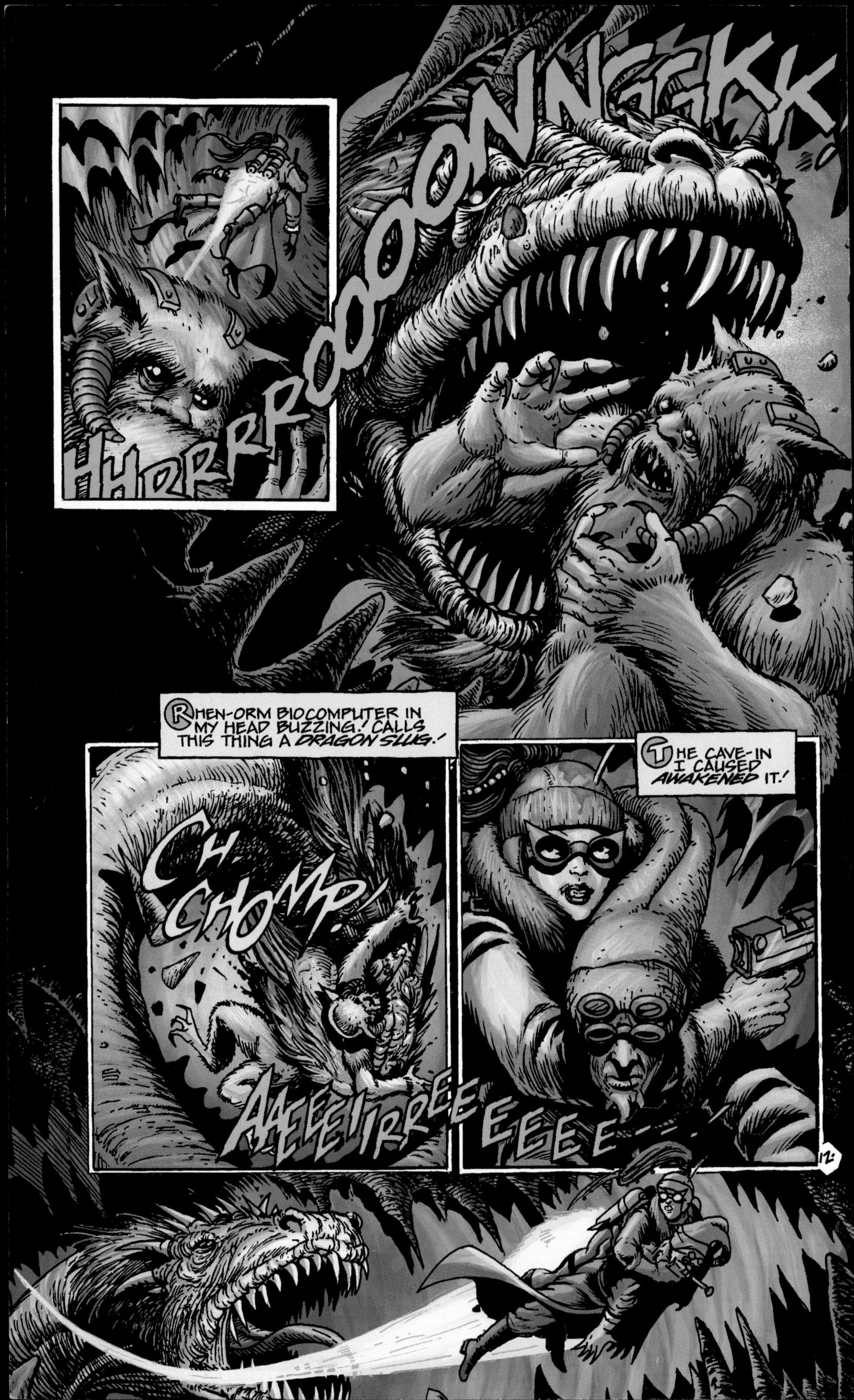
HHRRROOOOONNGKK!
RHEN-ORM BIOCOMPUTER IN MY HEAD BUZZING! CALLS THIS THING A DRAGON SLUG!
CH-CHOMP!
THE CAVE-IN I CAUSED AWAKENED IT!
AAEEIIRREEEEEEE---
12

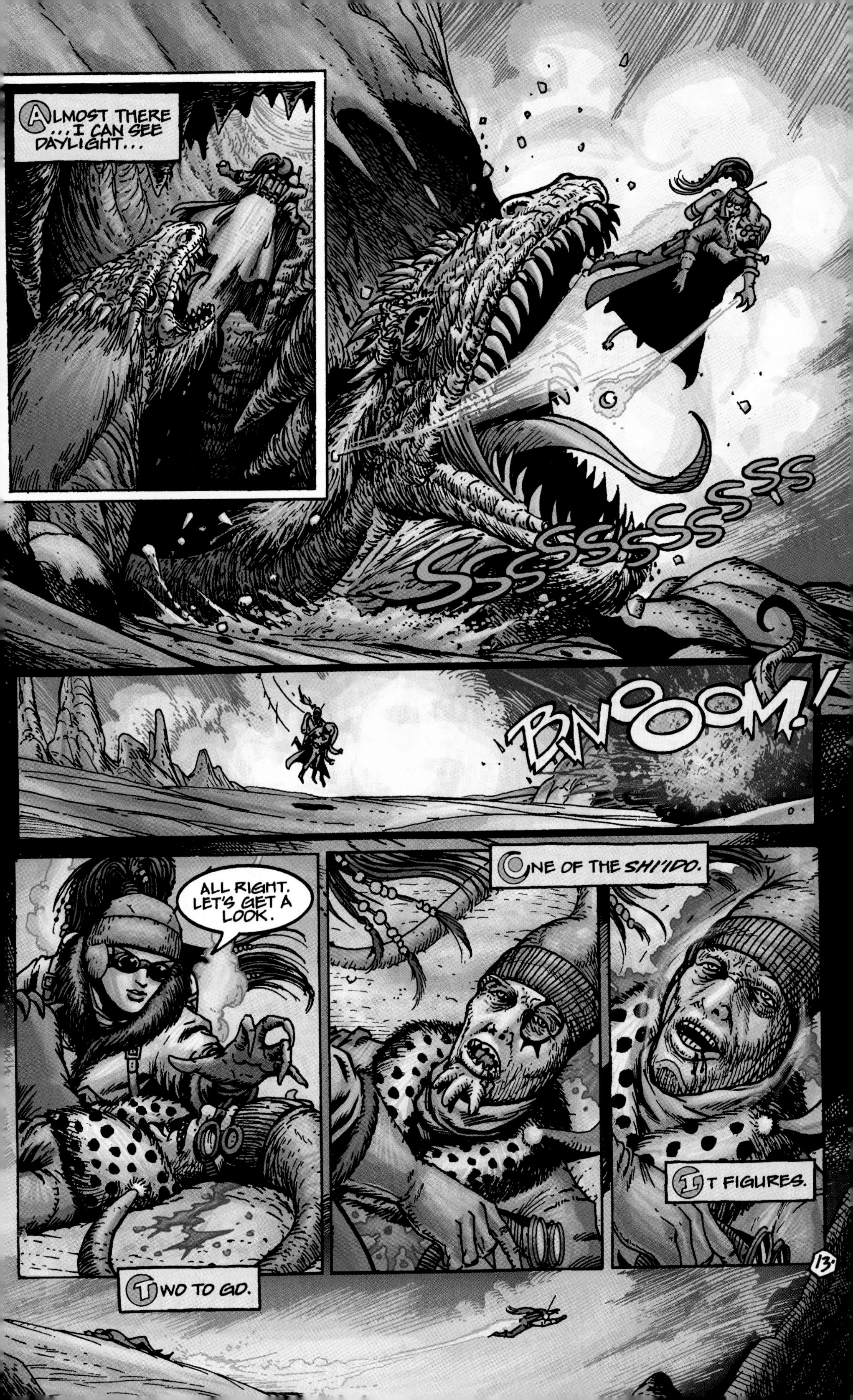
ALMOST THERE ...I CAN SEE DAYLIGHT...
SSSSSSSSSSSSSS
BNOOOM!
ALL RIGHT. LET'S GET A LOOK.
ONE OF THE SHI'IDO.
IT FIGURES.
TWO TO GO.

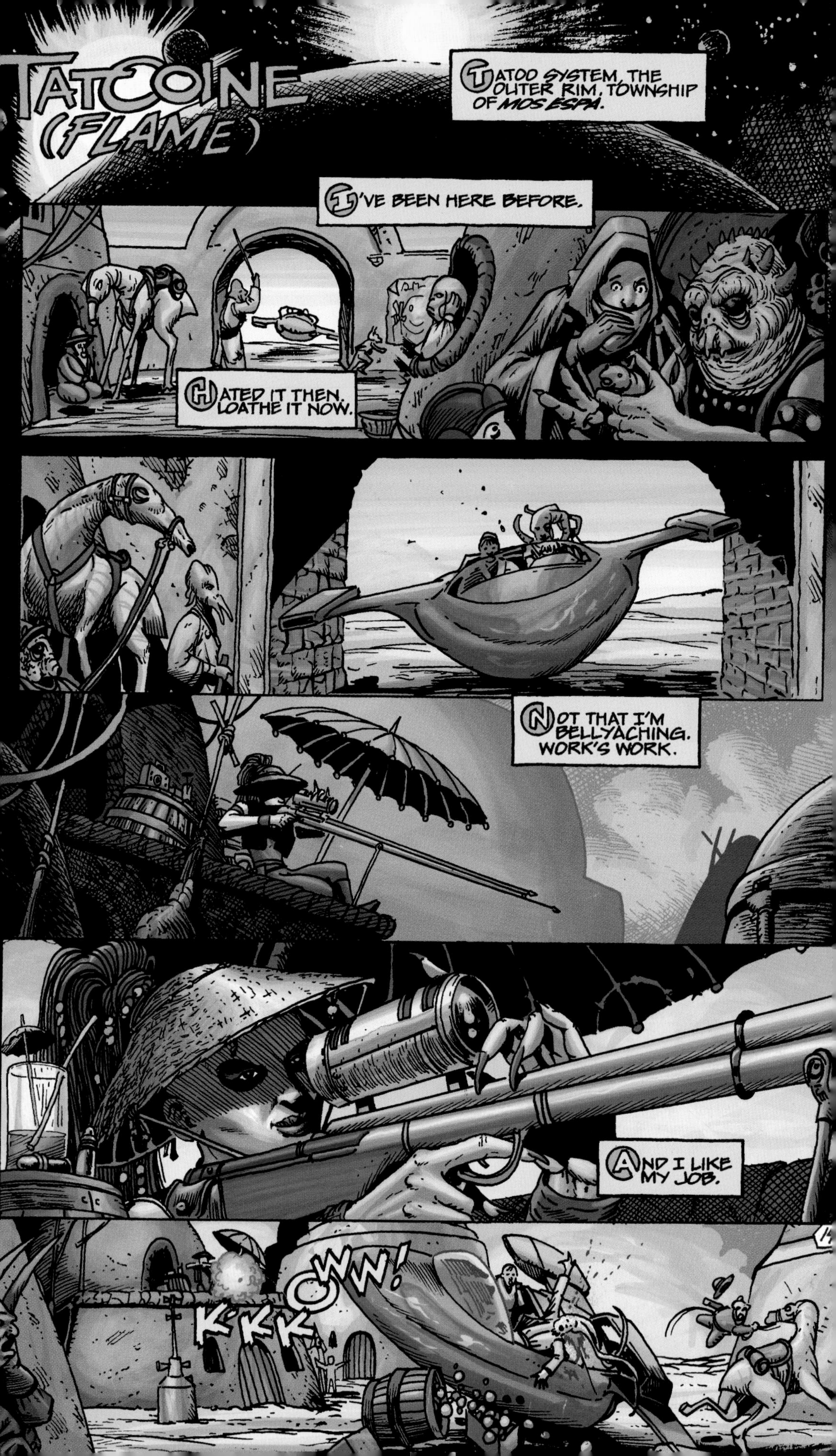
TATOOINE
(FLAME)
TATOOD SYSTEM, THE OUTER RIM, TOWNSHIP OF MOS ESPA.
I'VE BEEN HERE BEFORE.
HATED IT THEN. LOATHE IT NOW.
NOT THAT I'M BELLYACHING. WORK'S WORK.
AND I LIKE MY JOB.
K'K'KOWW!

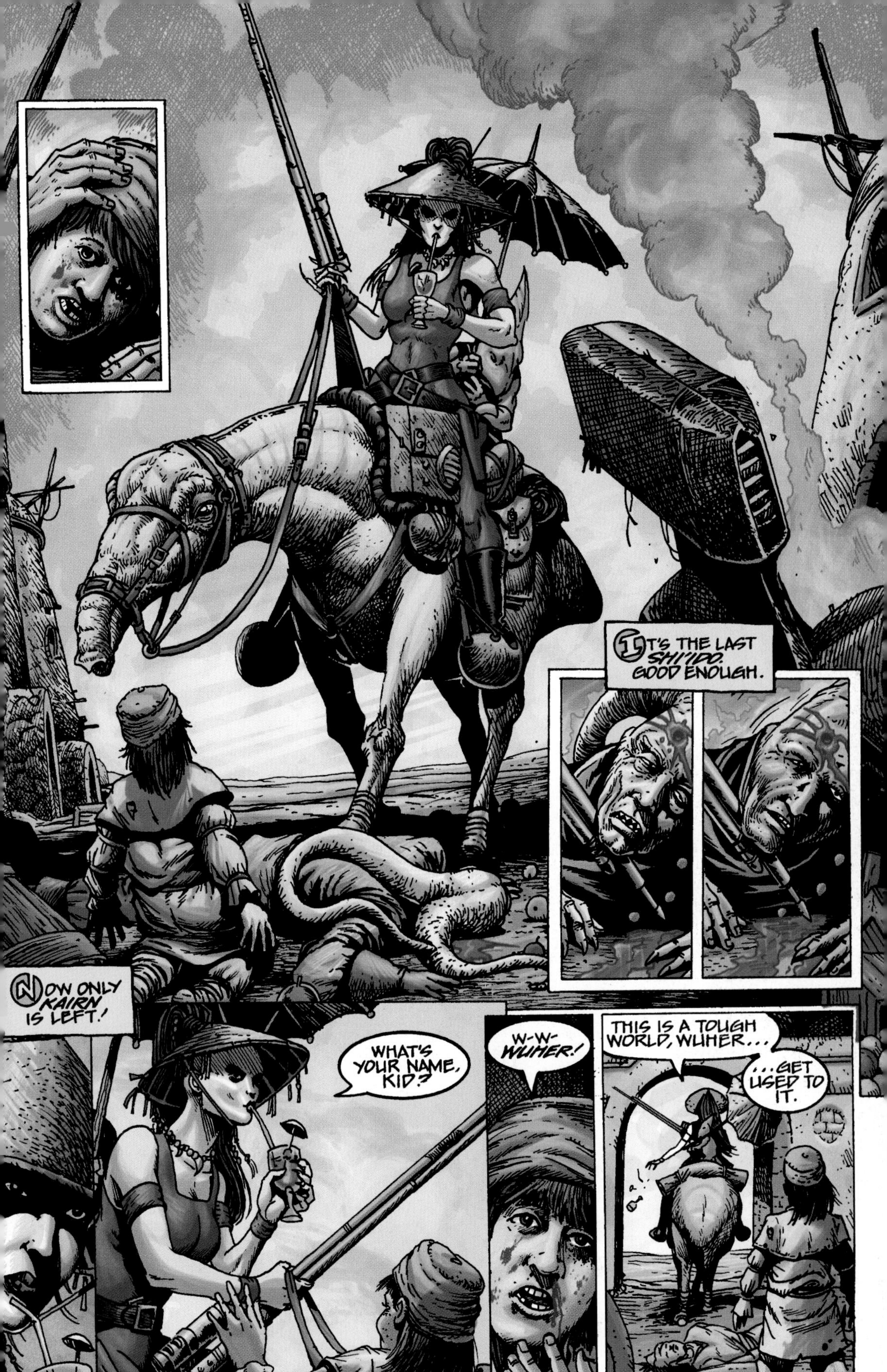

IT'S THE LAST SHI'IDO. GOOD ENOUGH.
NOW ONLY KAIRN IS LEFT!
WHAT'S YOUR NAME, KID?
W-W-WUHER!
THIS IS A TOUGH WORLD, WUHER...
...GET USED TO IT.

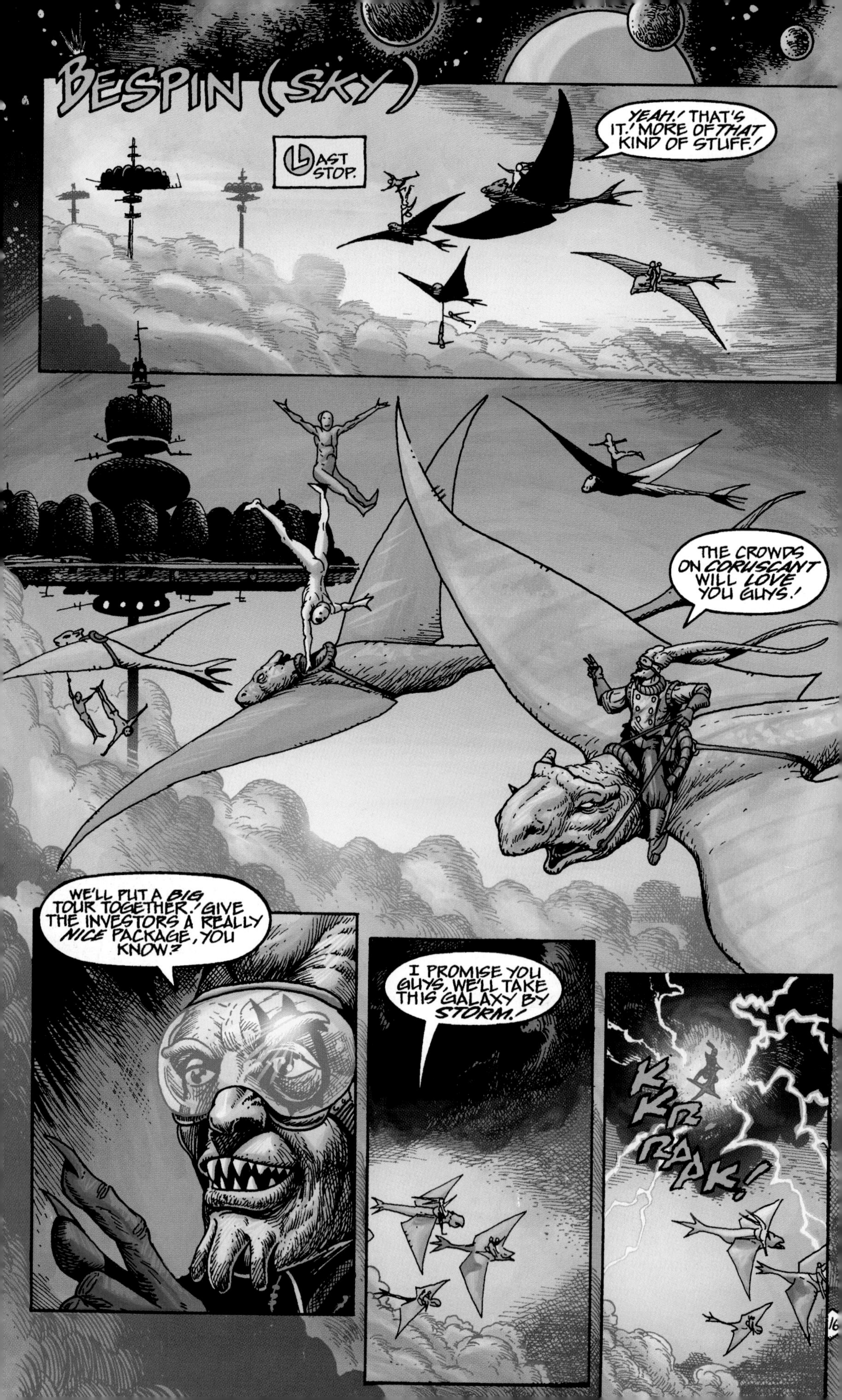
BESPIN (SKY)
LAST STOP.
YEAH! THAT'S IT! MORE OF THAT KIND OF STUFF!
THE CROWDS ON CORUSCANT WILL LOVE YOU GUYS!
WE'LL PUT A BIG TOUR TOGETHER! GIVE THE INVESTORS A REALLY NICE PACKAGE, YOU KNOW?
I PROMISE YOU GUYS, WE'LL TAKE THIS GALAXY BY STORM!
KKRRAAK!

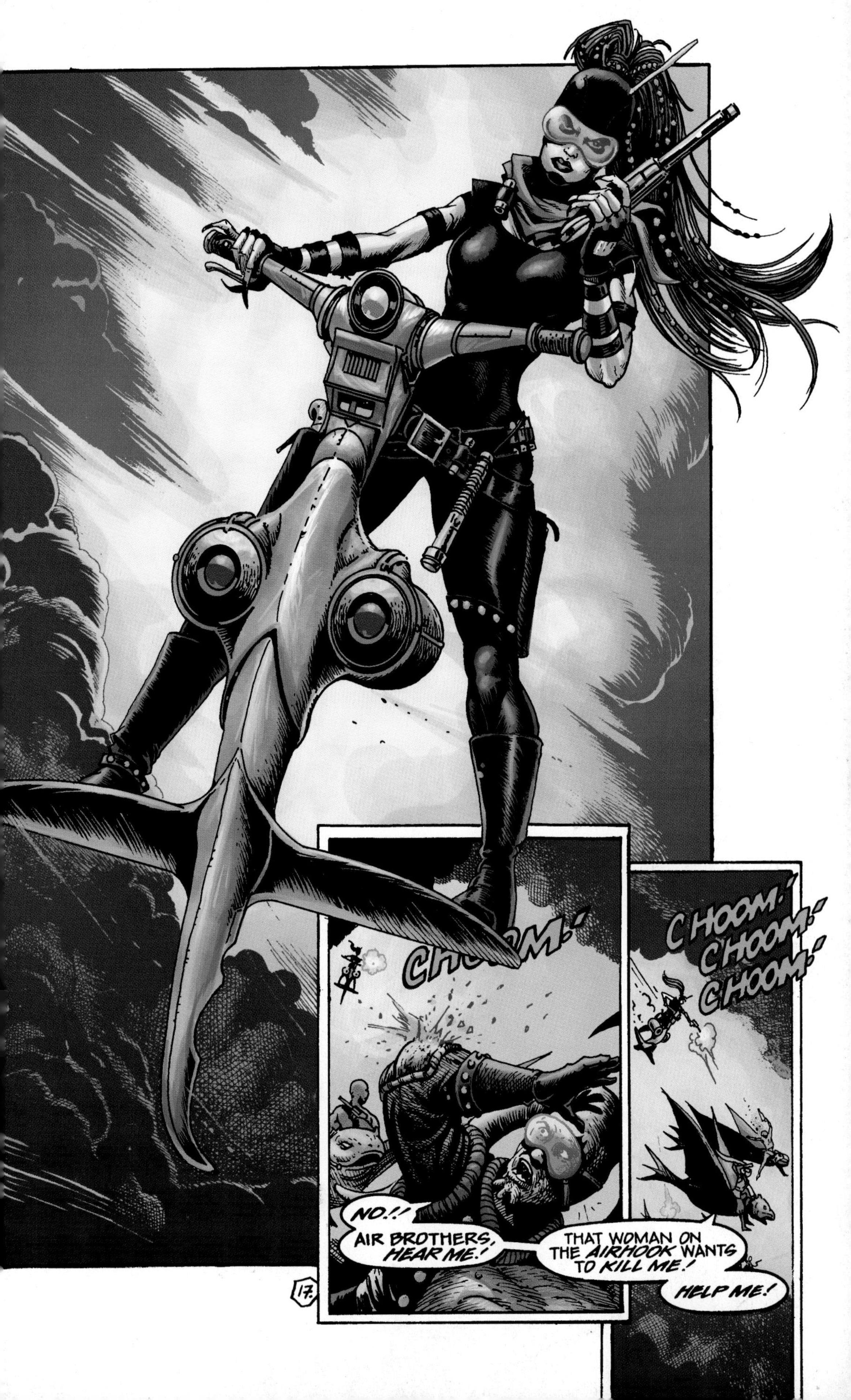
CHOOM!
NO!!
AIR BROTHERS, HEAR ME!
THAT WOMAN ON THE AIRHOOK WANTS TO KILL ME!
CHOOM! CHOOM! CHOOM!
HELP ME!

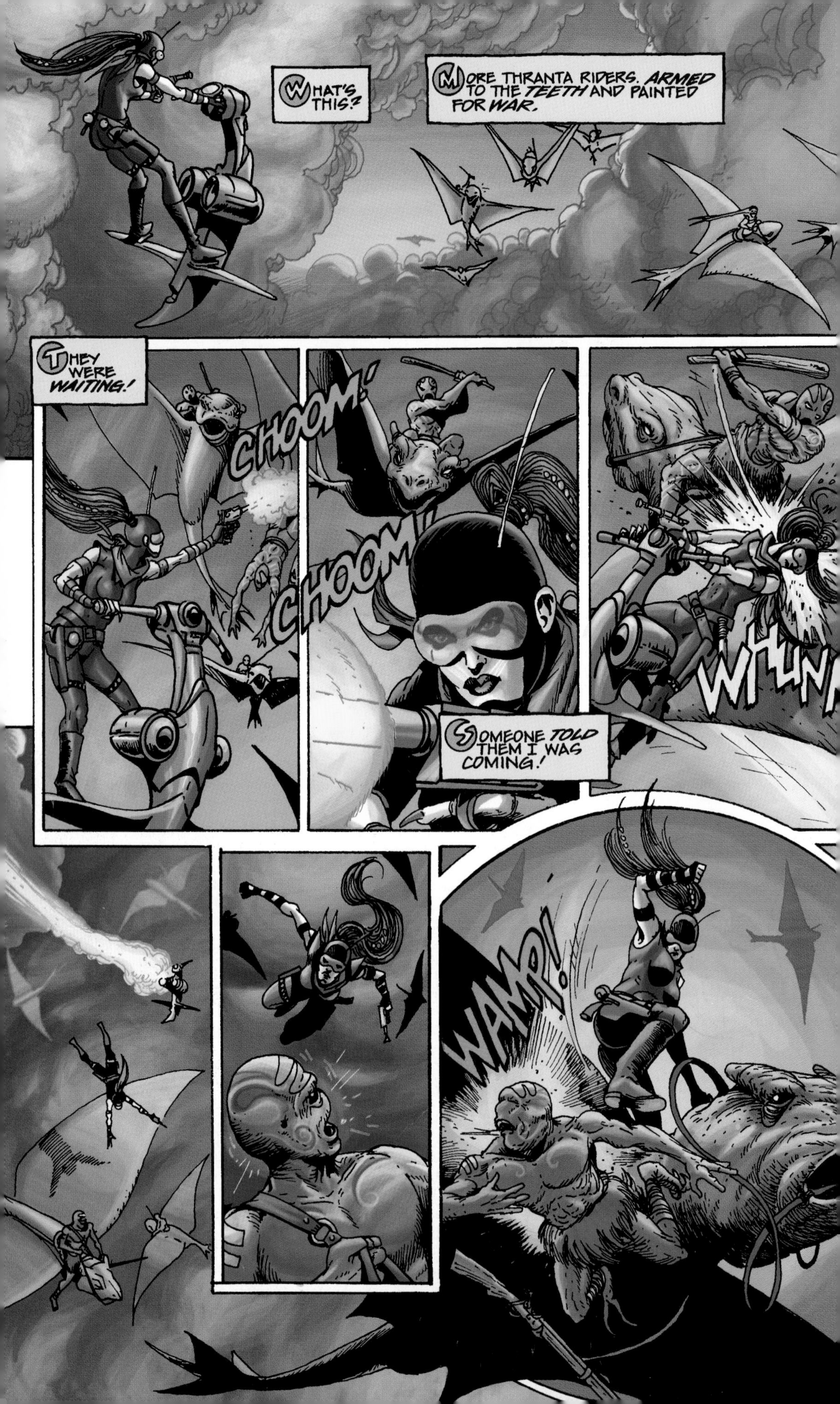
WHAT'S THIS?
MORE THRANTA RIDERS. ARMED TO THE TEETH AND PAINTED FOR WAR.
THEY WERE WAITING!
CHOOM!
CHOOM!
CHOOM!
SOMEONE TOLD THEM I WAS COMING!
WHUNK
WAMP!

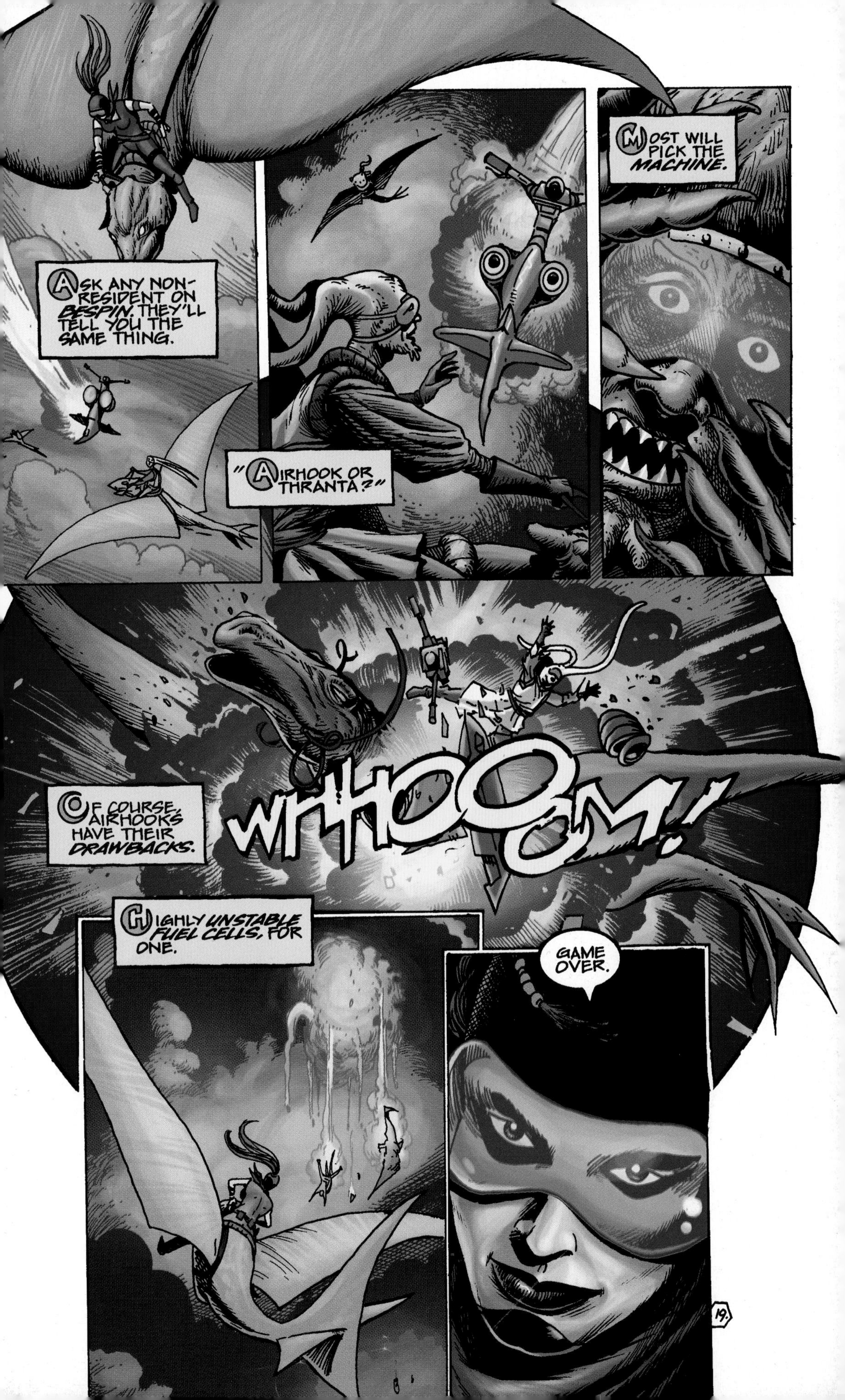
Ask any non-resident on Bespin. They'll tell you the same thing.
"Airhook or thranta?"
Most will pick the machine.
Of course, airhooks have their drawbacks.
WHHOOOOM!
Highly unstable fuel cells, for one.
Game over.
19.

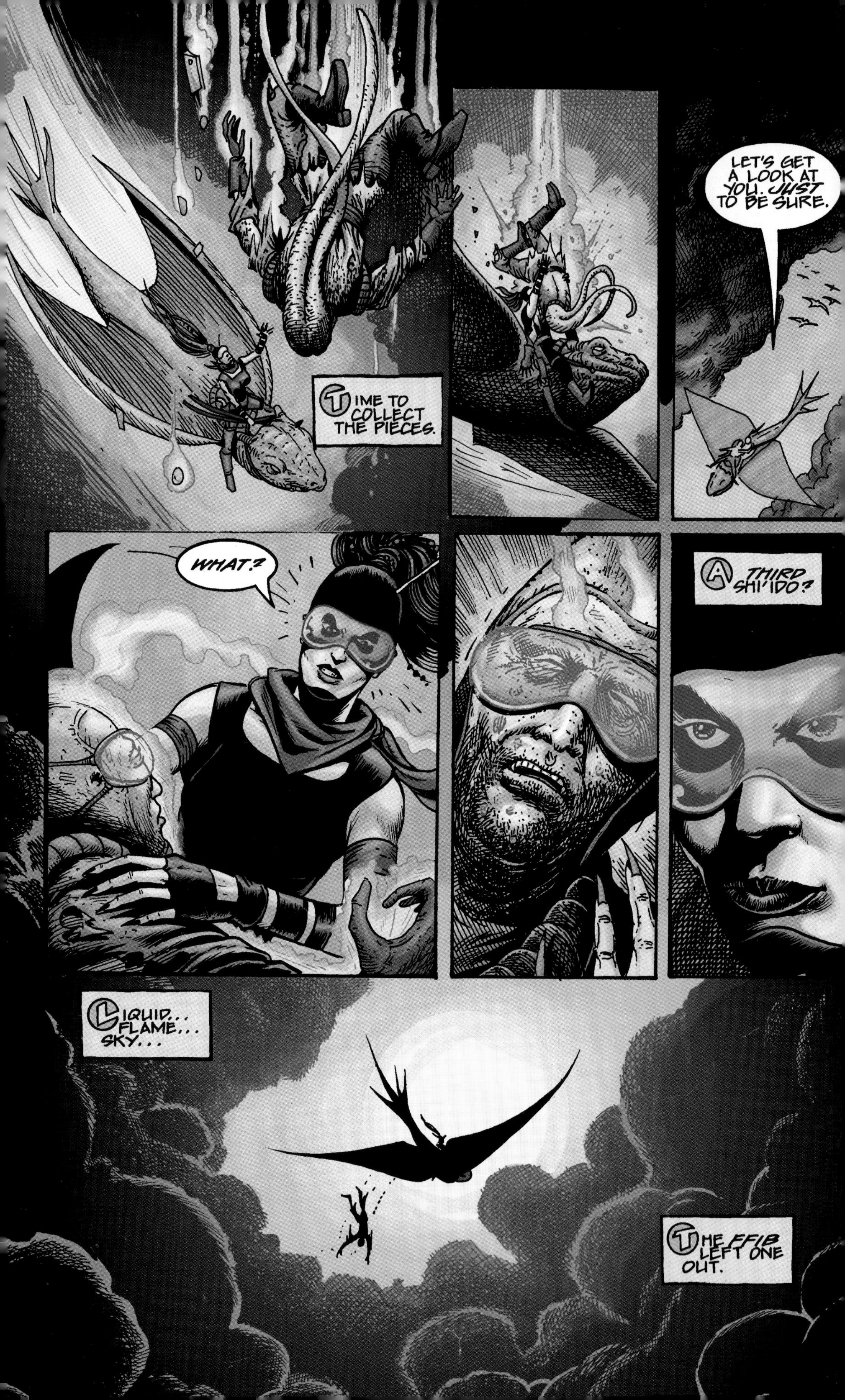
TIME TO COLLECT THE PIECES.
LET'S GET A LOOK AT YOU. JUST TO BE SURE.
WHAT?
A THIRD SHI'IDO?
LIQUID... FLAME... SKY...
THE FFIB LEFT ONE OUT.

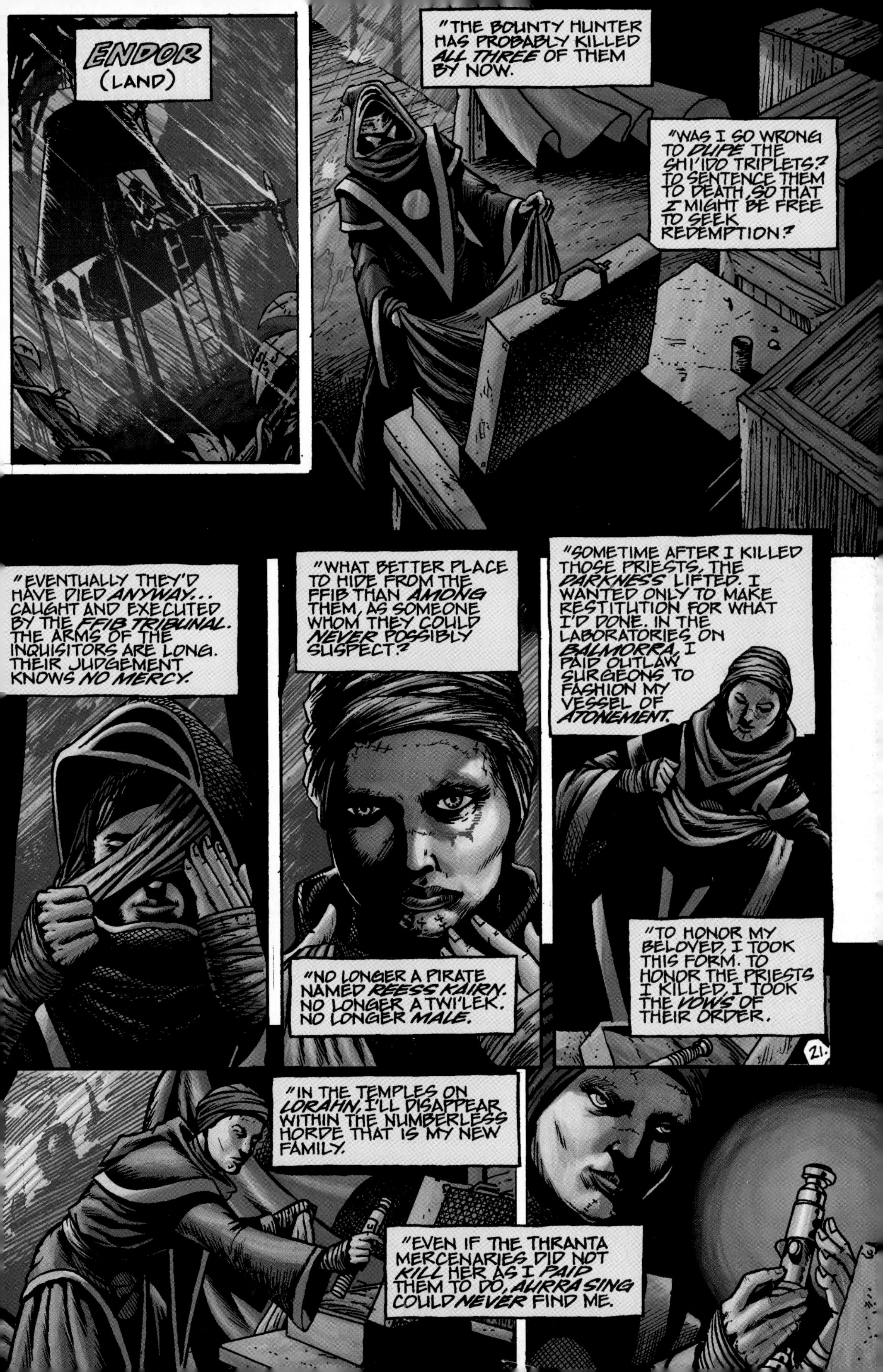

ENDOR (LAND)
"THE BOUNTY HUNTER HAS PROBABLY KILLED ALL THREE OF THEM BY NOW.
"WAS I SO WRONG TO DUPE THE SHI'IDO TRIPLETS? TO SENTENCE THEM TO DEATH, SO THAT I MIGHT BE FREE TO SEEK REDEMPTION?
"EVENTUALLY THEY'D HAVE DIED ANYWAY... CAUGHT AND EXECUTED BY THE FFIB TRIBUNAL. THE ARMS OF THE INQUISITORS ARE LONG. THEIR JUDGEMENT KNOWS NO MERCY.
"WHAT BETTER PLACE TO HIDE FROM THE FFIB THAN AMONG THEM, AS SOMEONE WHOM THEY COULD NEVER POSSIBLY SUSPECT?
"NO LONGER A PIRATE NAMED REESS KAIRN. NO LONGER A TWI'LEK. NO LONGER MALE.
"SOMETIME AFTER I KILLED THOSE PRIESTS, THE DARKNESS LIFTED. I WANTED ONLY TO MAKE RESTITUTION FOR WHAT I'D DONE. IN THE LABORATORIES ON BALMORRA, I PAID OUTLAW SURGEONS TO FASHION MY VESSEL OF ATONEMENT.
"TO HONOR MY BELOVED, I TOOK THIS FORM. TO HONOR THE PRIESTS I KILLED, I TOOK THE VOWS OF THEIR ORDER.
21.
"IN THE TEMPLES ON LORAHN, I'LL DISAPPEAR WITHIN THE NUMBERLESS HORDE THAT IS MY NEW FAMILY.
"EVEN IF THE THRANTA MERCENARIES DID NOT KILL HER AS I PAID THEM TO DO, AURRA SING COULD NEVER FIND ME.

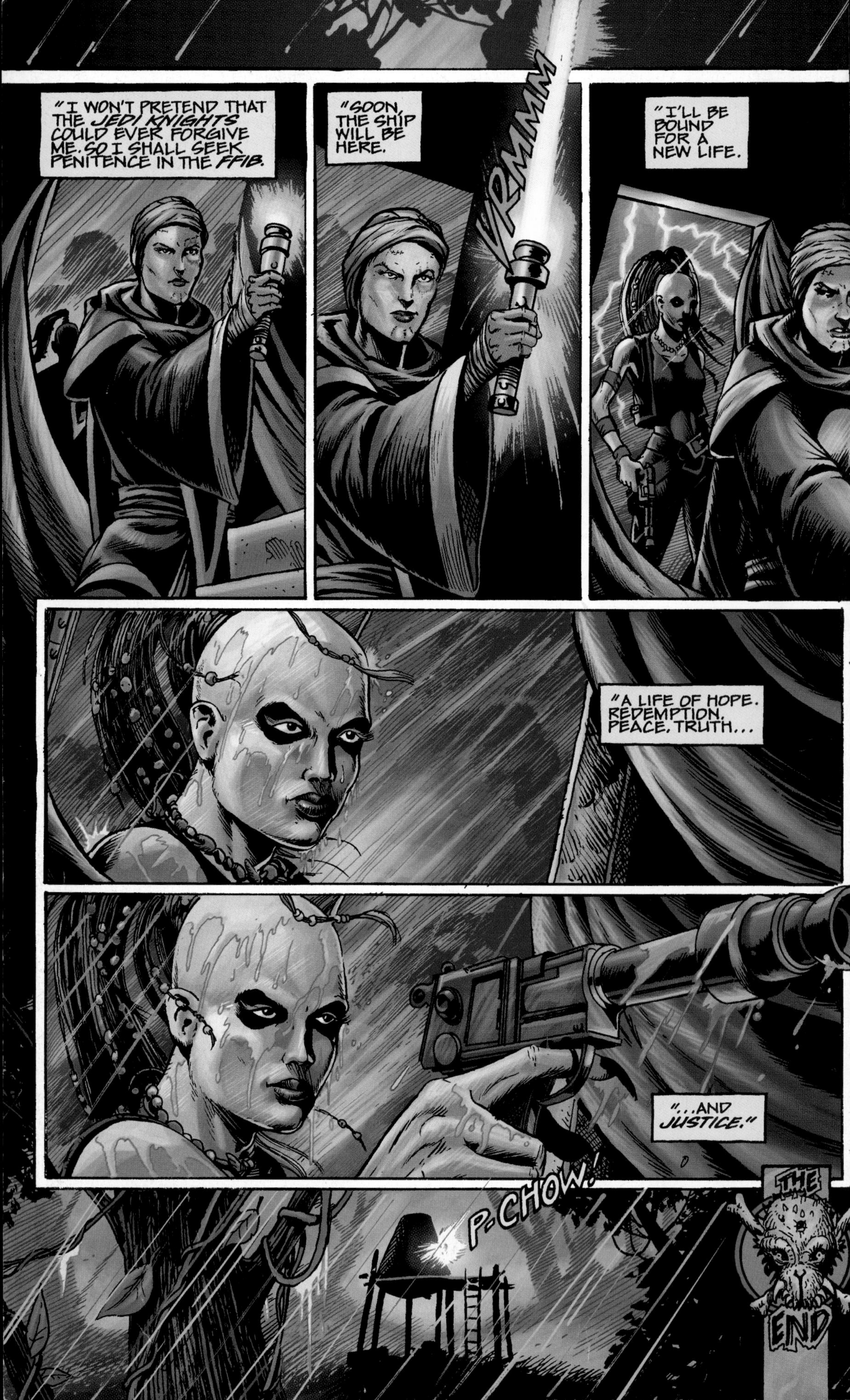
"I WON'T PRETEND THAT THE *JEDI KNIGHTS* COULD EVER FORGIVE ME. SO I SHALL SEEK PENITENCE IN THE *FFIB*.
"SOON, THE SHIP WILL BE HERE.
VRMMMM
"I'LL BE BOUND FOR A NEW LIFE.
"A LIFE OF HOPE. REDEMPTION. PEACE, TRUTH...
"...AND *JUSTICE*."
P-CHOW!
THE END

BOUNTY HUNTERS

SCOUNDREL'S WAGES

STORY
MARK SCHULTZ

PENCILS
MEL RUBI

INKS
ANDREW PEPOY

COLORS
DAN JACKSON

LETTERING
CLEM ROBINS

TITLE ART
MARC GABBANA

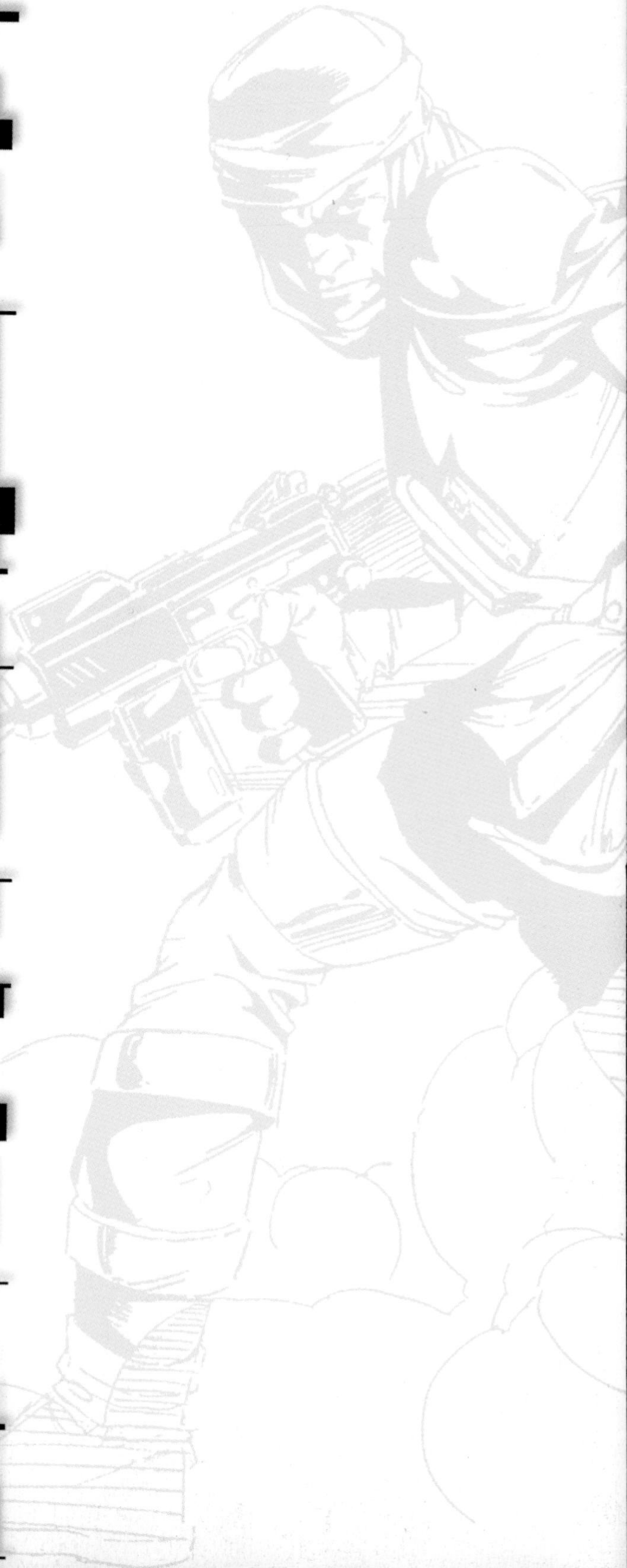

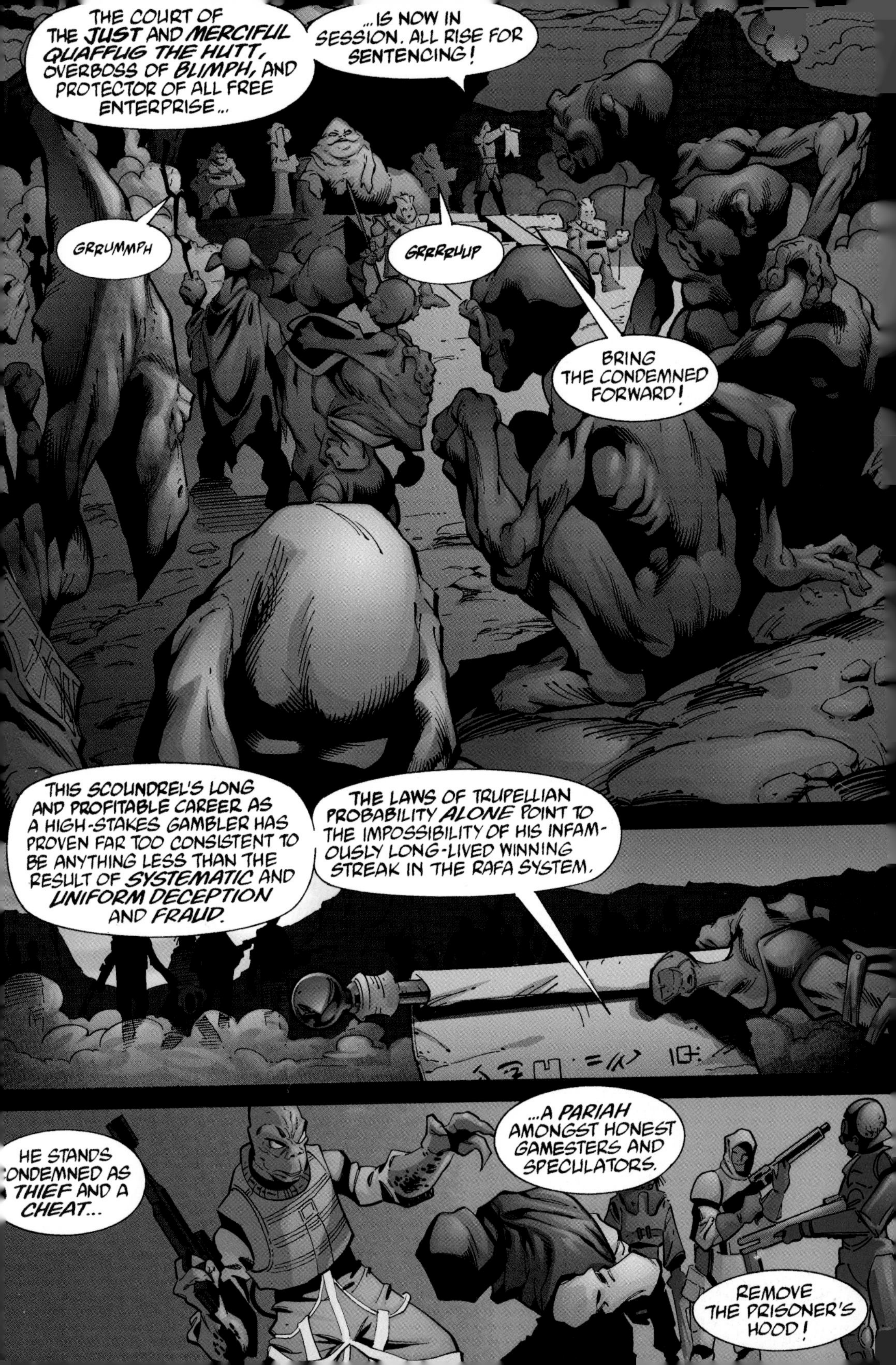
THE COURT OF THE JUST AND MERCIFUL QUAFFUG THE HUTT, OVERBOSS OF BLIMPH, AND PROTECTOR OF ALL FREE ENTERPRISE...
...IS NOW IN SESSION. ALL RISE FOR SENTENCING!
GRRUMMPH
GRRRRULP
BRING THE CONDEMNED FORWARD!
THIS SCOUNDREL'S LONG AND PROFITABLE CAREER AS A HIGH-STAKES GAMBLER HAS PROVEN FAR TOO CONSISTENT TO BE ANYTHING LESS THAN THE RESULT OF SYSTEMATIC AND UNIFORM DECEPTION AND FRAUD.
THE LAWS OF TRUPELLIAN PROBABILITY ALONE POINT TO THE IMPOSSIBILITY OF HIS INFAMOUSLY LONG-LIVED WINNING STREAK IN THE RAFA SYSTEM.
HE STANDS ONDEMNED AS THIEF AND A CHEAT...
...A PARIAH AMONGST HONEST GAMESTERS AND SPECULATORS.
REMOVE THE PRISONER'S HOOD!

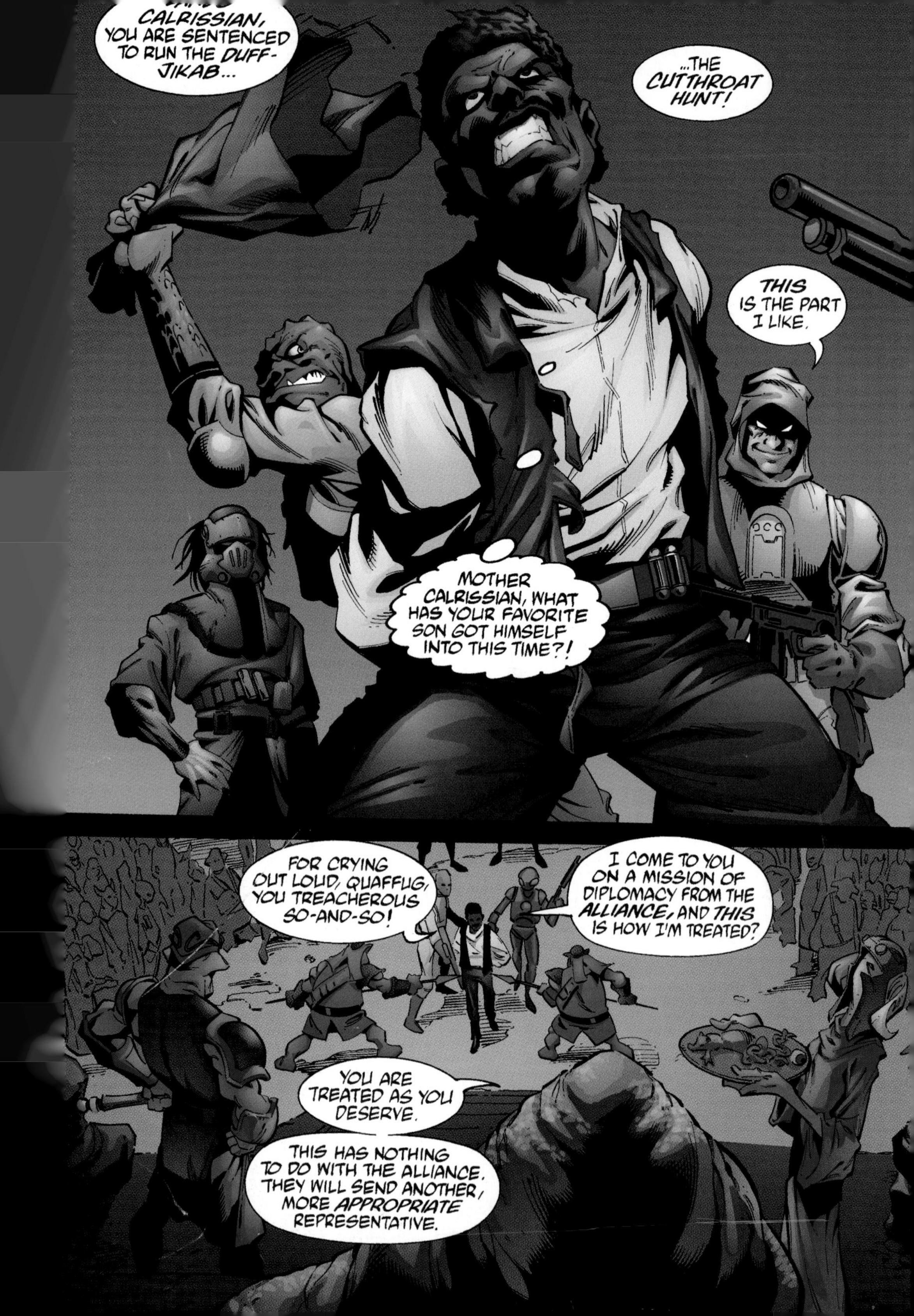
CALRISSIAN, YOU ARE SENTENCED TO RUN THE DUFF-JIKAB...
...THE CUTTHROAT HUNT!
THIS IS THE PART I LIKE.
MOTHER CALRISSIAN, WHAT HAS YOUR FAVORITE SON GOT HIMSELF INTO THIS TIME?!
FOR CRYING OUT LOUD, QUAFFUG, YOU TREACHEROUS SO-AND-SO!
I COME TO YOU ON A MISSION OF DIPLOMACY FROM THE ALLIANCE, AND THIS IS HOW I'M TREATED?
YOU ARE TREATED AS YOU DESERVE.
THIS HAS NOTHING TO DO WITH THE ALLIANCE. THEY WILL SEND ANOTHER, MORE APPROPRIATE REPRESENTATIVE.

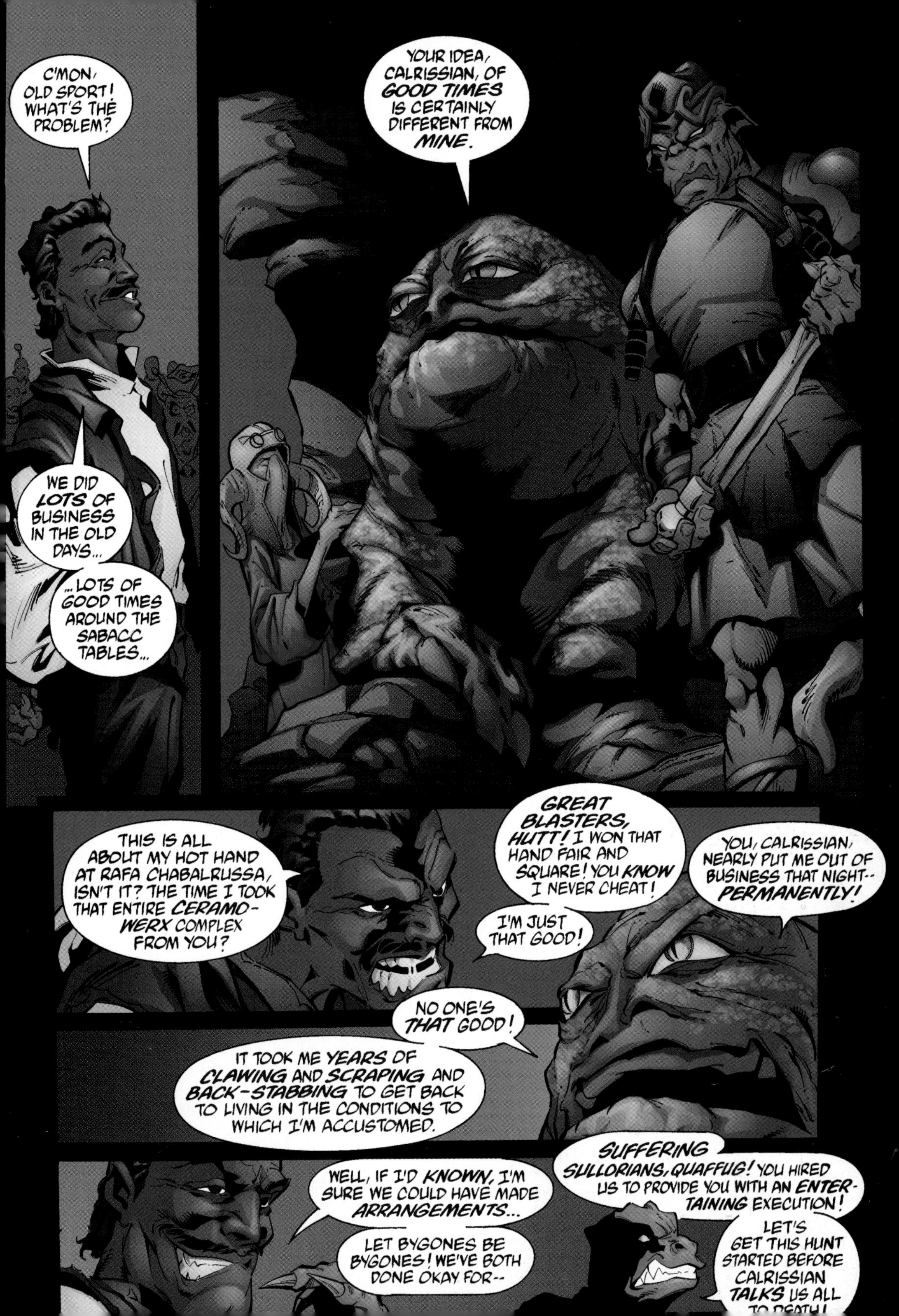
C'MON, OLD SPORT! WHAT'S THE PROBLEM?
YOUR IDEA, CALRISSIAN, OF GOOD TIMES IS CERTAINLY DIFFERENT FROM MINE.
WE DID LOTS OF BUSINESS IN THE OLD DAYS...
...LOTS OF GOOD TIMES AROUND THE SABACC TABLES...
THIS IS ALL ABOUT MY HOT HAND AT RAFA CHABALRUSSA, ISN'T IT? THE TIME I TOOK THAT ENTIRE CERAMO-WERX COMPLEX FROM YOU?
GREAT BLASTERS, HUTT! I WON THAT HAND FAIR AND SQUARE! YOU KNOW I NEVER CHEAT!
I'M JUST THAT GOOD!
YOU, CALRISSIAN, NEARLY PUT ME OUT OF BUSINESS THAT NIGHT-- PERMANENTLY!
NO ONE'S THAT GOOD!
IT TOOK ME YEARS OF CLAWING AND SCRAPING AND BACK-STABBING TO GET BACK TO LIVING IN THE CONDITIONS TO WHICH I'M ACCUSTOMED.
WELL, IF I'D KNOWN, I'M SURE WE COULD HAVE MADE ARRANGEMENTS...
LET BYGONES BE BYGONES! WE'VE BOTH DONE OKAY FOR--
SUFFERING SULLORIANS, QUAFFUG! YOU HIRED US TO PROVIDE YOU WITH AN ENTERTAINING EXECUTION!
LET'S GET THIS HUNT STARTED BEFORE CALRISSIAN TALKS US ALL

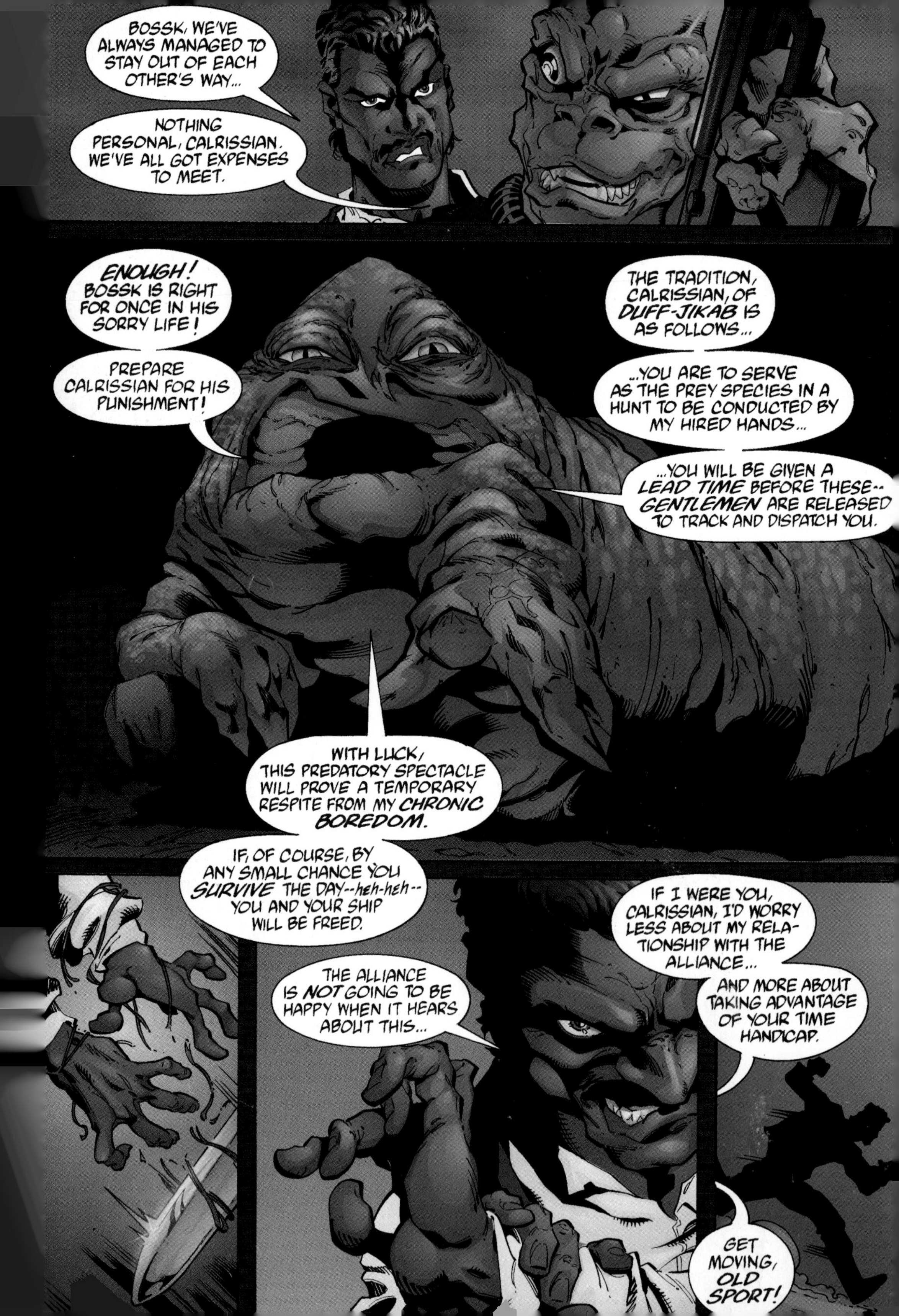
BOSSK, WE'VE ALWAYS MANAGED TO STAY OUT OF EACH OTHER'S WAY...
NOTHING PERSONAL, CALRISSIAN. WE'VE ALL GOT EXPENSES TO MEET.
ENOUGH! BOSSK IS RIGHT FOR ONCE IN HIS SORRY LIFE!
PREPARE CALRISSIAN FOR HIS PUNISHMENT!
THE TRADITION, CALRISSIAN, OF DUFF-JIKAB IS AS FOLLOWS...
...YOU ARE TO SERVE AS THE PREY SPECIES IN A HUNT TO BE CONDUCTED BY MY HIRED HANDS...
...YOU WILL BE GIVEN A LEAD TIME BEFORE THESE--GENTLEMEN ARE RELEASED TO TRACK AND DISPATCH YOU.
WITH LUCK, THIS PREDATORY SPECTACLE WILL PROVE A TEMPORARY RESPITE FROM MY CHRONIC BOREDOM.
IF, OF COURSE, BY ANY SMALL CHANCE YOU SURVIVE THE DAY--heh-heh--YOU AND YOUR SHIP WILL BE FREED.
THE ALLIANCE IS NOT GOING TO BE HAPPY WHEN IT HEARS ABOUT THIS...
IF I WERE YOU, CALRISSIAN, I'D WORRY LESS ABOUT MY RELA-TIONSHIP WITH THE ALLIANCE...
AND MORE ABOUT TAKING ADVANTAGE OF YOUR TIME HANDICAP.
GET MOVING, OLD SPORT!

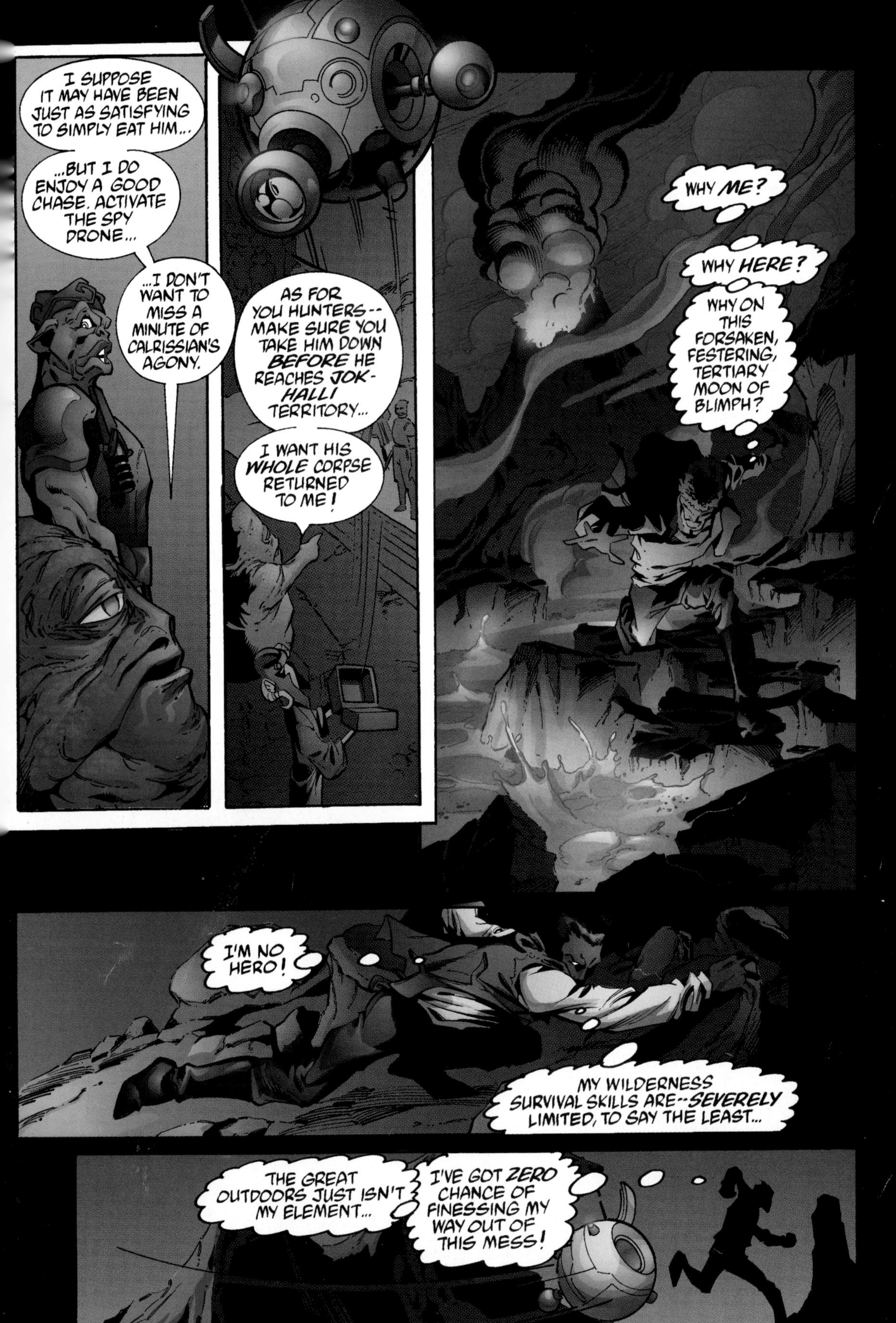
I SUPPOSE IT MAY HAVE BEEN JUST AS SATISFYING TO SIMPLY EAT HIM...
...BUT I DO ENJOY A GOOD CHASE. ACTIVATE THE SPY DRONE...
...I DON'T WANT TO MISS A MINUTE OF CALRISSIAN'S AGONY.
AS FOR YOU HUNTERS--MAKE SURE YOU TAKE HIM DOWN BEFORE HE REACHES JOK-HALLI TERRITORY...
I WANT HIS WHOLE CORPSE RETURNED TO ME!
WHY ME?
WHY HERE?
WHY ON THIS FORSAKEN, FESTERING, TERTIARY MOON OF BLIMPH?
I'M NO HERO!
MY WILDERNESS SURVIVAL SKILLS ARE--SEVERELY LIMITED, TO SAY THE LEAST...
THE GREAT OUTDOORS JUST ISN'T MY ELEMENT...
I'VE GOT ZERO CHANCE OF FINESSING MY WAY OUT OF THIS MESS!

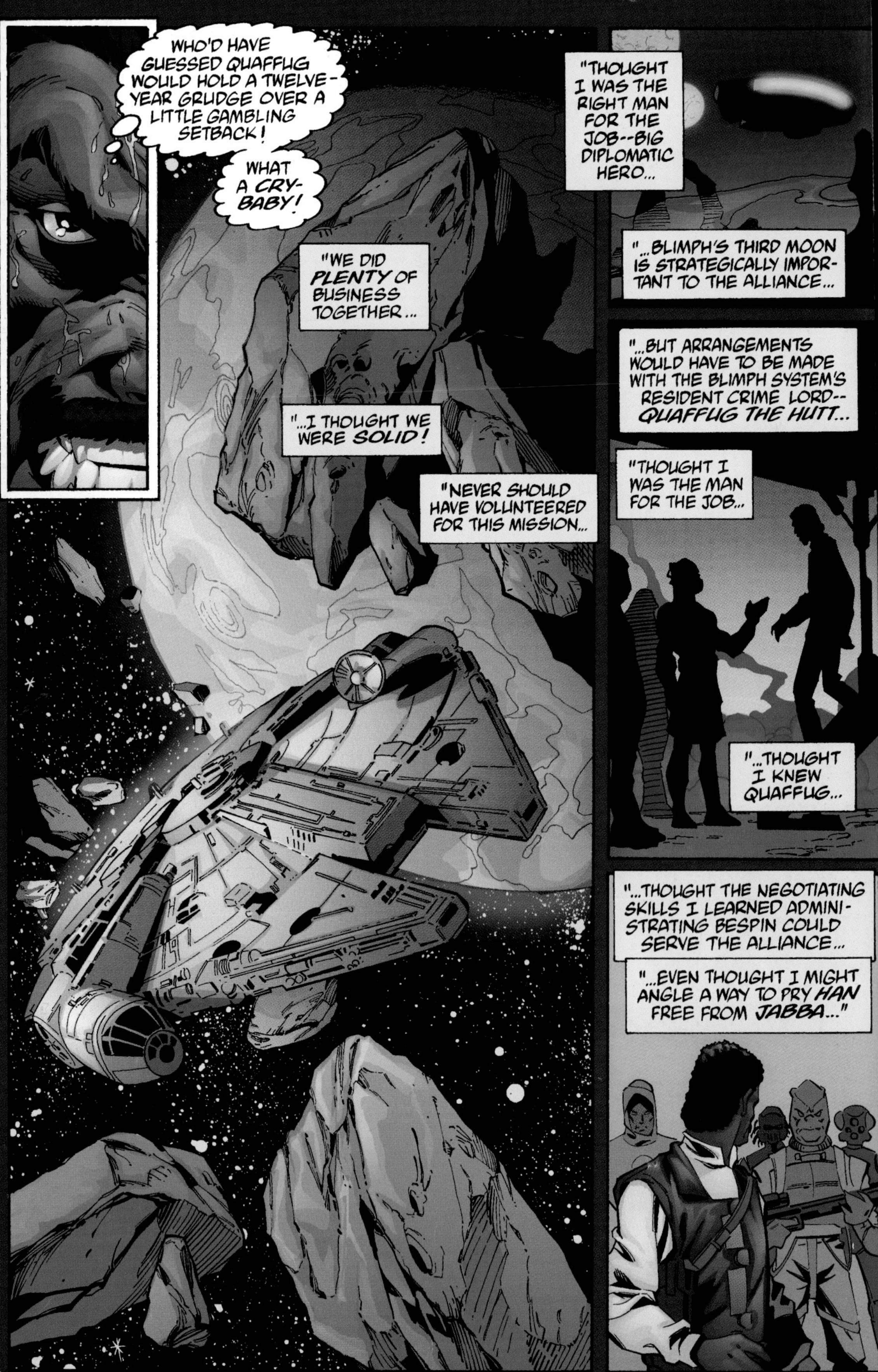
WHO'D HAVE GUESSED QUAFFUG WOULD HOLD A TWELVE-YEAR GRUDGE OVER A LITTLE GAMBLING SETBACK!
WHAT A CRY-BABY!
"WE DID PLENTY OF BUSINESS TOGETHER...
"...I THOUGHT WE WERE SOLID!
"NEVER SHOULD HAVE VOLUNTEERED FOR THIS MISSION...
"THOUGHT I WAS THE RIGHT MAN FOR THE JOB--BIG DIPLOMATIC HERO...
"...BLIMPH'S THIRD MOON IS STRATEGICALLY IMPORTANT TO THE ALLIANCE...
"...BUT ARRANGEMENTS WOULD HAVE TO BE MADE WITH THE BLIMPH SYSTEM'S RESIDENT CRIME LORD-- QUAFFUG THE HUTT...
"THOUGHT I WAS THE MAN FOR THE JOB...
"...THOUGHT I KNEW QUAFFUG...
"...THOUGHT THE NEGOTIATING SKILLS I LEARNED ADMINISTRATING BESPIN COULD SERVE THE ALLIANCE...
"...EVEN THOUGHT I MIGHT ANGLE A WAY TO PRY HAN FREE FROM JABBA..."

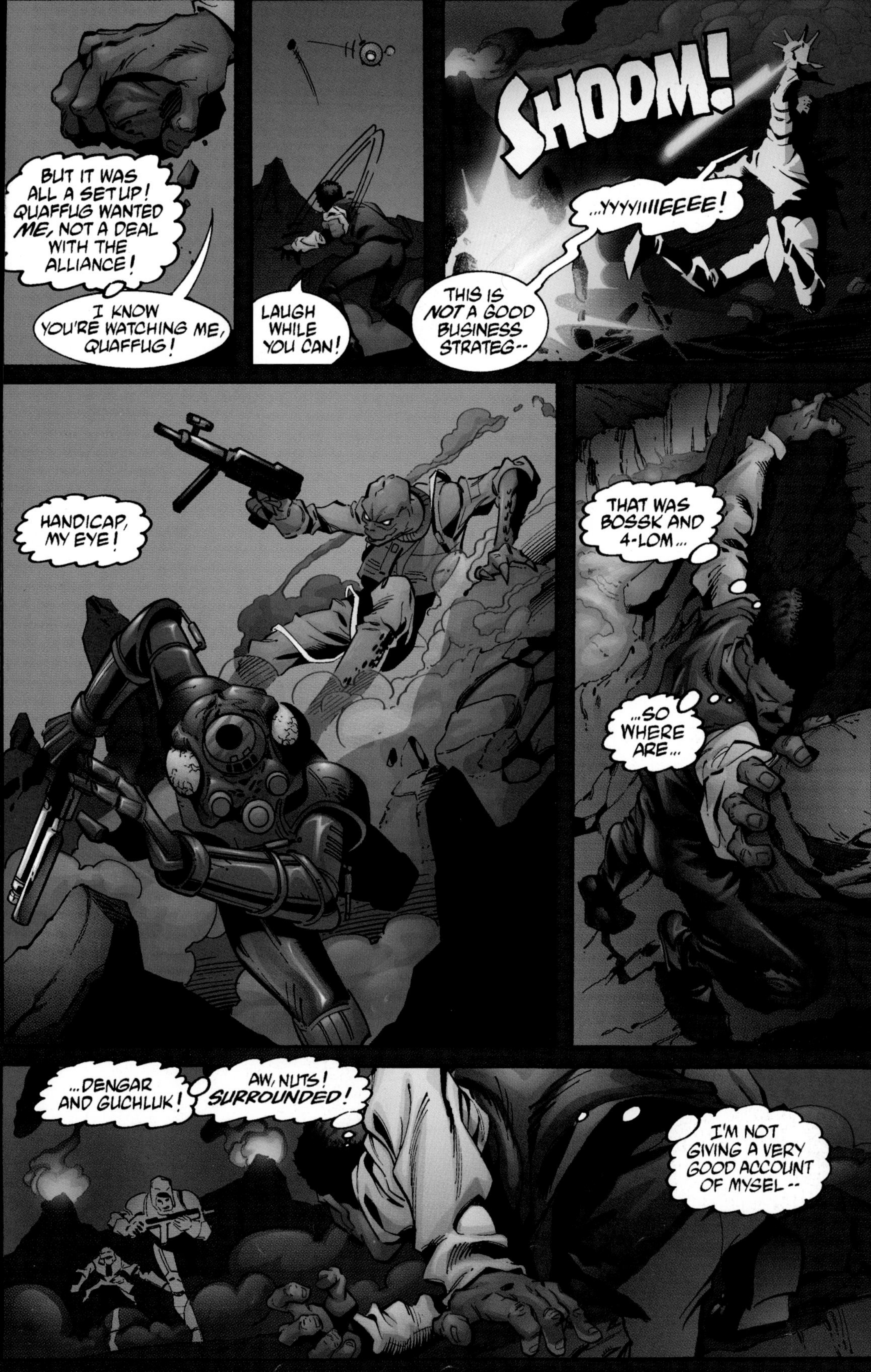
BUT IT WAS ALL A SETUP! QUAFFUG WANTED *ME*, NOT A DEAL WITH THE ALLIANCE!
I KNOW YOU'RE WATCHING ME, QUAFFUG!
LAUGH WHILE YOU CAN!
SHOOM!
...YYYYIIIIIEEEE!
THIS IS *NOT* A GOOD BUSINESS STRATEG--
HANDICAP, MY EYE!
THAT WAS BOSSK AND 4-LOM...
...SO WHERE ARE...
...DENGAR AND GUCHLUK!
AW, NUTS! *SURROUNDED*!
I'M NOT GIVING A VERY GOOD ACCOUNT OF MYSEL--

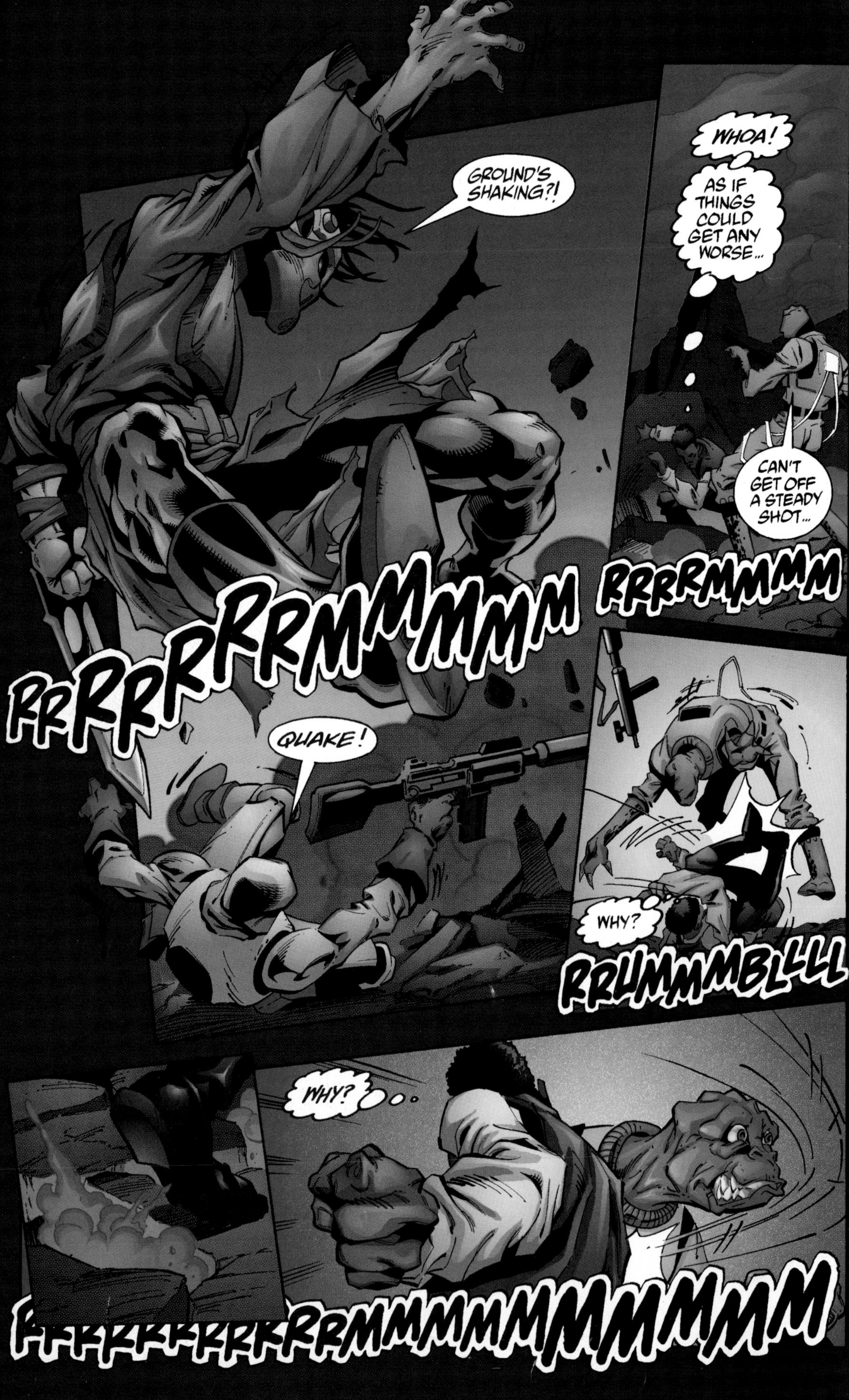
GROUND'S SHAKING?!
WHOA!
AS IF THINGS COULD GET ANY WORSE...
CAN'T GET OFF A STEADY SHOT...
RRRRRRMMMMMMM RRRRMMMM
QUAKE!
WHY?
RRUMMMBLLLL
WHY?
RRMMMMMMMMMMMMMMM

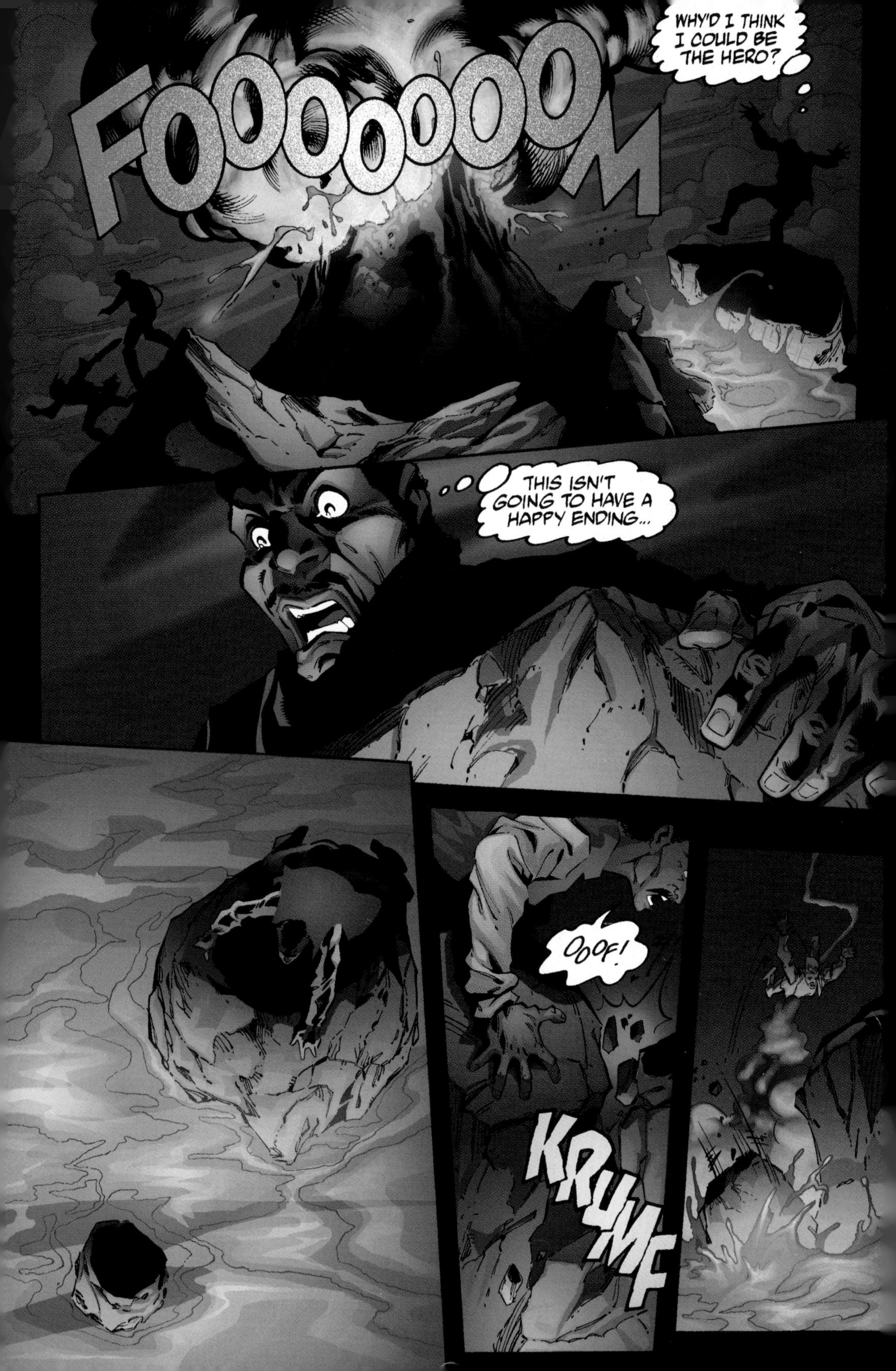
FOOOOOOOM
WHY'D I THINK I COULD BE THE HERO?
THIS ISN'T GOING TO HAVE A HAPPY ENDING...
OOOF!
KRUMF

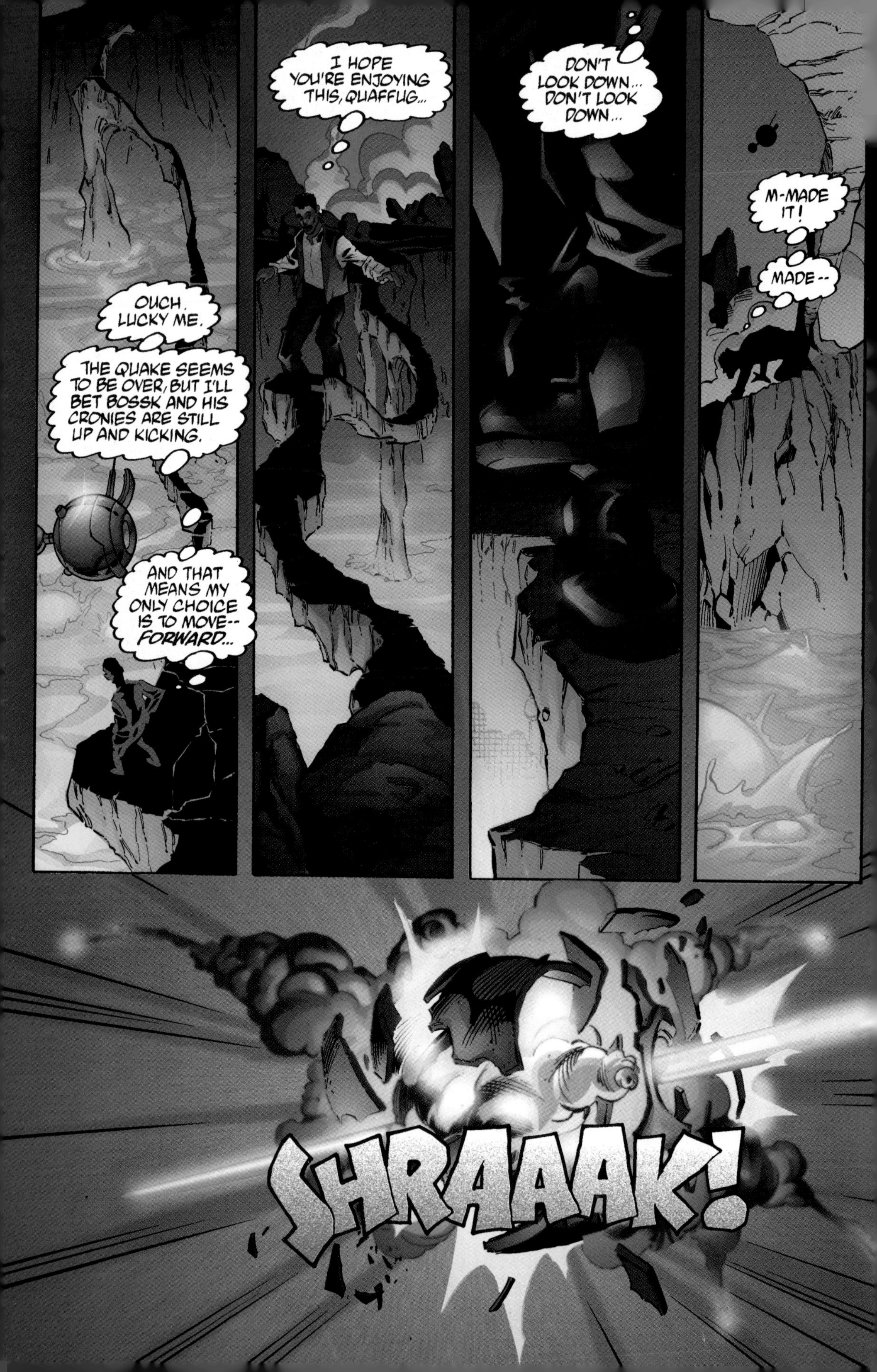
OUCH. LUCKY ME.
THE QUAKE SEEMS TO BE OVER, BUT I'LL BET BOSSK AND HIS CRONIES ARE STILL UP AND KICKING.
AND THAT MEANS MY ONLY CHOICE IS TO MOVE-- *FORWARD*...
I HOPE YOU'RE ENJOYING THIS, QUAFFUG...
DON'T LOOK DOWN... DON'T LOOK DOWN...
M-MADE IT!
MADE--
SHRAAAK!

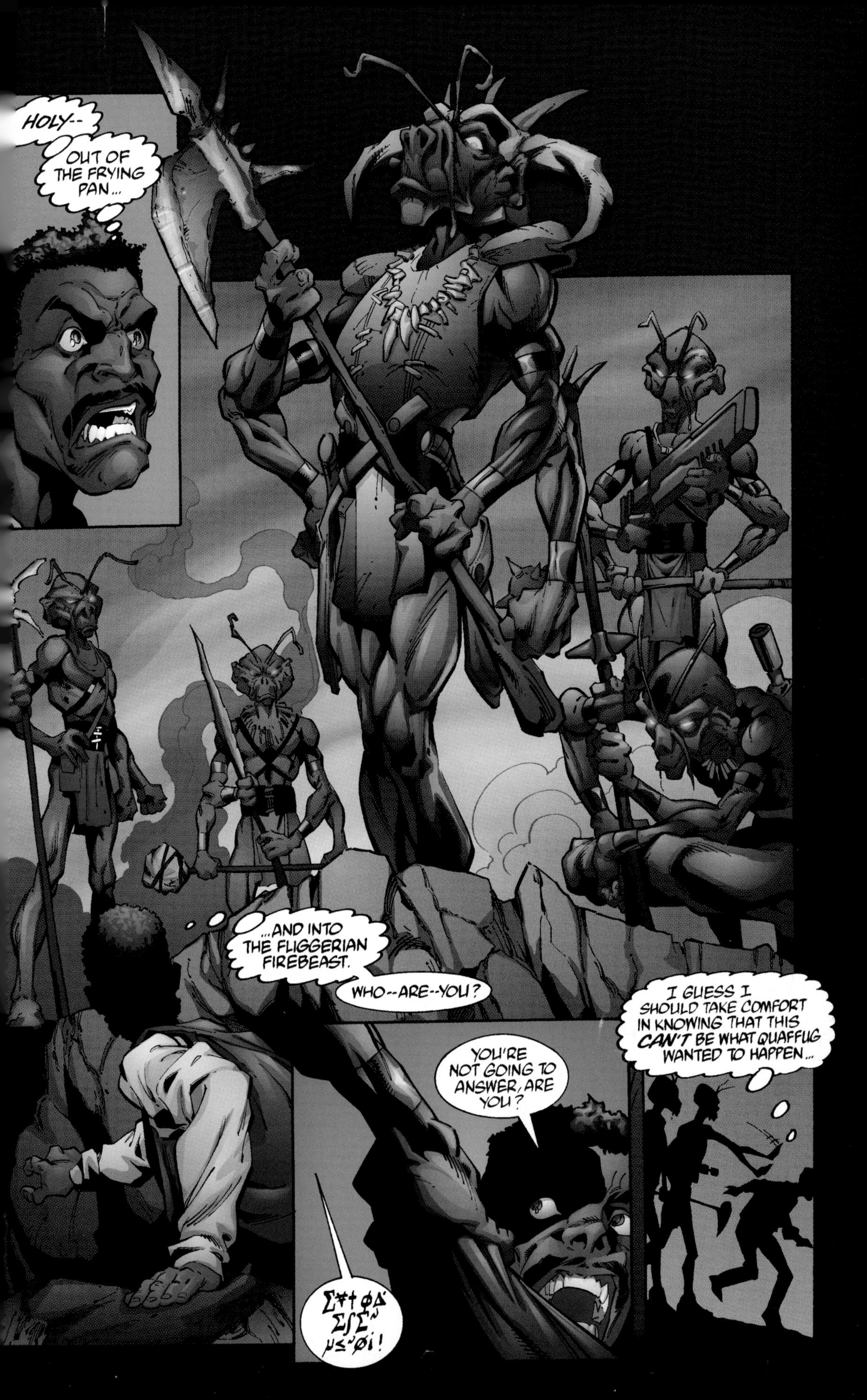
HOLY--
OUT OF THE FRYING PAN...
...AND INTO THE FLIGGERIAN FIREBEAST.
WHO--ARE--YOU?
YOU'RE NOT GOING TO ANSWER, ARE YOU?
I GUESS I SHOULD TAKE COMFORT IN KNOWING THAT THIS CAN'T BE WHAT QUAFFUG WANTED TO HAPPEN...

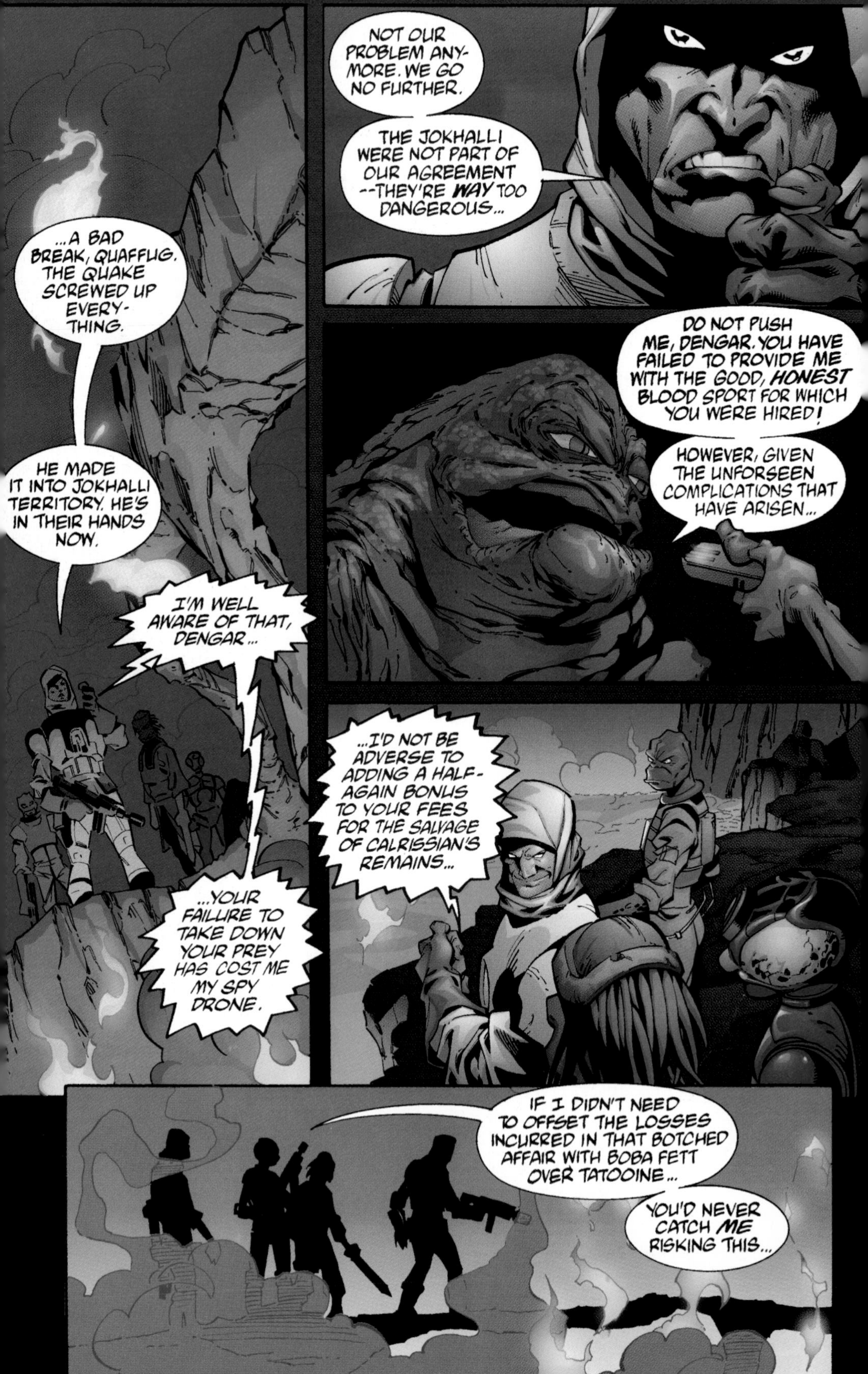

...A BAD BREAK, QUAFFUG. THE QUAKE SCREWED UP EVERY-THING.
HE MADE IT INTO JOKHALLI TERRITORY. HE'S IN THEIR HANDS NOW.
NOT OUR PROBLEM ANY-MORE. WE GO NO FURTHER.
THE JOKHALLI WERE NOT PART OF OUR AGREEMENT --THEY'RE WAY TOO DANGEROUS...
I'M WELL AWARE OF THAT, DENGAR...
...YOUR FAILURE TO TAKE DOWN YOUR PREY HAS COST ME MY SPY DRONE.
DO NOT PUSH ME, DENGAR. YOU HAVE FAILED TO PROVIDE ME WITH THE GOOD, HONEST BLOOD SPORT FOR WHICH YOU WERE HIRED!
HOWEVER, GIVEN THE UNFORSEEN COMPLICATIONS THAT HAVE ARISEN...
...I'D NOT BE ADVERSE TO ADDING A HALF-AGAIN BONUS TO YOUR FEES FOR THE SALVAGE OF CALRISSIAN'S REMAINS...
IF I DIDN'T NEED TO OFFSET THE LOSSES INCURRED IN THAT BOTCHED AFFAIR WITH BOBA FETT OVER TATOOINE...
YOU'D NEVER CATCH ME RISKING THIS...

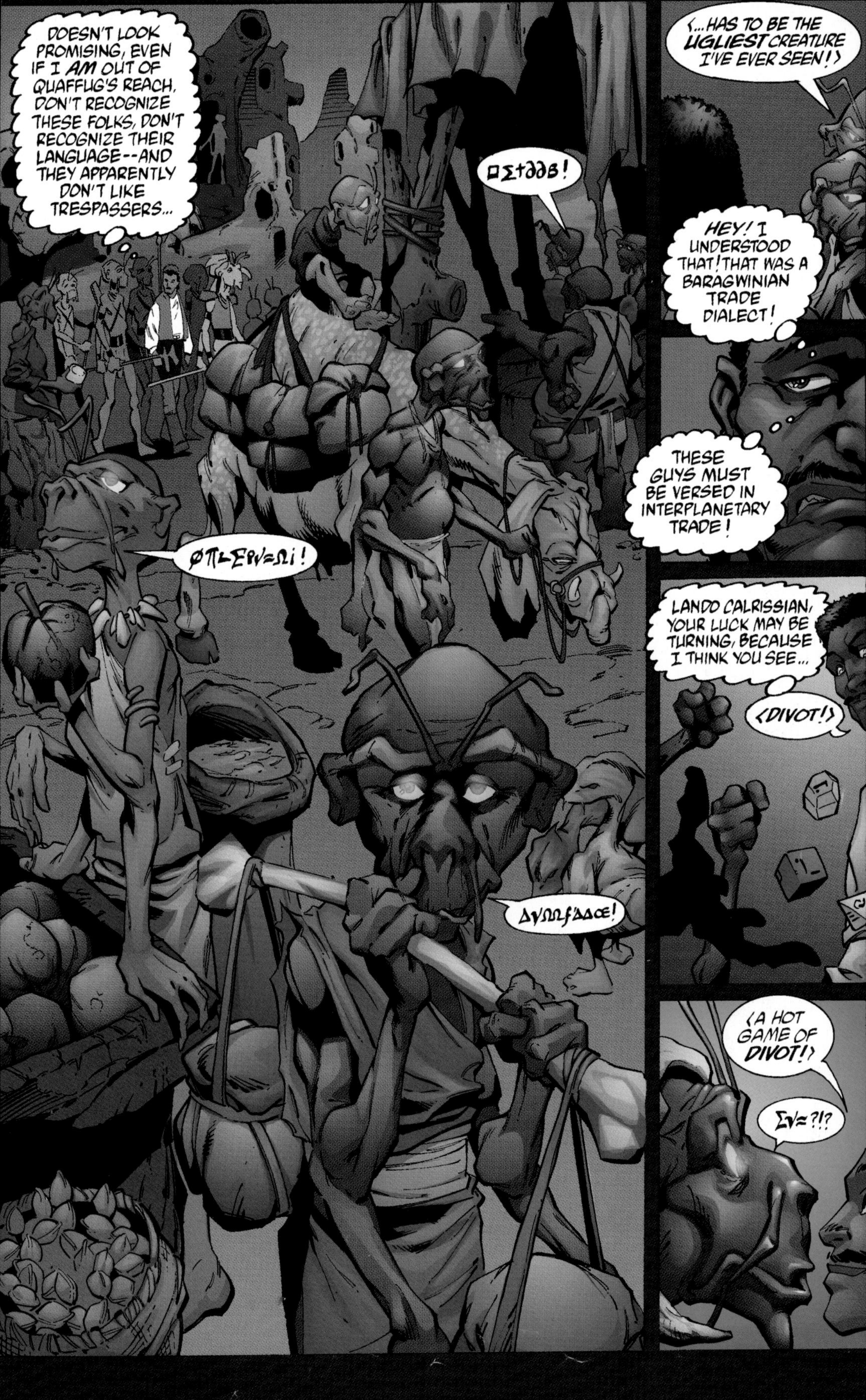
DOESN'T LOOK PROMISING, EVEN IF I *AM* OUT OF QUAFFUG'S REACH. DON'T RECOGNIZE THESE FOLKS, DON'T RECOGNIZE THEIR LANGUAGE--AND THEY APPARENTLY DON'T LIKE TRESPASSERS...
<...HAS TO BE THE ***UGLIEST*** CREATURE I'VE EVER SEEN!>
HEY! I UNDERSTOOD THAT! THAT WAS A BARAGWINIAN TRADE DIALECT!
THESE GUYS MUST BE VERSED IN INTERPLANETARY TRADE!
LANDO CALRISSIAN, YOUR LUCK MAY BE TURNING, BECAUSE I THINK YOU SEE...
<DIVOT!>
<A HOT GAME OF ***DIVOT!***>

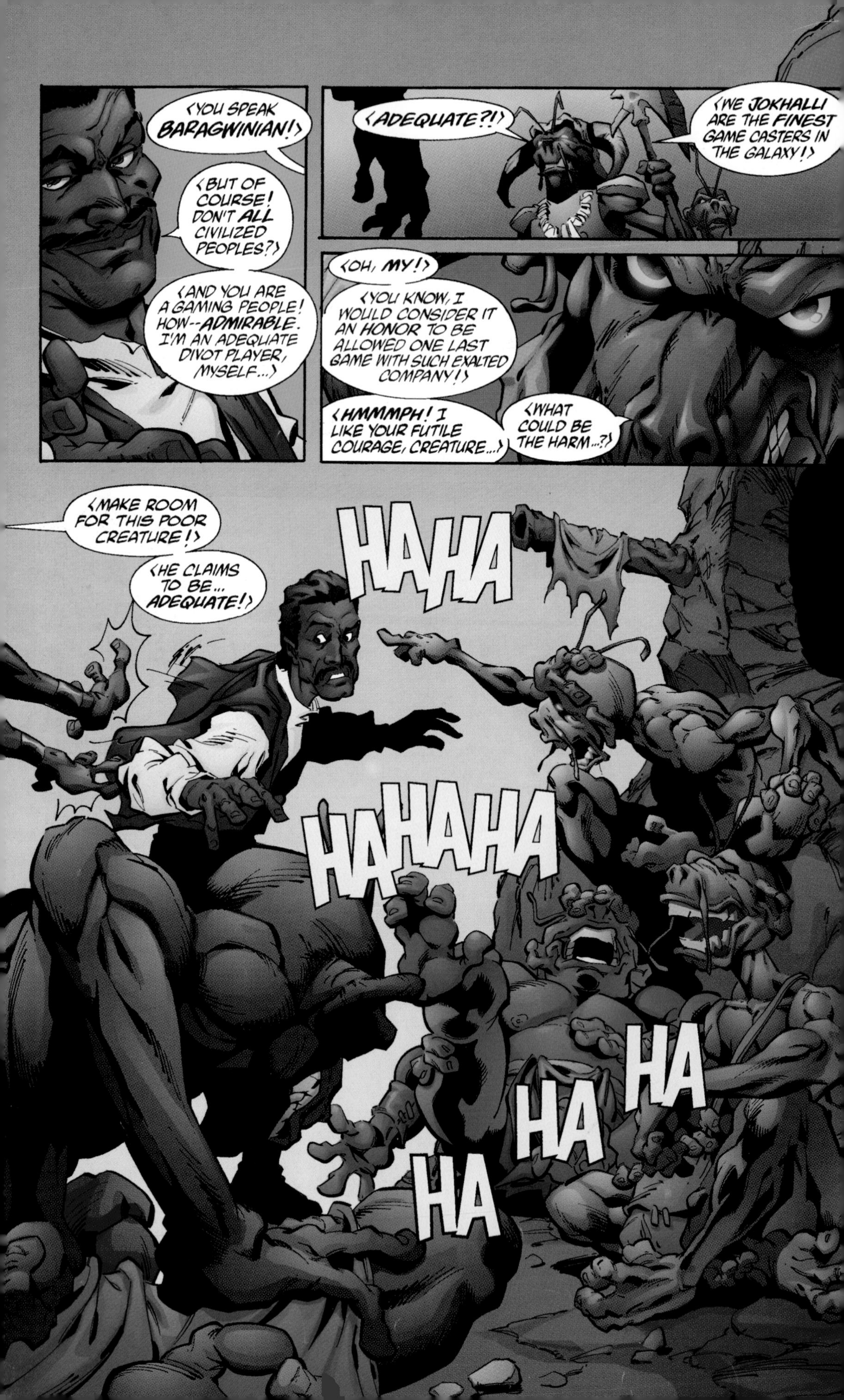

‹YOU SPEAK BARAGWINIAN!›
‹BUT OF COURSE! DON'T ALL CIVILIZED PEOPLES?›
‹AND YOU ARE A GAMING PEOPLE! HOW--ADMIRABLE. I'M AN ADEQUATE DIVOT PLAYER, MYSELF...›
‹ADEQUATE?!›
‹WE JOKHALLI ARE THE FINEST GAME CASTERS IN THE GALAXY!›
‹OH, MY!›
‹YOU KNOW, I WOULD CONSIDER IT AN HONOR TO BE ALLOWED ONE LAST GAME WITH SUCH EXALTED COMPANY!›
‹HMMMPH! I LIKE YOUR FUTILE COURAGE, CREATURE...›
‹WHAT COULD BE THE HARM...?›
‹MAKE ROOM FOR THIS POOR CREATURE!›
‹HE CLAIMS TO BE... ADEQUATE!›
HAHA
HAHAHA
HA
HA
HA

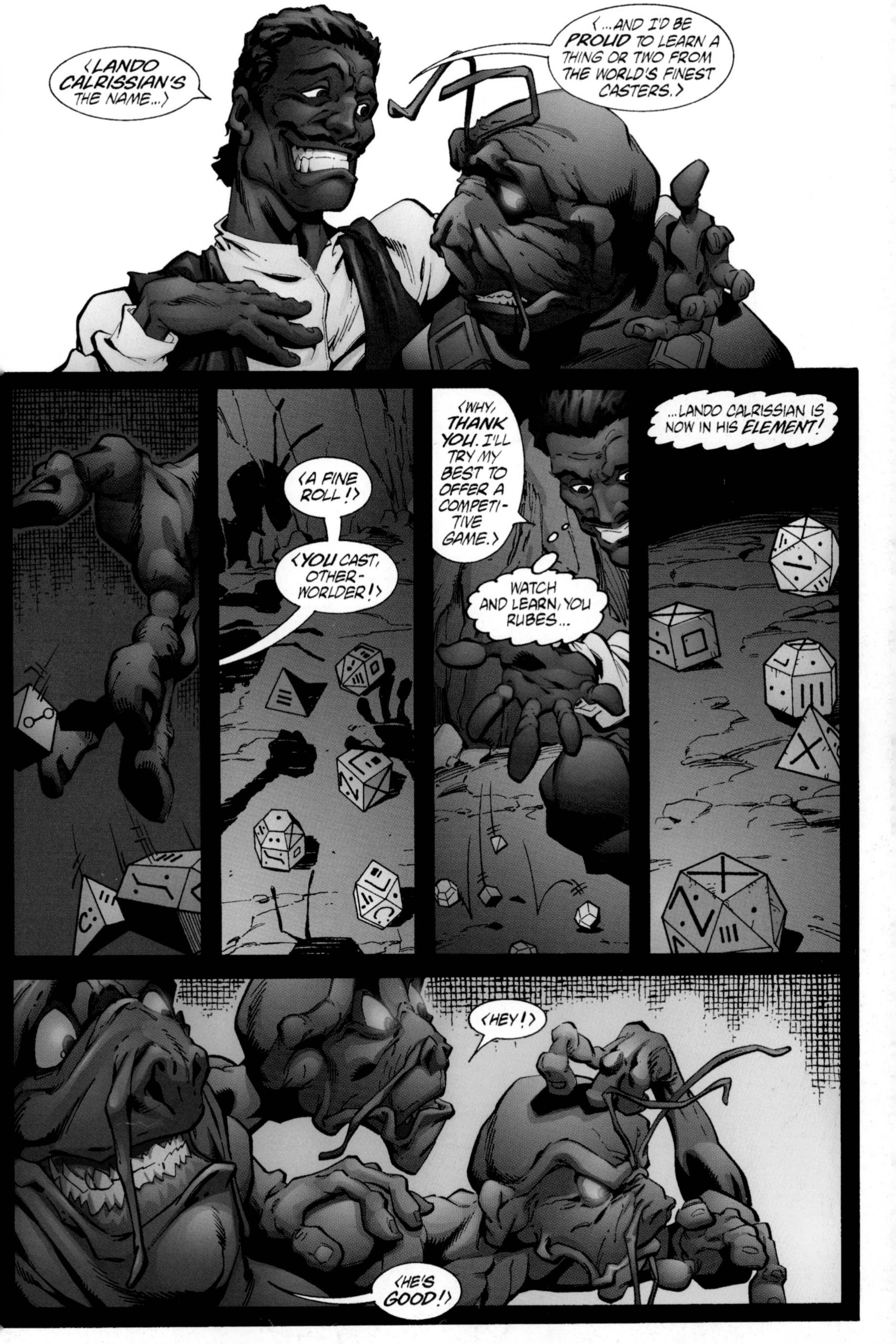
<LANDO CALRISSIAN'S THE NAME...>
<...AND I'D BE PROUD TO LEARN A THING OR TWO FROM THE WORLD'S FINEST CASTERS.>
<A FINE ROLL!>
<YOU CAST, OTHER-WORLDER!>
<WHY, THANK YOU. I'LL TRY MY BEST TO OFFER A COMPETI-TIVE GAME.>
WATCH AND LEARN, YOU RUBES...
...LANDO CALRISSIAN IS NOW IN HIS ELEMENT!
<HEY!>
<HE'S GOOD!>

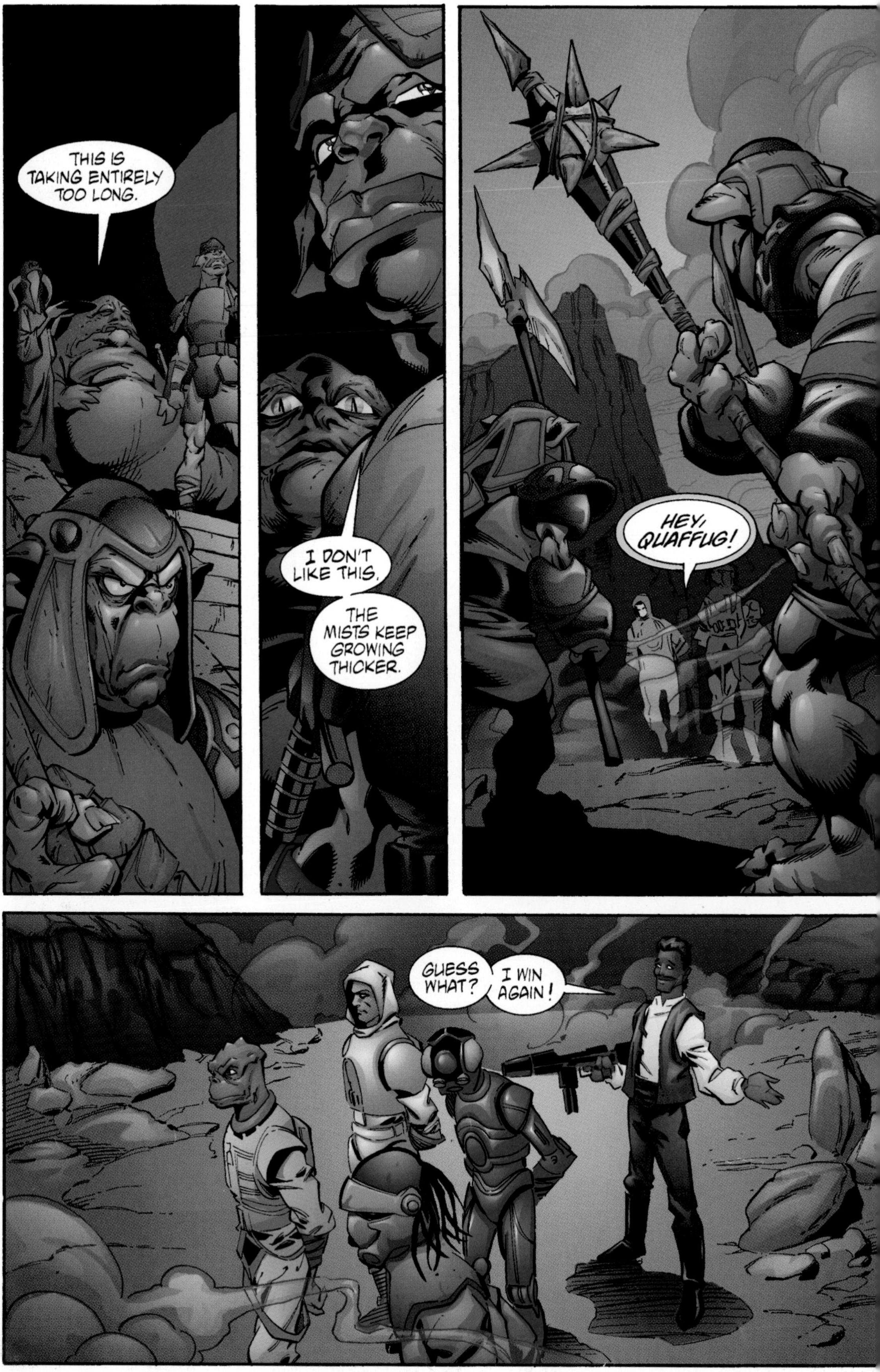
THIS IS TAKING ENTIRELY TOO LONG.
I DON'T LIKE THIS.
THE MISTS KEEP GROWING THICKER.
HEY, QUAFFUG!
GUESS WHAT?
I WIN AGAIN!

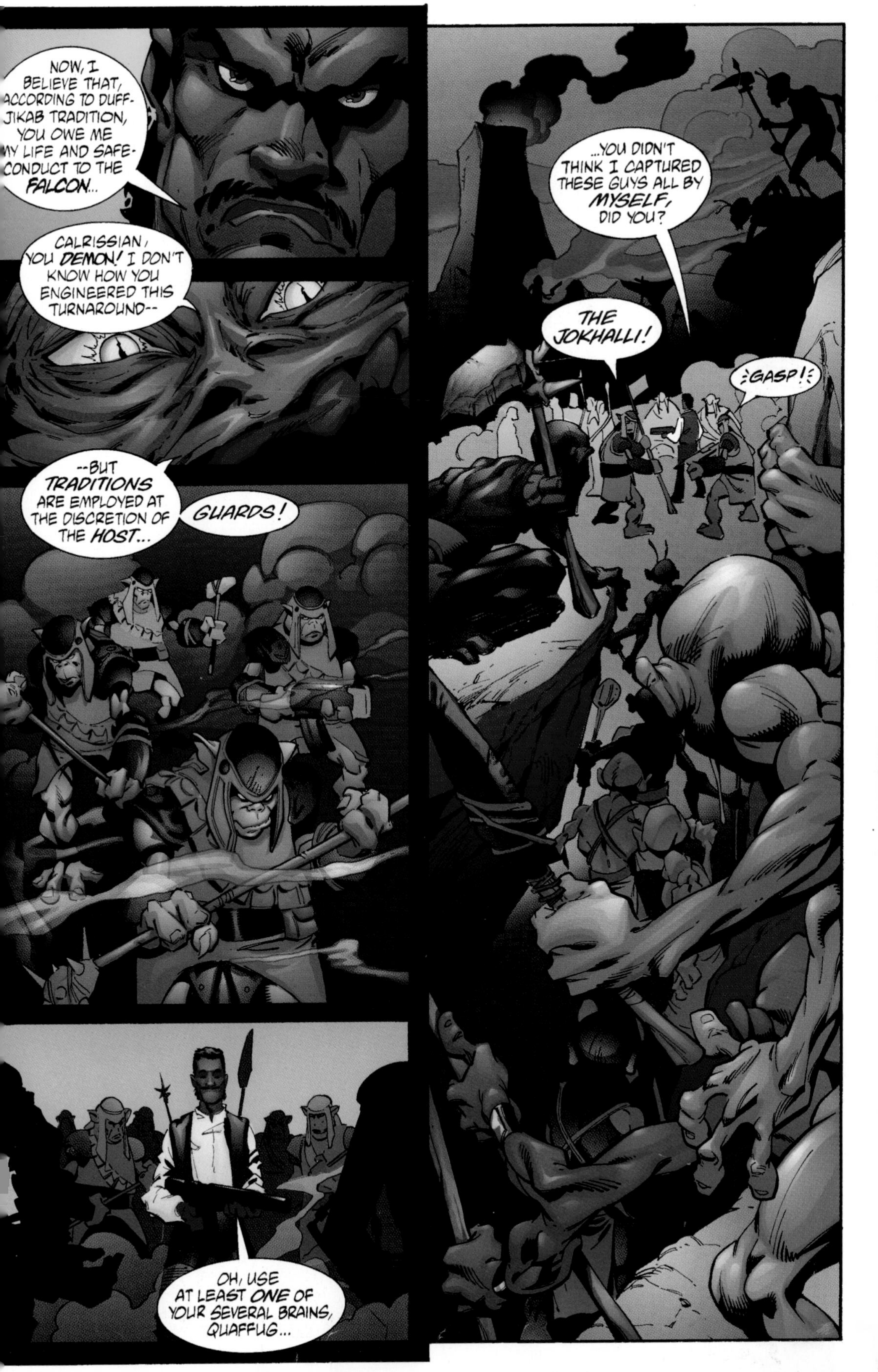

NOW, I BELIEVE THAT, ACCORDING TO DUFF-JIKAB TRADITION, YOU OWE ME MY LIFE AND SAFE-CONDUCT TO THE FALCON...
CALRISSIAN, YOU DEMON! I DON'T KNOW HOW YOU ENGINEERED THIS TURNAROUND--
--BUT TRADITIONS ARE EMPLOYED AT THE DISCRETION OF THE HOST...
GUARDS!
OH, USE AT LEAST ONE OF YOUR SEVERAL BRAINS, QUAFFUG...
...YOU DIDN'T THINK I CAPTURED THESE GUYS ALL BY MYSELF, DID YOU?
THE JOKHALLI!
GASP!

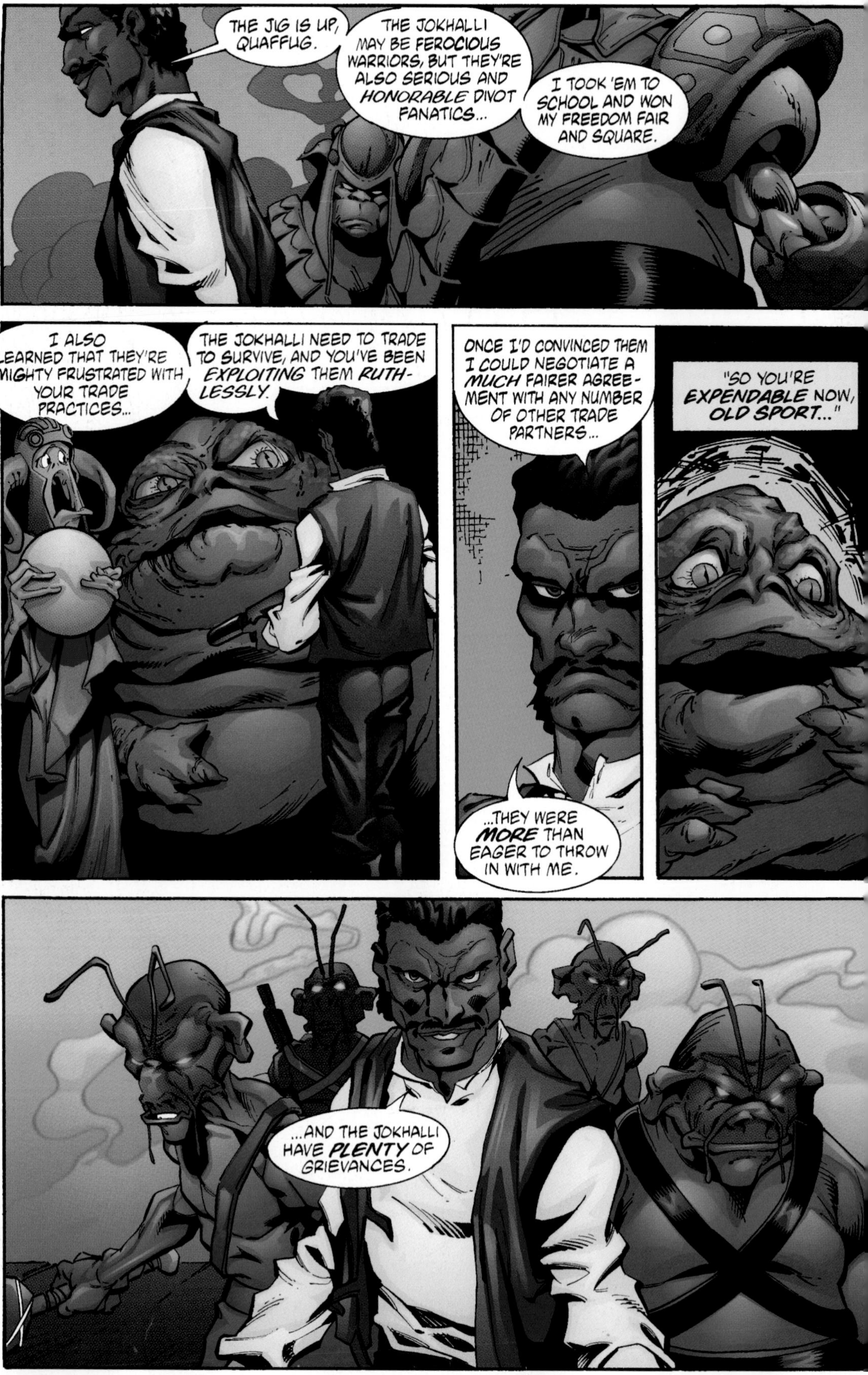
THE JIG IS UP, QUAFFUG.
THE JOKHALLI MAY BE FEROCIOUS WARRIORS, BUT THEY'RE ALSO SERIOUS AND HONORABLE DIVOT FANATICS...
I TOOK 'EM TO SCHOOL AND WON MY FREEDOM FAIR AND SQUARE.
I ALSO LEARNED THAT THEY'RE MIGHTY FRUSTRATED WITH YOUR TRADE PRACTICES...
THE JOKHALLI NEED TO TRADE TO SURVIVE, AND YOU'VE BEEN EXPLOITING THEM RUTH-LESSLY.
ONCE I'D CONVINCED THEM I COULD NEGOTIATE A MUCH FAIRER AGREE-MENT WITH ANY NUMBER OF OTHER TRADE PARTNERS...
...THEY WERE MORE THAN EAGER TO THROW IN WITH ME.
"SO YOU'RE EXPENDABLE NOW, OLD SPORT..."
...AND THE JOKHALLI HAVE PLENTY OF GRIEVANCES.

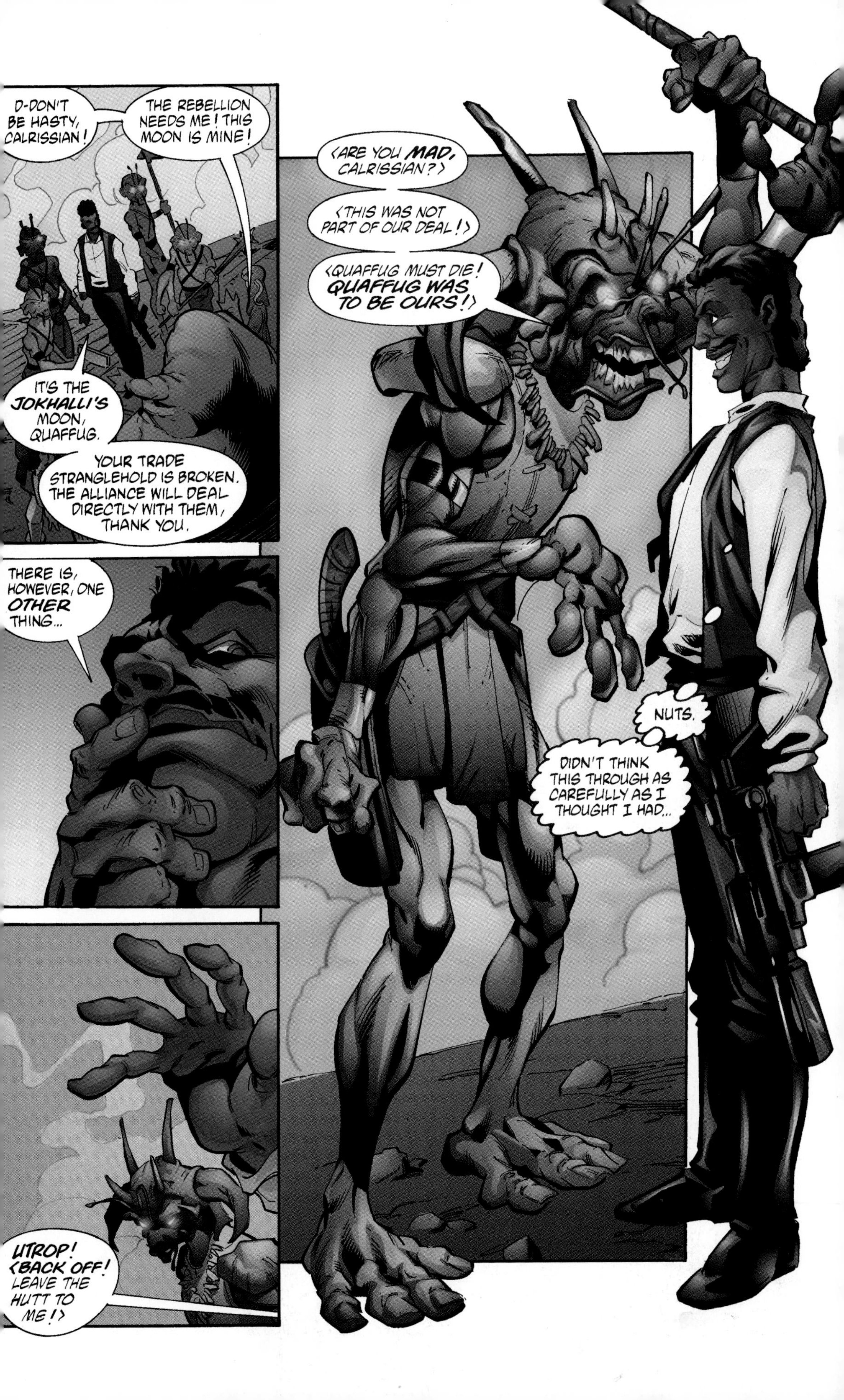
D-DON'T BE HASTY, CALRISSIAN!
THE REBELLION NEEDS ME! THIS MOON IS MINE!
IT'S THE **JOKHALLI'S** MOON, QUAFFUG.
YOUR TRADE STRANGLEHOLD IS BROKEN. THE ALLIANCE WILL DEAL DIRECTLY WITH THEM, THANK YOU.
THERE IS, HOWEVER, ONE **OTHER** THING...
UTROP! <**BACK OFF!** LEAVE THE HUTT TO ME!>
<ARE YOU **MAD,** CALRISSIAN?>
<THIS WAS NOT PART OF OUR DEAL!>
<QUAFFUG MUST DIE! **QUAFFUG WAS TO BE OURS!**>
NUTS.
DIDN'T THINK THIS THROUGH AS CAREFULLY AS I THOUGHT I HAD...

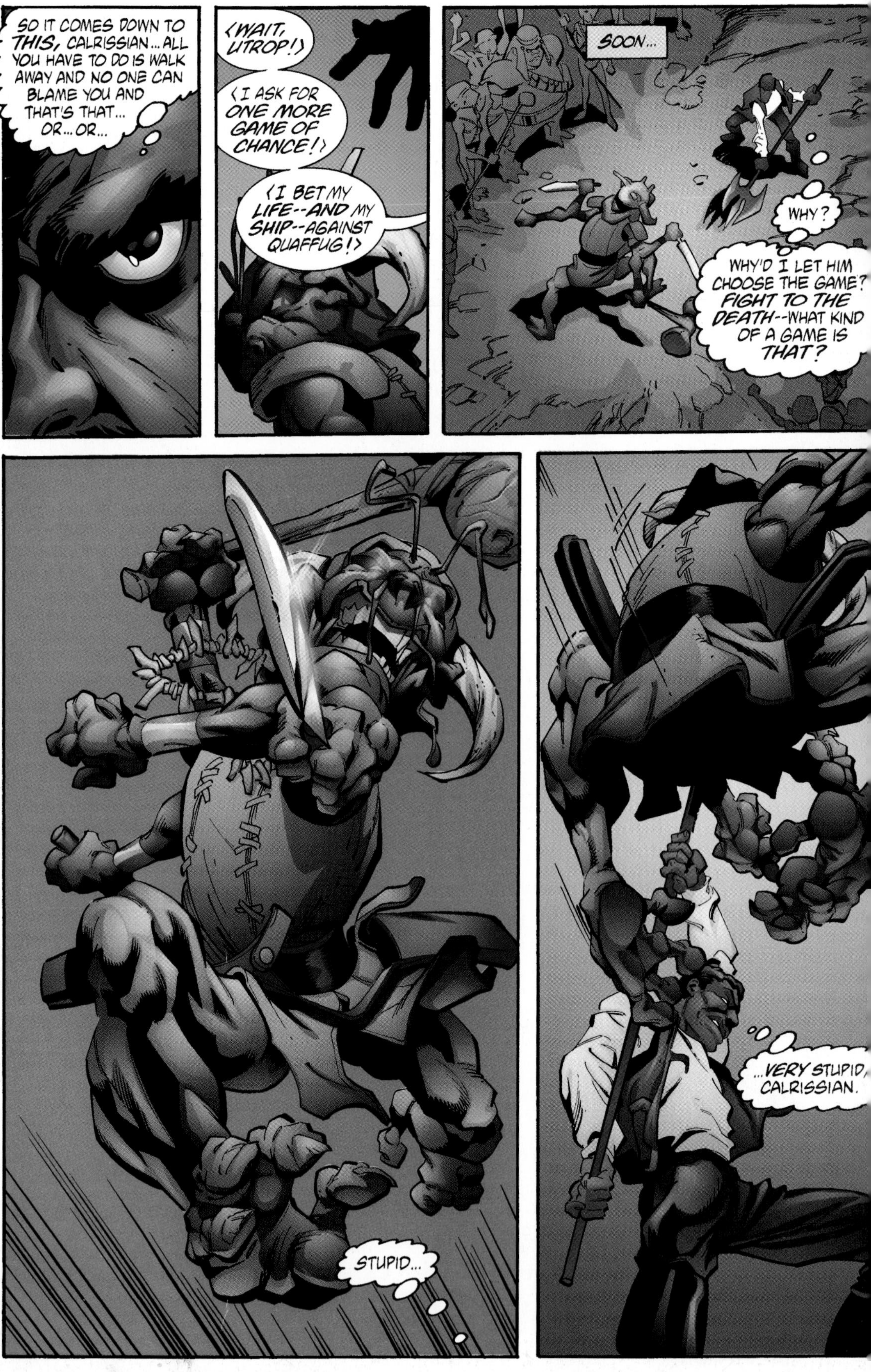
SO IT COMES DOWN TO THIS, CALRISSIAN... ALL YOU HAVE TO DO IS WALK AWAY AND NO ONE CAN BLAME YOU AND THAT'S THAT... OR... OR...
‹WAIT, UTROP!›
‹I ASK FOR ONE MORE GAME OF CHANCE!›
‹I BET MY LIFE--AND MY SHIP--AGAINST QUAFFUG!›
SOON...
WHY?
WHY'D I LET HIM CHOOSE THE GAME? FIGHT TO THE DEATH--WHAT KIND OF A GAME IS THAT?
STUPID...
...VERY STUPID, CALRISSIAN.

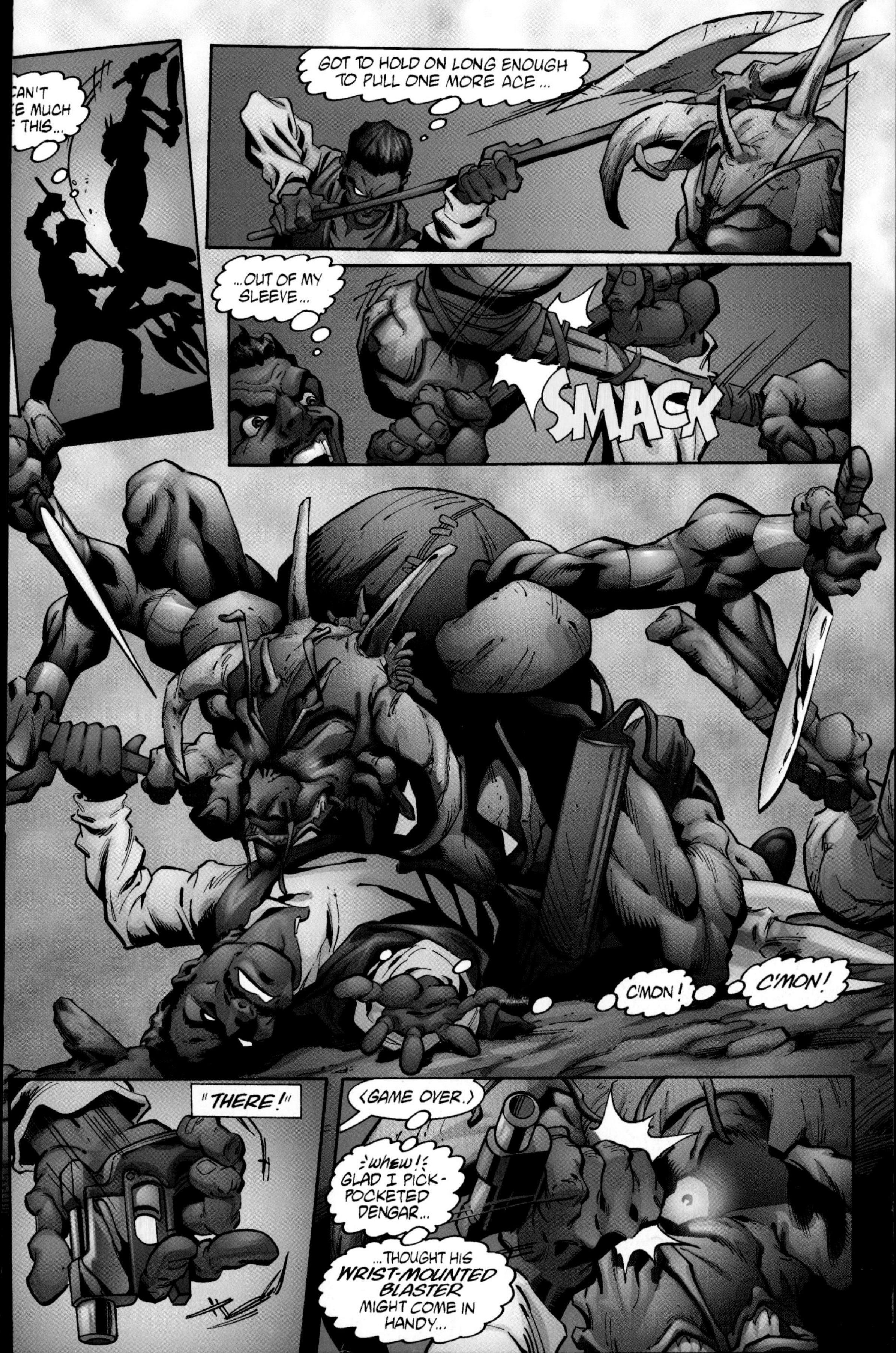
CAN'T E MUCH F THIS...
GOT TO HOLD ON LONG ENOUGH TO PULL ONE MORE ACE ...
...OUT OF MY SLEEVE...
SMACK
C'MON!
C'MON!
"THERE!"
‹GAME OVER.›
WHEW! GLAD I PICK-POCKETED DENGAR...
...THOUGHT HIS WRIST-MOUNTED BLASTER MIGHT COME IN HANDY...

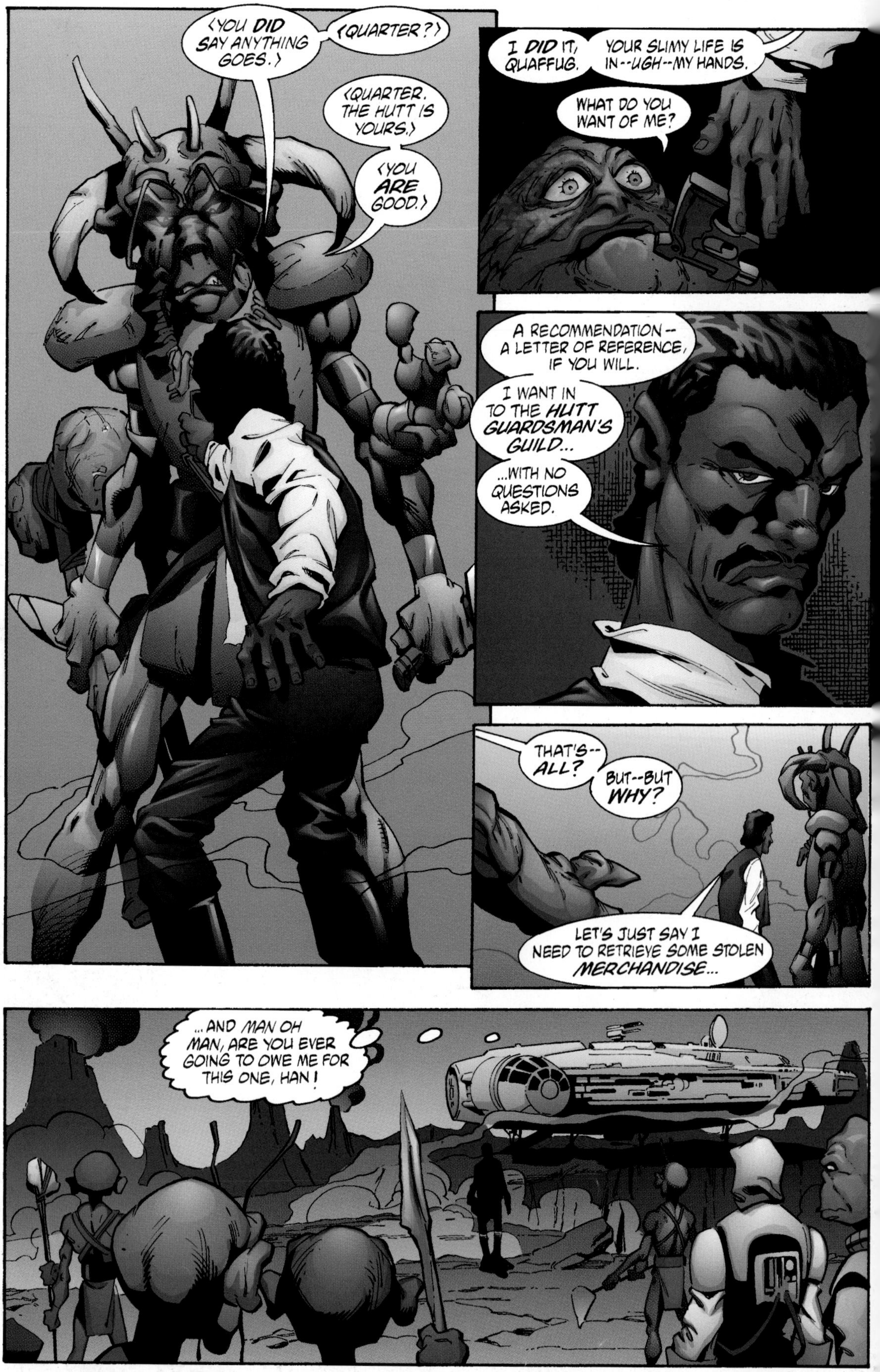
‹YOU DID SAY ANYTHING GOES.›
‹QUARTER?›
‹QUARTER. THE HUTT IS YOURS.›
‹YOU ARE GOOD.›
I DID IT, QUAFFUG.
YOUR SLIMY LIFE IS IN--UGH--MY HANDS.
WHAT DO YOU WANT OF ME?
A RECOMMENDATION -- A LETTER OF REFERENCE, IF YOU WILL.
I WANT IN TO THE HUTT GUARDSMAN'S GUILD...
...WITH NO QUESTIONS ASKED.
THAT'S-- ALL?
BUT--BUT WHY?
LET'S JUST SAY I NEED TO RETRIEVE SOME STOLEN MERCHANDISE...
...AND MAN OH MAN, ARE YOU EVER GOING TO OWE ME FOR THIS ONE, HAN!

THE END

BOBA FETT
TWIN ENGINES OF DESTRUCTION

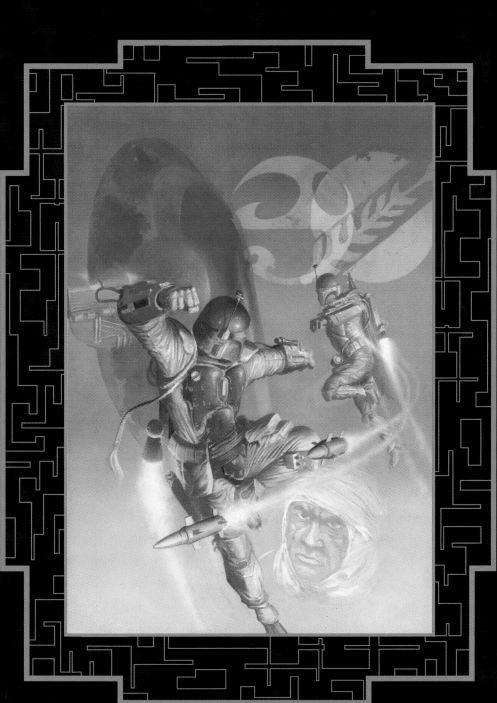

STORY
ANDY MANGELS

PENCILS
JOHN NADEAU

INKS
JORDI ENSIGN

LETTERING
MICHAEL TAYLOR

COLORS
CARY PORTER

TITLE ART
JOHN NADEAU

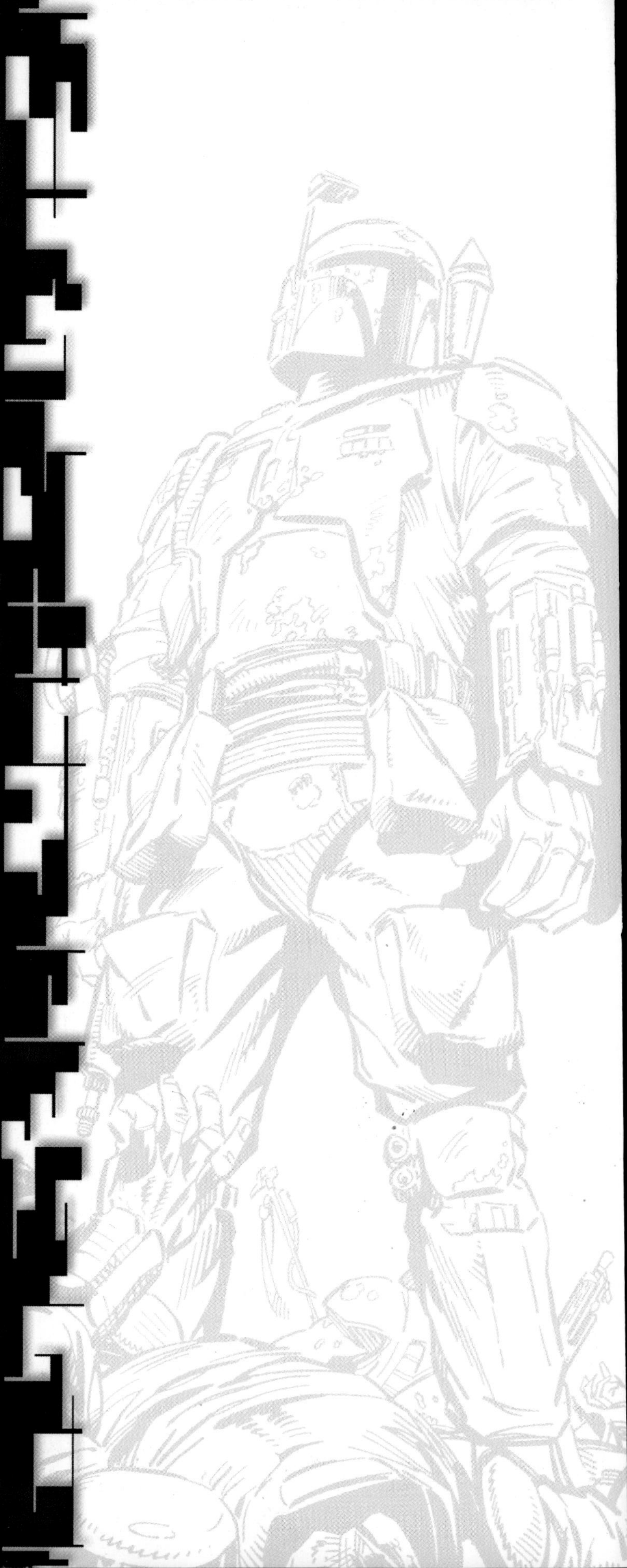

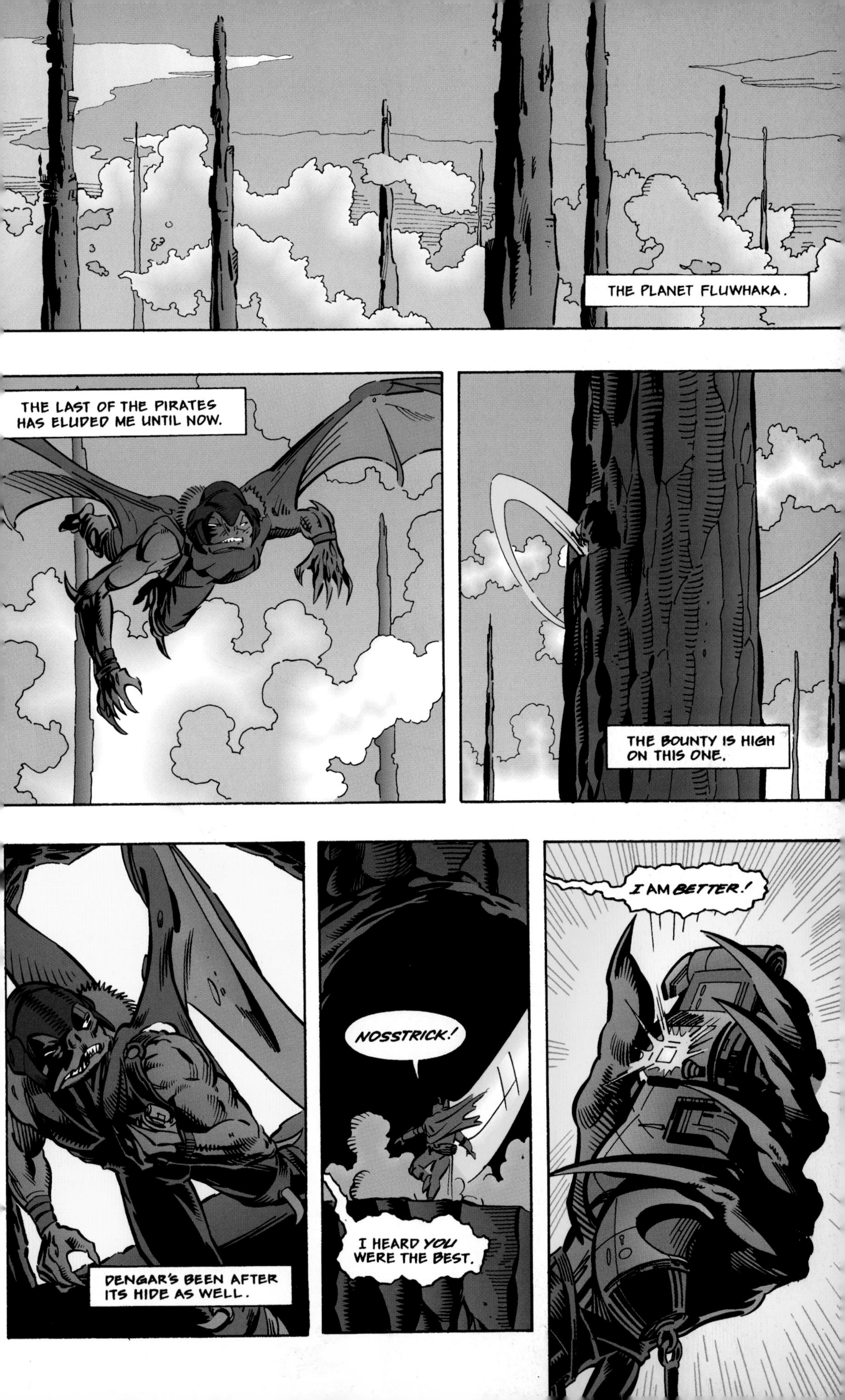
THE PLANET FLUWHAKA.
THE LAST OF THE PIRATES HAS ELUDED ME UNTIL NOW.
THE BOUNTY IS HIGH ON THIS ONE.
DENGAR'S BEEN AFTER ITS HIDE AS WELL.
NOSSTRICK!
I HEARD YOU WERE THE BEST.
I AM BETTER!

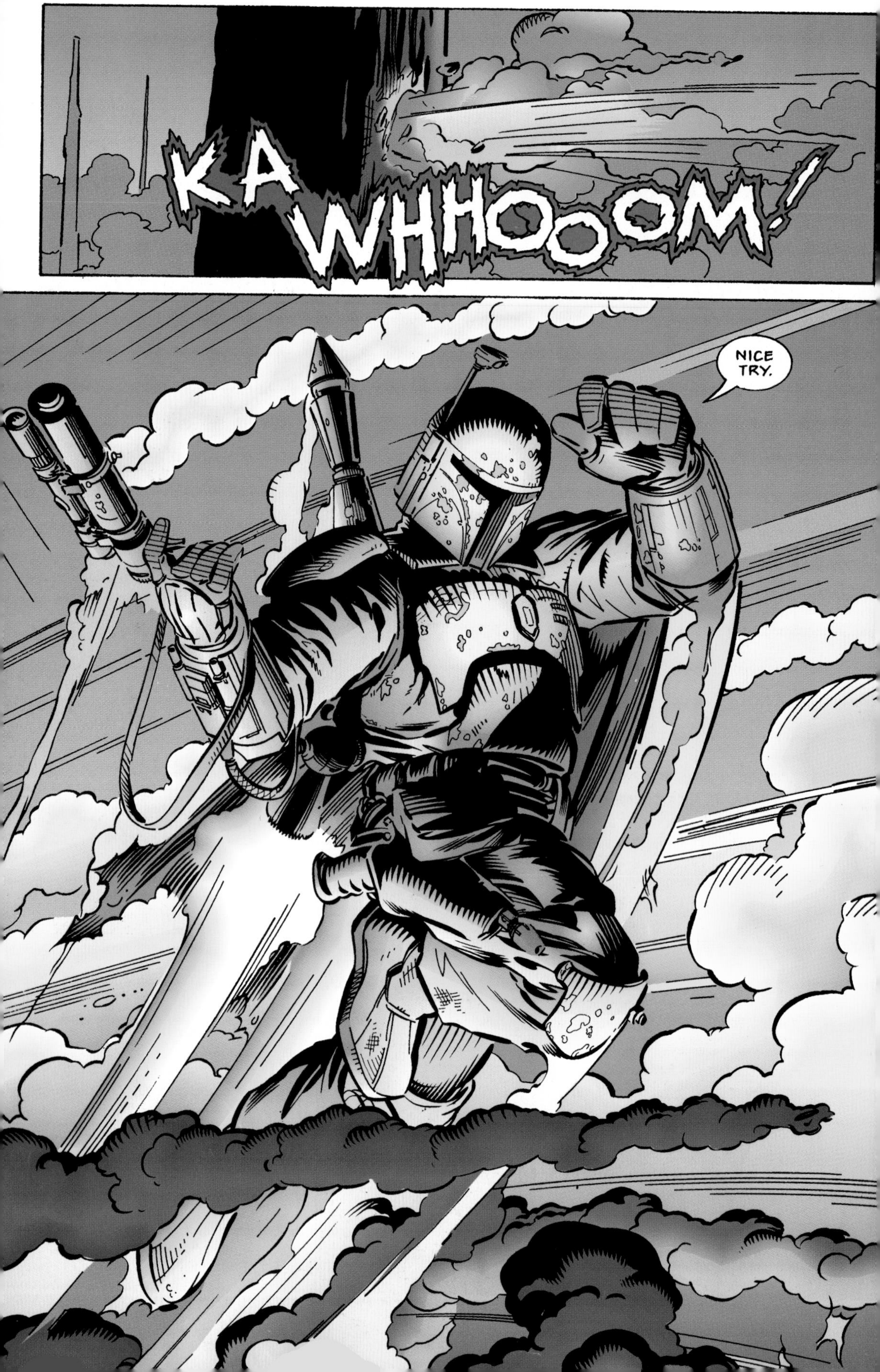
KA
WHHOOOM!
NICE TRY.

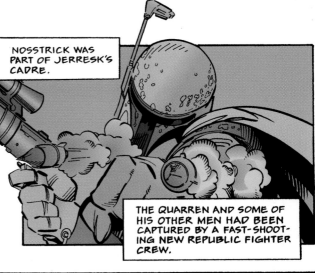

NOSSTRICK WAS PART OF JERRESK'S CADRE.

THE QUARREN AND SOME OF HIS OTHER MEN HAD BEEN CAPTURED BY A FAST-SHOOTING NEW REPUBLIC FIGHTER CREW.

IDENTITY CONFIRMED.

FSSSSTTTT!

ACCCCKK!

KONNNG!

THE CADRE ATTACKED SEVERAL NEW REPUBLIC SUPPLY SHIPMENTS AND GOT A PRICE ON THEIR HEADS. THAT GOT THEM OUT OF THE *HUNDRED CLUB*, AND ONTO THE *MOST WANTED* LIST.

GOT IT.

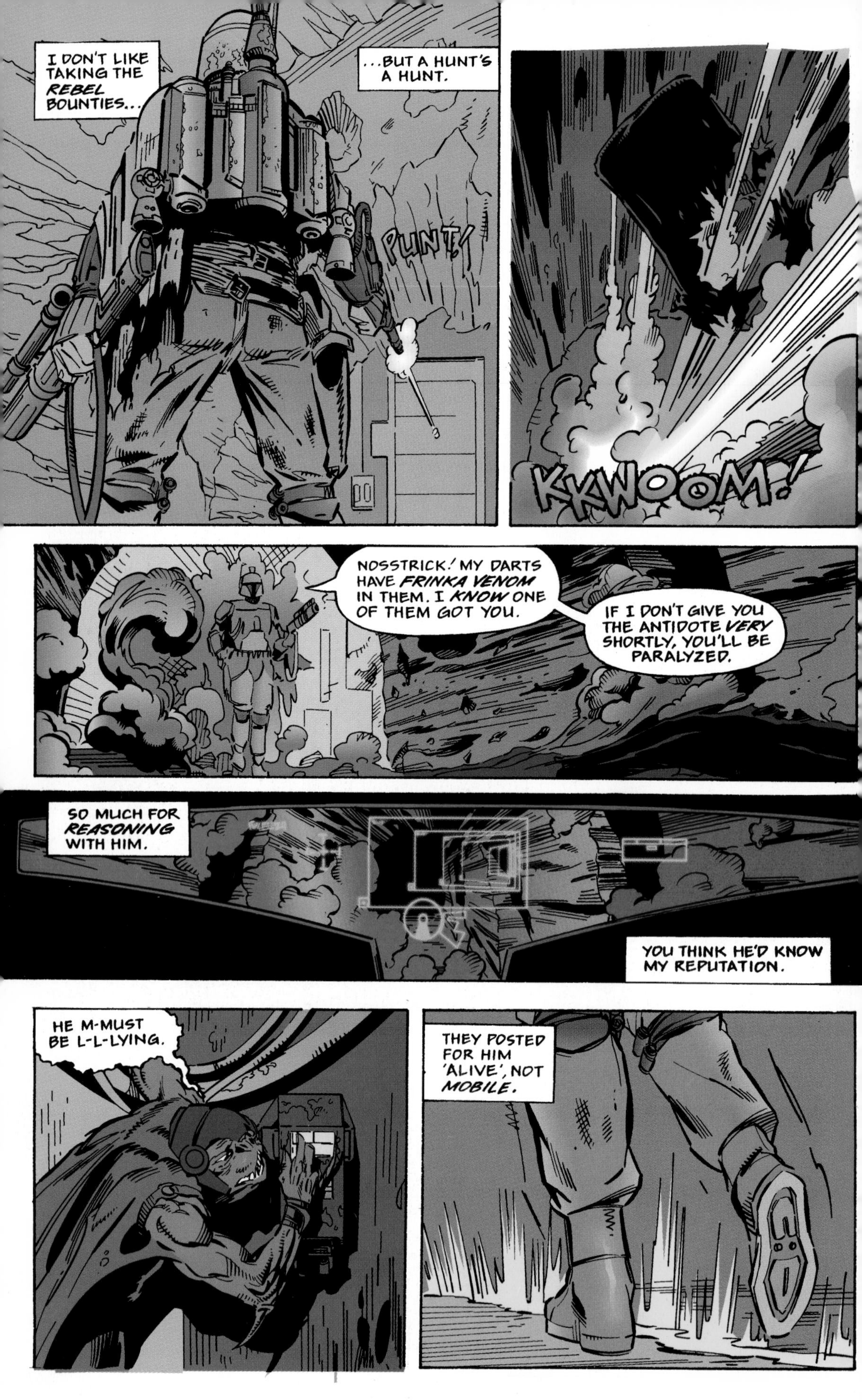
I DON'T LIKE TAKING THE *REBEL* BOUNTIES...
...BUT A HUNT'S A HUNT.
PUNT!
KKWOOM!
NOSSTRICK! MY DARTS HAVE *FRINKA VENOM* IN THEM. I *KNOW* ONE OF THEM GOT YOU.
IF I DON'T GIVE YOU THE ANTIDOTE *VERY* SHORTLY, YOU'LL BE PARALYZED.
SO MUCH FOR *REASONING* WITH HIM.
YOU THINK HE'D KNOW MY REPUTATION.
HE M-MUST BE L-L-LYING.
THEY POSTED FOR HIM 'ALIVE', NOT *MOBILE*.

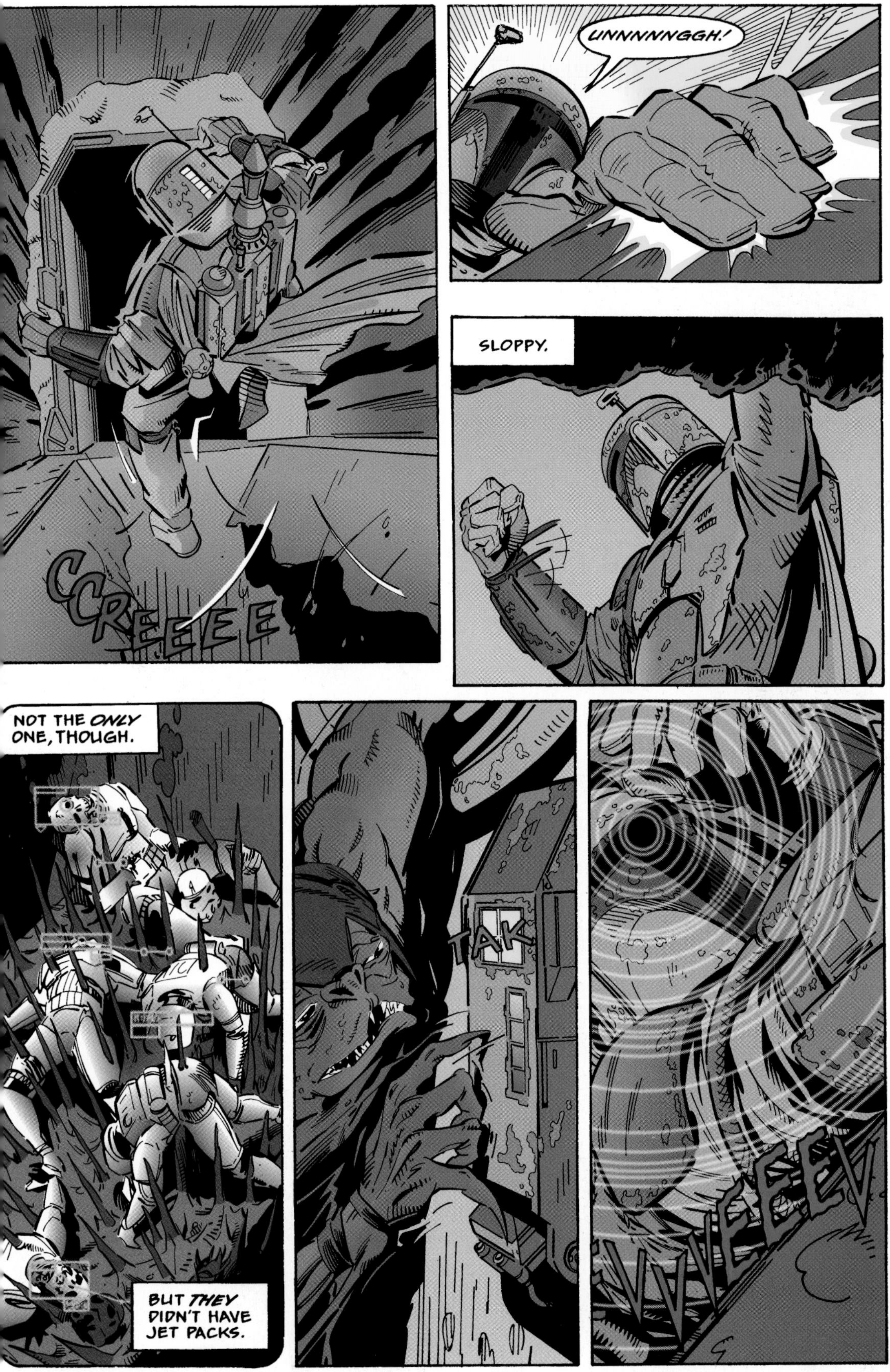
CCREEEEE
UNNNNNGGH!
SLOPPY.
NOT THE ONLY ONE, THOUGH.
BUT THEY DIDN'T HAVE JET PACKS.
TAK
VVVEEEV

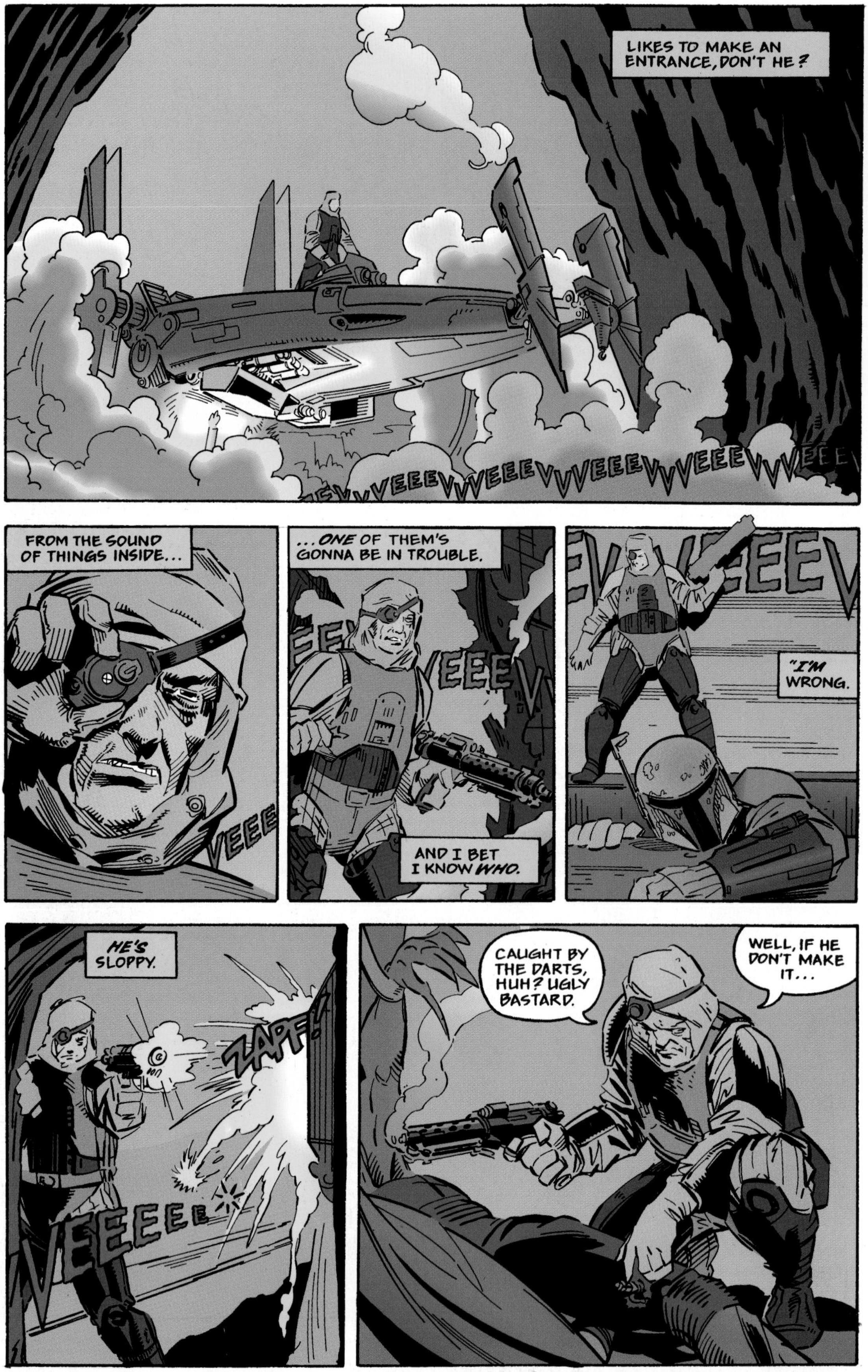
LIKES TO MAKE AN ENTRANCE, DON'T HE?
VVEEEVVVEEEVVVEEEVVVEEEVVVEEE
FROM THE SOUND OF THINGS INSIDE...
VEEE
...ONE OF THEM'S GONNA BE IN TROUBLE.
EEEV
AND I BET I KNOW WHO.
"I'M WRONG.
HE'S SLOPPY.
ZAPF!
VEEEEEE
CAUGHT BY THE DARTS, HUH? UGLY BASTARD.
WELL, IF HE DON'T MAKE IT...

...I GOT MYSELF A BOUNTY.

YOU'VE GOT YOURSELF A *HOLE* IN THE HEAD IF YOU DON'T STEP AWAY.

DROP THE BLASTER.

I PROB'LY SAVED YOUR LIFE, FETT. *AGAIN.*

AND *THIS* IS THE THANKS I--

YOU AIN'T *FETT.*

WHAT MAKES YOU THINK THAT?

BESIDES THE SLOPPY ENTRANCE AND THE CLIFF-HANGIN' HE WAS DOIN', FETT WOULD *NEVER* PULL A BLASTER ON ANOTHER HUNTER.

WELL, *ALMOST* NEVER.

YOU'RE THAT *KAST* GUY, AIN'T YOU? *JODO KAST.*

YOU CAN LOWER THE BLASTER, I'M NOT GONNA RUSH YOU.

NOT *MY* STYLE.

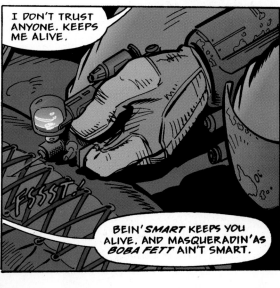

I DON'T TRUST ANYONE. KEEPS ME ALIVE.

FSSST.

BEIN' *SMART* KEEPS YOU ALIVE. AND MASQUERADIN' AS *BOBA FETT* AIN'T SMART.

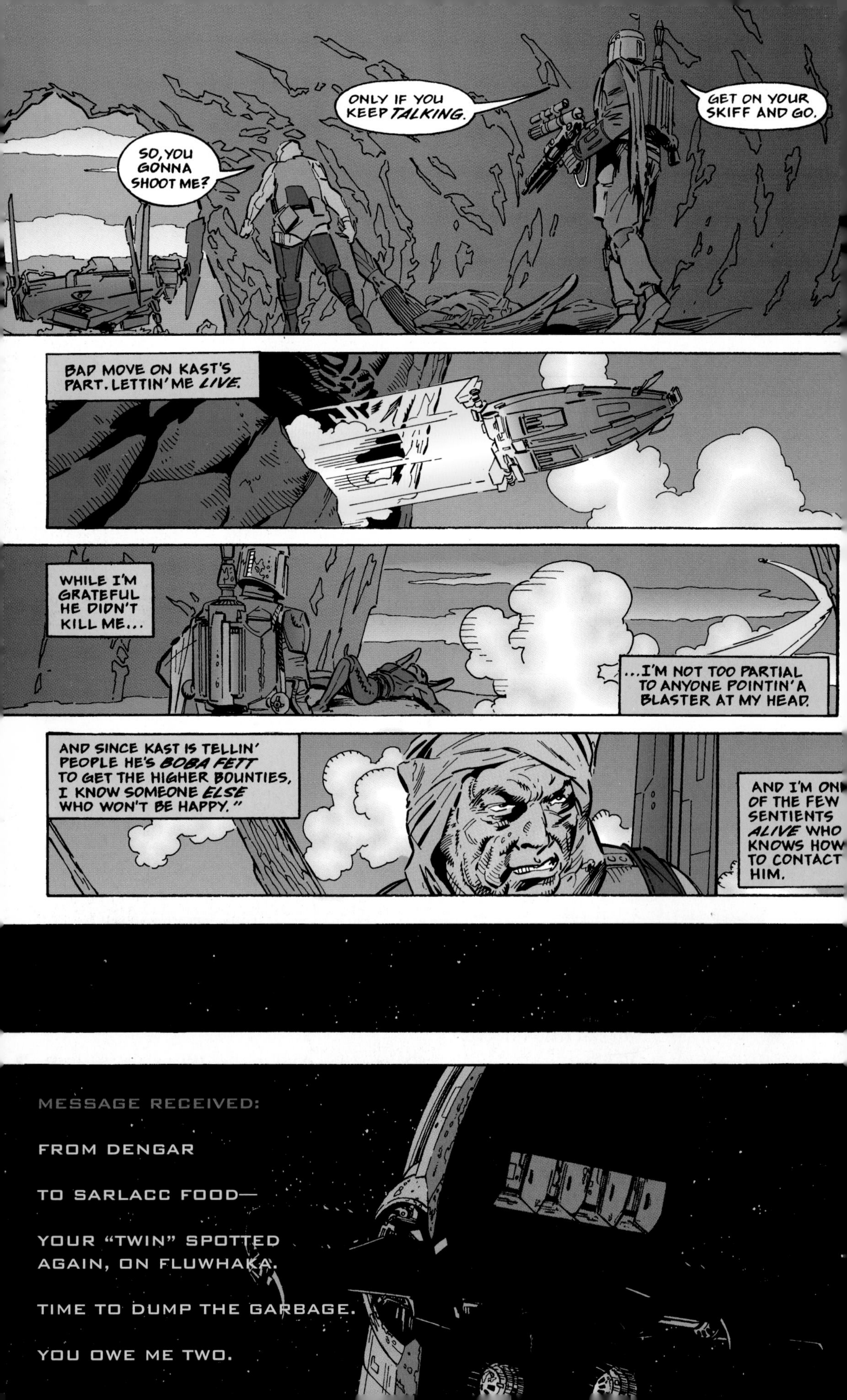
SO, YOU GONNA SHOOT ME?
ONLY IF YOU KEEP *TALKING*.
GET ON YOUR SKIFF AND GO.
BAD MOVE ON KAST'S PART. LETTIN' ME *LIVE*.
WHILE I'M GRATEFUL HE DIDN'T KILL ME...
...I'M NOT TOO PARTIAL TO ANYONE POINTIN' A BLASTER AT MY HEAD.
AND SINCE KAST IS TELLIN' PEOPLE HE'S *BOBA FETT* TO GET THE HIGHER BOUNTIES, I KNOW SOMEONE *ELSE* WHO WON'T BE HAPPY."
AND I'M ONE OF THE FEW SENTIENTS *ALIVE* WHO KNOWS HOW TO CONTACT HIM.
MESSAGE RECEIVED:
FROM DENGAR
TO SARLACC FOOD—
YOUR "TWIN" SPOTTED AGAIN, ON FLUWHAKA.
TIME TO DUMP THE GARBAGE.
YOU OWE ME TWO.

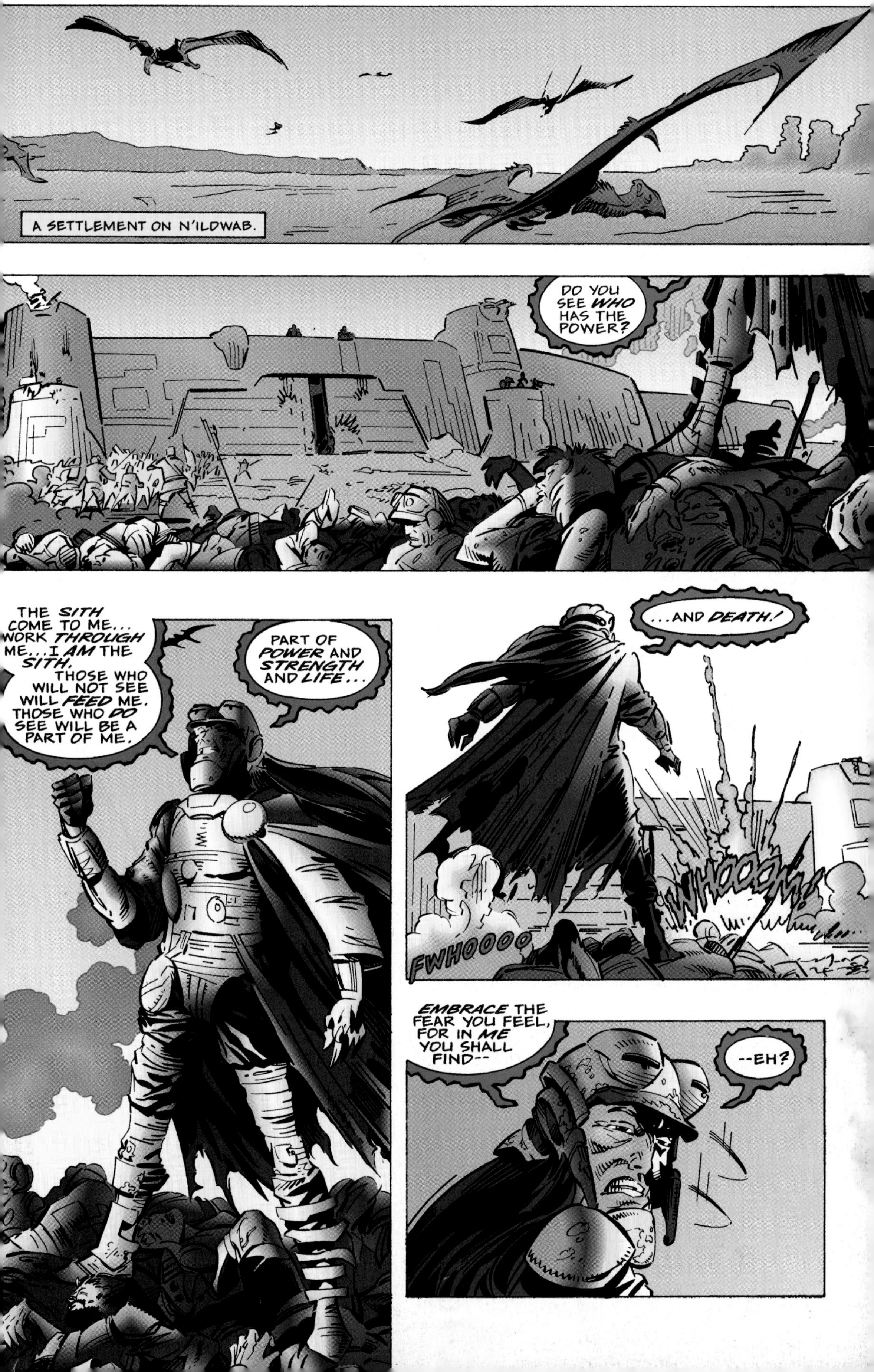
A SETTLEMENT ON N'ILDWAB.
DO YOU SEE WHO HAS THE POWER?
THE SITH COME TO ME... WORK THROUGH ME... I AM THE SITH. THOSE WHO WILL NOT SEE WILL FEED ME. THOSE WHO DO SEE WILL BE A PART OF ME.
PART OF POWER AND STRENGTH AND LIFE...
...AND DEATH!
FWHOOOO
WHOOOM!
EMBRACE THE FEAR YOU FEEL, FOR IN ME YOU SHALL FIND--
--EH?

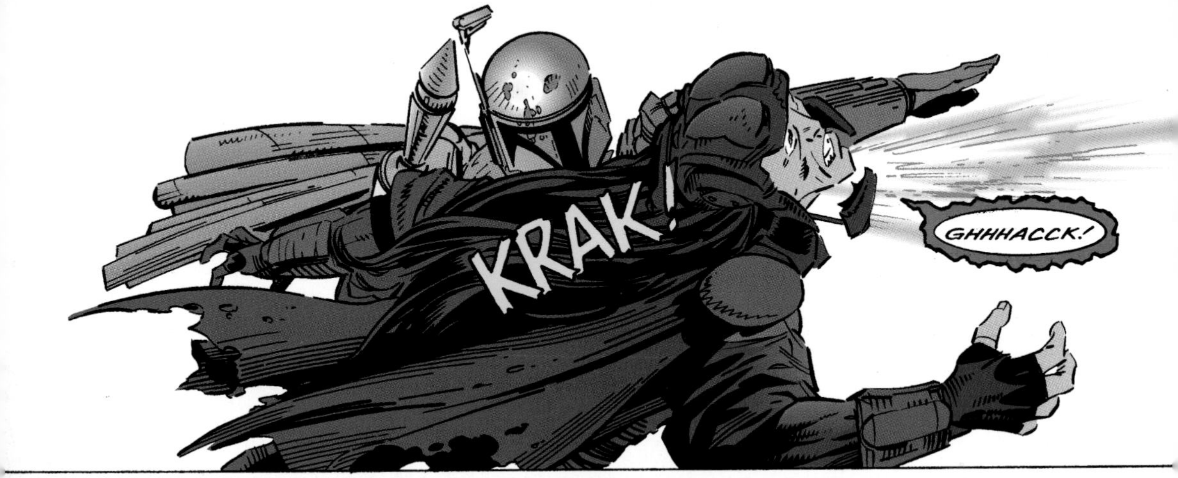
KRAK!
GHHHACCK!

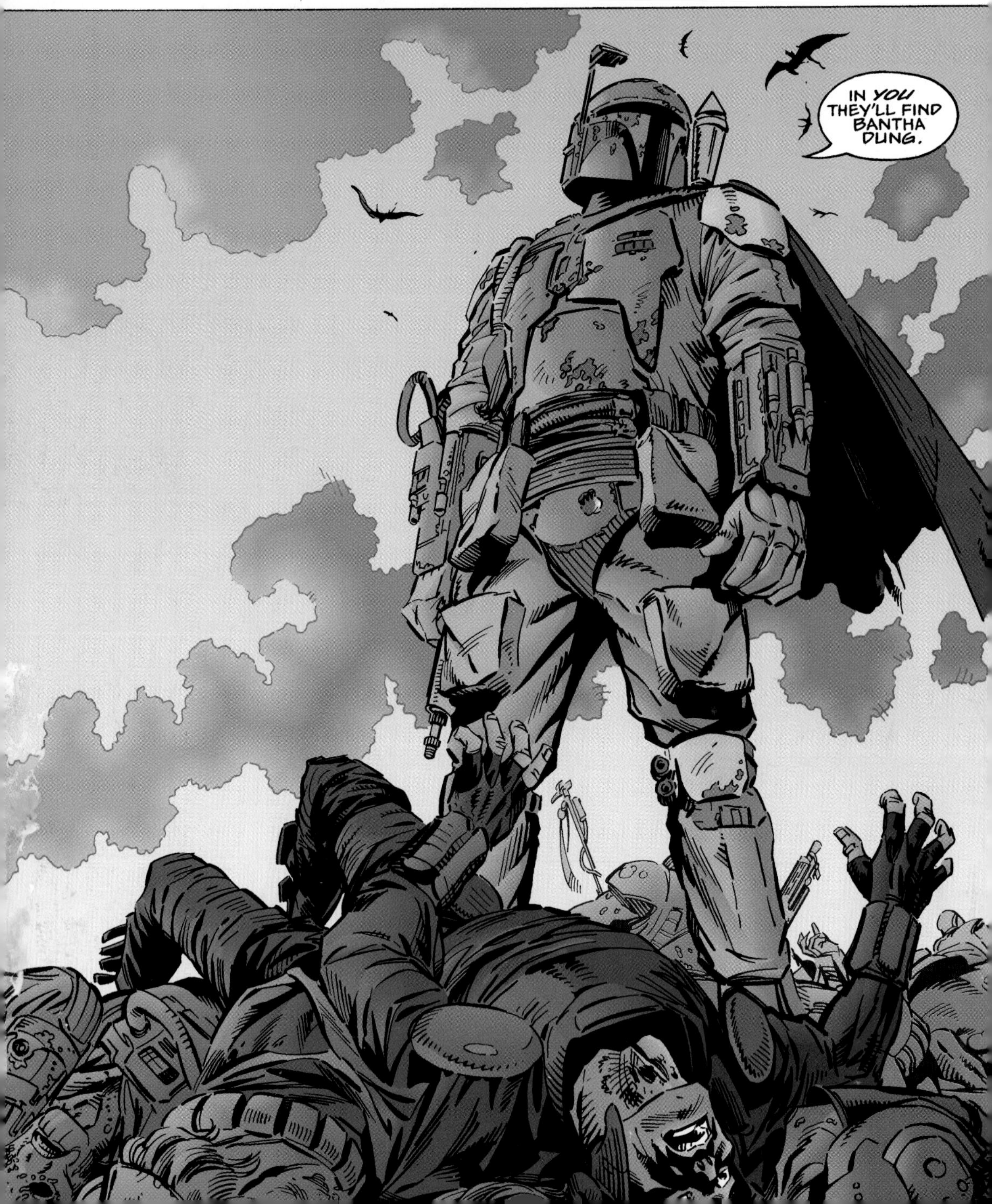
IN YOU THEY'LL FIND BANTHA DUNG.

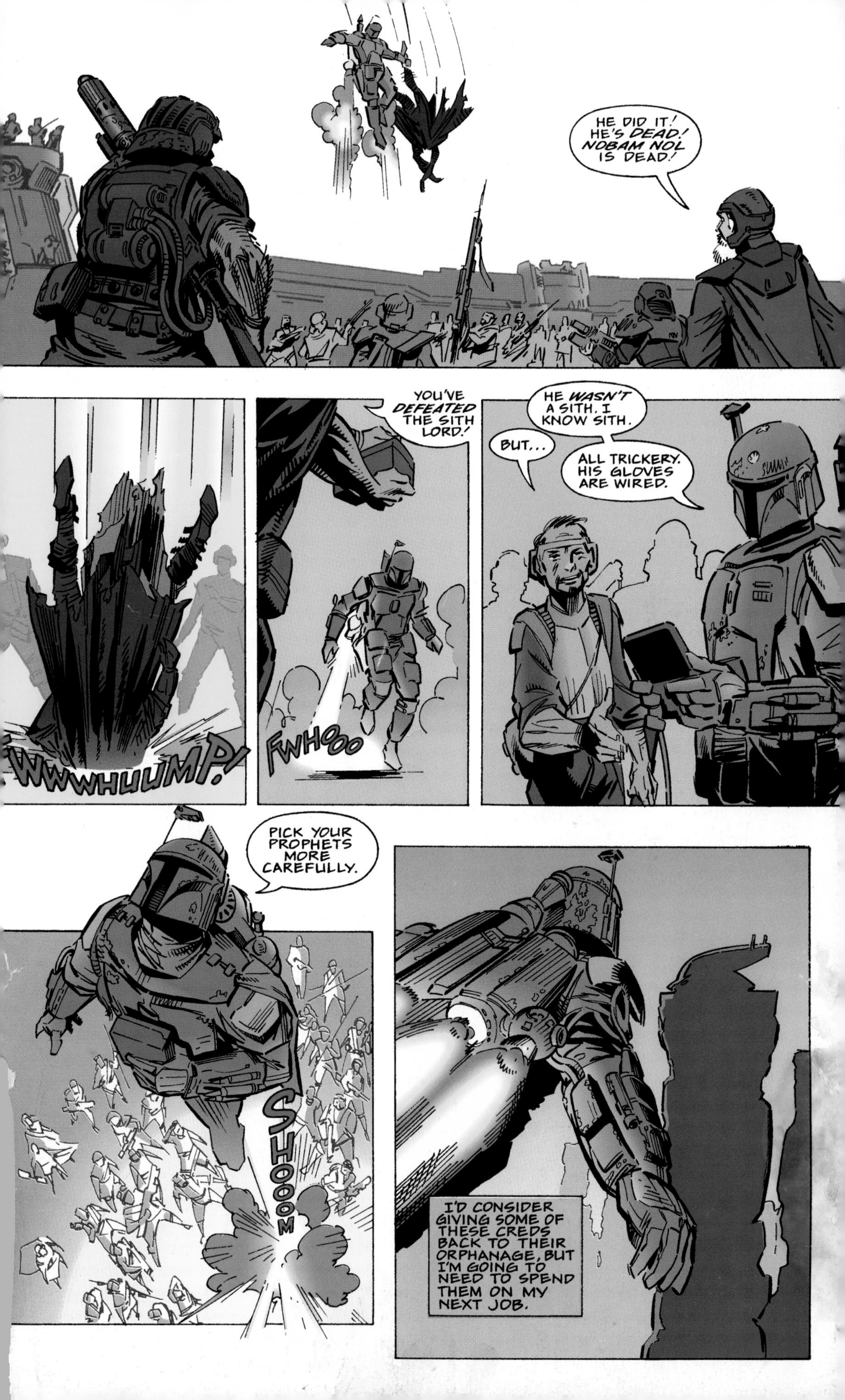
HE DID IT! HE'S DEAD! NOBAM NOL IS DEAD!
WWWHUUMP!
YOU'VE DEFEATED THE SITH LORD!
FWHOOO
HE WASN'T A SITH. I KNOW SITH.
BUT...
ALL TRICKERY. HIS GLOVES ARE WIRED.
PICK YOUR PROPHETS MORE CAREFULLY.
SHOOOM
I'D CONSIDER GIVING SOME OF THESE CREDS BACK TO THEIR ORPHANAGE, BUT I'M GOING TO NEED TO SPEND THEM ON MY NEXT JOB.

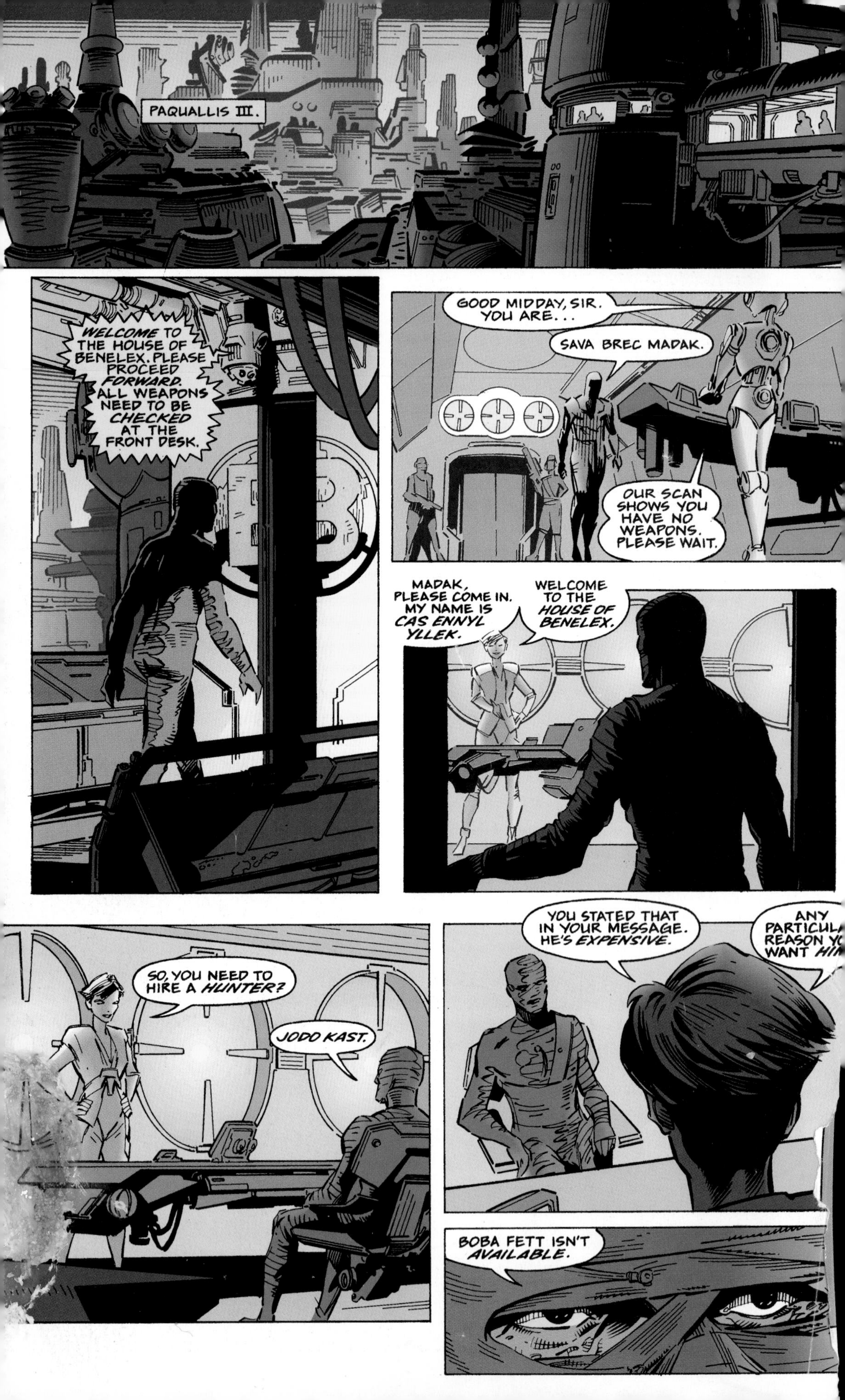
PAQUALLIS III.
WELCOME TO THE HOUSE OF BENELEX. PLEASE PROCEED FORWARD. ALL WEAPONS NEED TO BE CHECKED AT THE FRONT DESK.
GOOD MIDDAY, SIR. YOU ARE...
SAVA BREC MADAK.
OUR SCAN SHOWS YOU HAVE NO WEAPONS. PLEASE WAIT.
MADAK, PLEASE COME IN. MY NAME IS CAS ENNYL YLLEK.
WELCOME TO THE HOUSE OF BENELEX.
SO, YOU NEED TO HIRE A HUNTER?
JODO KAST.
YOU STATED THAT IN YOUR MESSAGE. HE'S EXPENSIVE.
ANY PARTICUL REASON Y WANT HI
BOBA FETT ISN'T AVAILABLE.

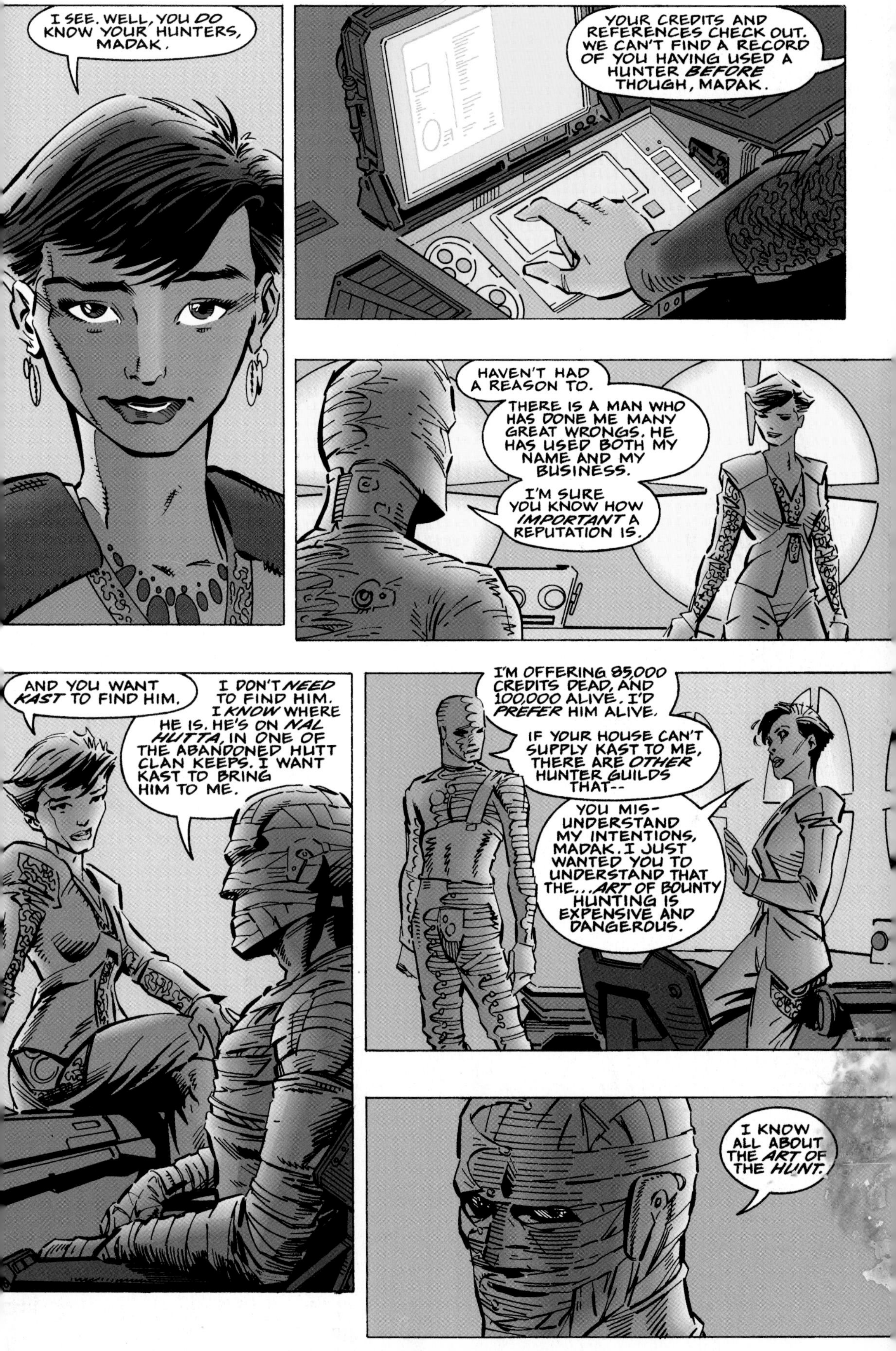
I SEE. WELL, YOU *DO* KNOW YOUR HUNTERS, MADAK.
YOUR CREDITS AND REFERENCES CHECK OUT. WE CAN'T FIND A RECORD OF YOU HAVING USED A HUNTER *BEFORE* THOUGH, MADAK.
HAVEN'T HAD A REASON TO.
THERE IS A MAN WHO HAS DONE ME MANY GREAT WRONGS. HE HAS USED BOTH MY NAME AND MY BUSINESS.
I'M SURE YOU KNOW HOW *IMPORTANT* A REPUTATION IS.
AND YOU WANT *KAST* TO FIND HIM.
I DON'T *NEED* TO FIND HIM. I *KNOW* WHERE HE IS. HE'S ON *NAL HUTTA*, IN ONE OF THE ABANDONED HUTT CLAN KEEPS. I WANT KAST TO BRING HIM TO ME.
I'M OFFERING 85,000 CREDITS DEAD, AND 100,000 ALIVE. I'D *PREFER* HIM ALIVE.
IF YOUR HOUSE CAN'T SUPPLY KAST TO ME, THERE ARE *OTHER* HUNTER GUILDS THAT--
YOU MIS-UNDERSTAND MY INTENTIONS, MADAK. I JUST WANTED YOU TO UNDERSTAND THAT THE... *ART* OF BOUNTY HUNTING IS EXPENSIVE AND DANGEROUS.
I KNOW ALL ABOUT THE *ART* OF THE *HUNT*.

THANK YOU FOR YOUR VISIT TO THE HOUSE OF BENELEX.

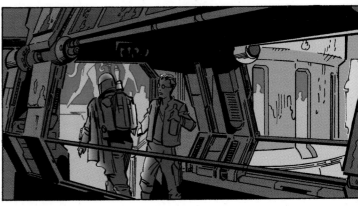

THERE YOU *ARE.* I WONDERED WHAT WAS TAKIN' YOU SO LONG.

A MAN COULD GET *HOPPED UP* ON THESE SYNTH DRINKS.

GWEEZHHA FROOG TABBA *SYNTHALE* ER *STIMULANTS?*

NAW, BABE. WE'RE GONNA HEAD OUT.

SO YOU *HIRED* KAST?

YES.

URRRRRRRP.

BACK TO THE SHIP THEN, IS IT?

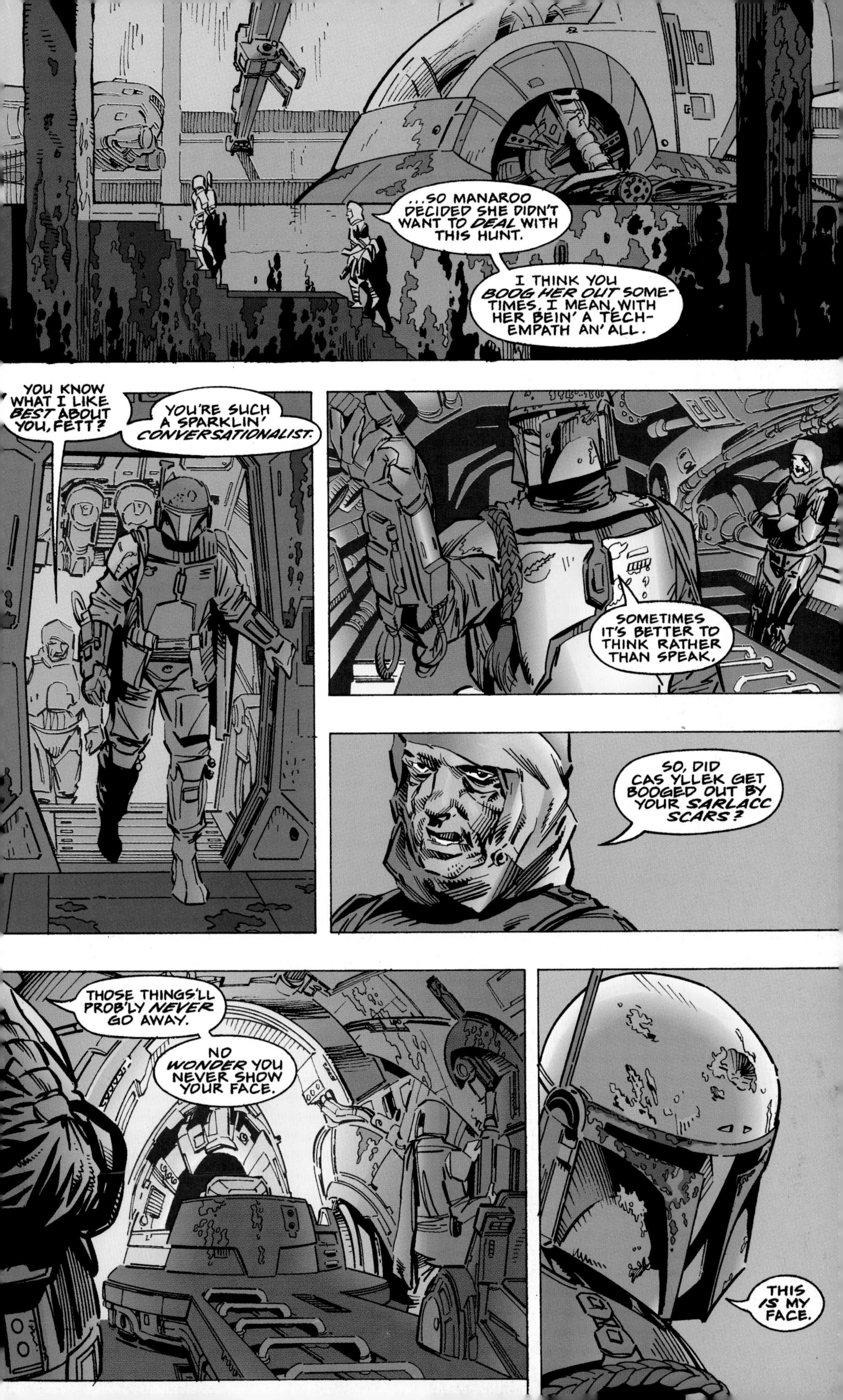
...SO MANAROO DECIDED SHE DIDN'T WANT TO *DEAL* WITH THIS HUNT.
I THINK YOU *BOOG HER OUT* SOMETIMES. I MEAN, WITH HER BEIN' A TECH-EMPATH AN' ALL.
YOU KNOW WHAT I LIKE *BEST* ABOUT YOU, FETT?
YOU'RE SUCH A SPARKLIN' *CONVERSATIONALIST.*
SOMETIMES IT'S BETTER TO THINK RATHER THAN SPEAK.
SO, DID CAS YLLEK GET BOOGED OUT BY YOUR *SARLACC SCARS?*
THOSE THINGS'LL PROB'LY *NEVER* GO AWAY.
NO *WONDER* YOU NEVER SHOW YOUR FACE.
THIS *IS* MY FACE.

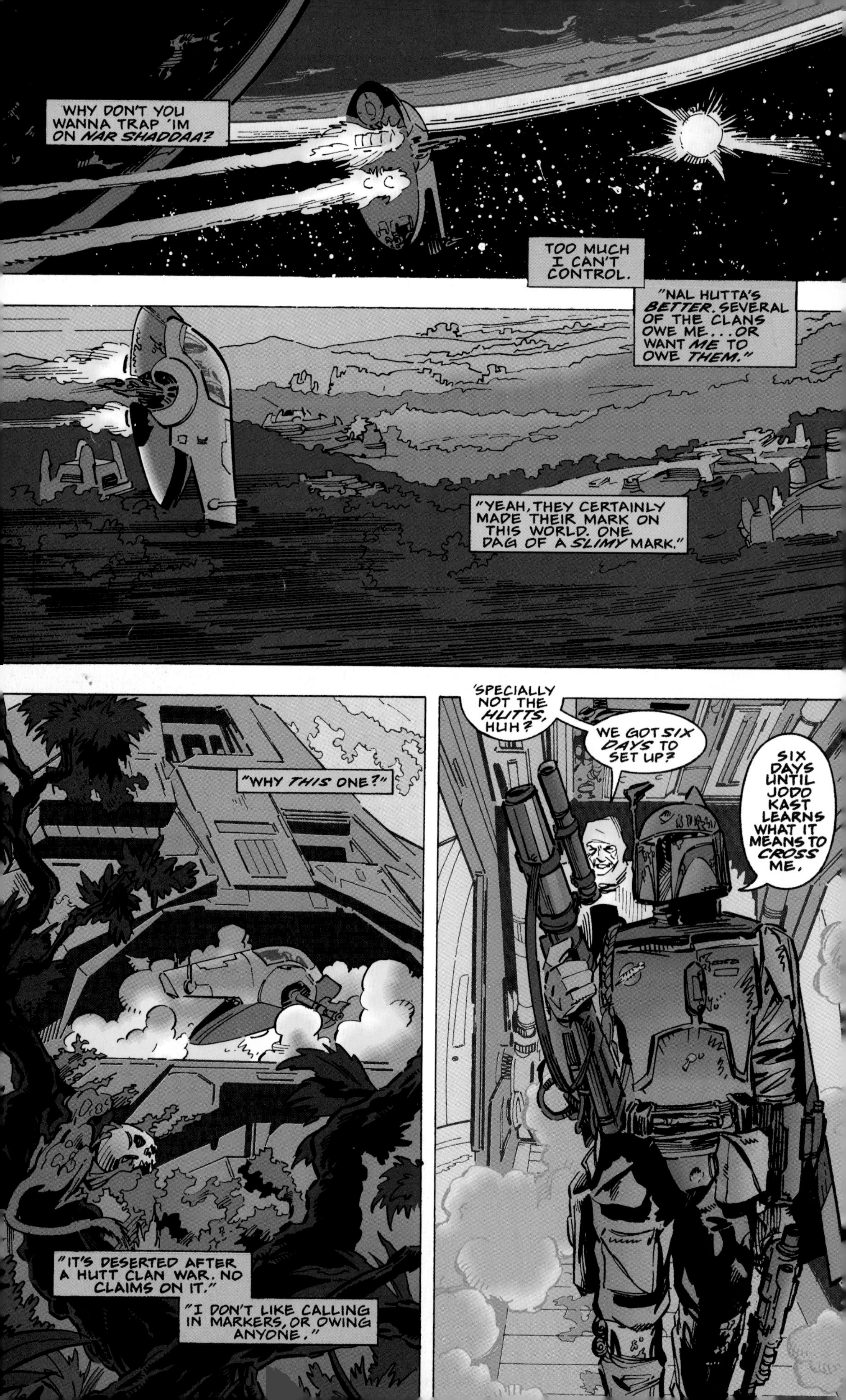

WHY DON'T YOU WANNA TRAP 'IM ON *NAR SHADDAA?*
TOO MUCH I CAN'T CONTROL.
"NAL HUTTA'S *BETTER*. SEVERAL OF THE CLANS OWE ME . . . OR WANT *ME* TO OWE *THEM.*"
"YEAH, THEY CERTAINLY MADE THEIR MARK ON THIS WORLD. ONE DAG OF A *SLIMY* MARK."
"WHY *THIS* ONE?"
"IT'S DESERTED AFTER A HUTT CLAN WAR. NO CLAIMS ON IT."
"I DON'T LIKE CALLING IN MARKERS, OR OWING ANYONE."
'SPECIALLY NOT THE *HUTTS,* HUH?
WE GOT *SIX DAYS* TO SET UP?
SIX DAYS UNTIL JODO KAST LEARNS WHAT IT MEANS TO *CROSS* ME.

NAL HUTTA.

THE HUTT HOME-WORLD. THEY *RENAMED* IT AFTER THEY DROVE ALL THE EVOCII OFF-PLANET.

THE NAME MEANS '*GLORIOUS JEWEL*' IN HUTTESE.

CERTAIN PARTS OF THE PLANET STILL *ARE* BEAUTIFUL IF YOU LIKE PLANTS, BUT THE HUTTS HAVE ERECTED ALL SORTS OF PALACES, PLEASURE GARDENS, AND CLAN HOUSES.

BUT I'M NOT HERE FOR *SIGHT-SEEING*.

SOME RICH GUY NAMED *MADAK* HAS HIRED ME TO CAPTURE SATNIK HIICROP.

HIICROP HAS APPARENTLY BEEN MASQUERADING *AS* MADAK AND SCREWING UP SOME JOBS.

BENELEX GUILD TOLD ME I GOT HIRED BECAUSE BOBA FETT WASN'T AVAILABLE.

THE *IRONY* DIDN'T ESCAPE THEM OR ME. I'VE GOTTEN *MORE* THAN A FEW JOBS BECAUSE I'VE GOT THE SAME MANDALORIAN ARMOR AS FETT.

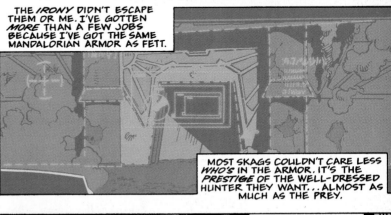

MOST SKAGS COULDN'T CARE LESS WHO'S IN THE ARMOR. IT'S THE *PRESTIGE* OF THE WELL-DRESSED HUNTER THEY WANT... ALMOST AS MUCH AS THE PREY.

SO WHAT IF A FEW OF THEM THINK I'M *FETT*? I'M *BETTER* THAN THAT OLD FOSSIL, ANYHOW.

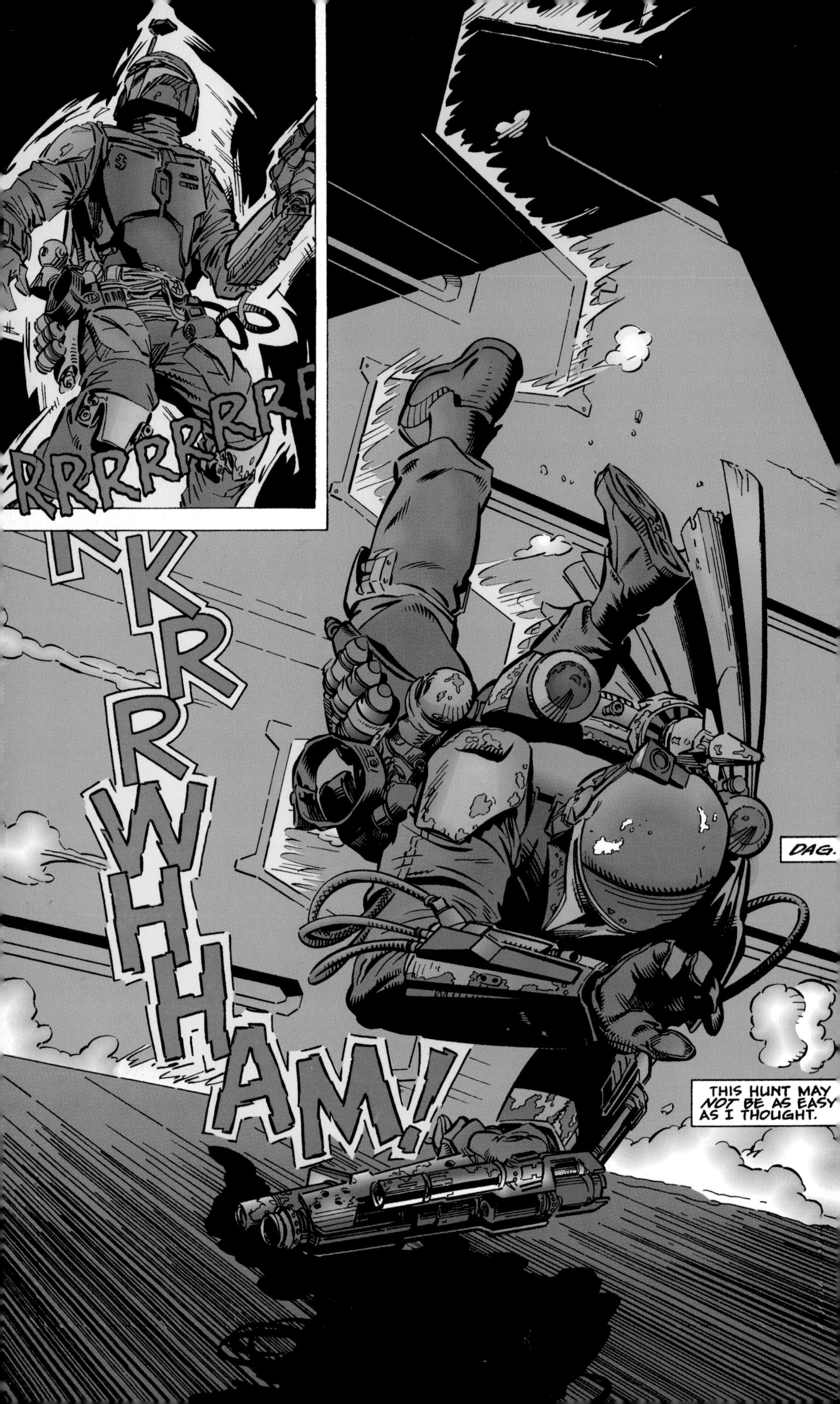
RRRRRRRRR
KRRWHHHAM!
DAG.
THIS HUNT MAY *NOT* BE AS EASY AS I THOUGHT.

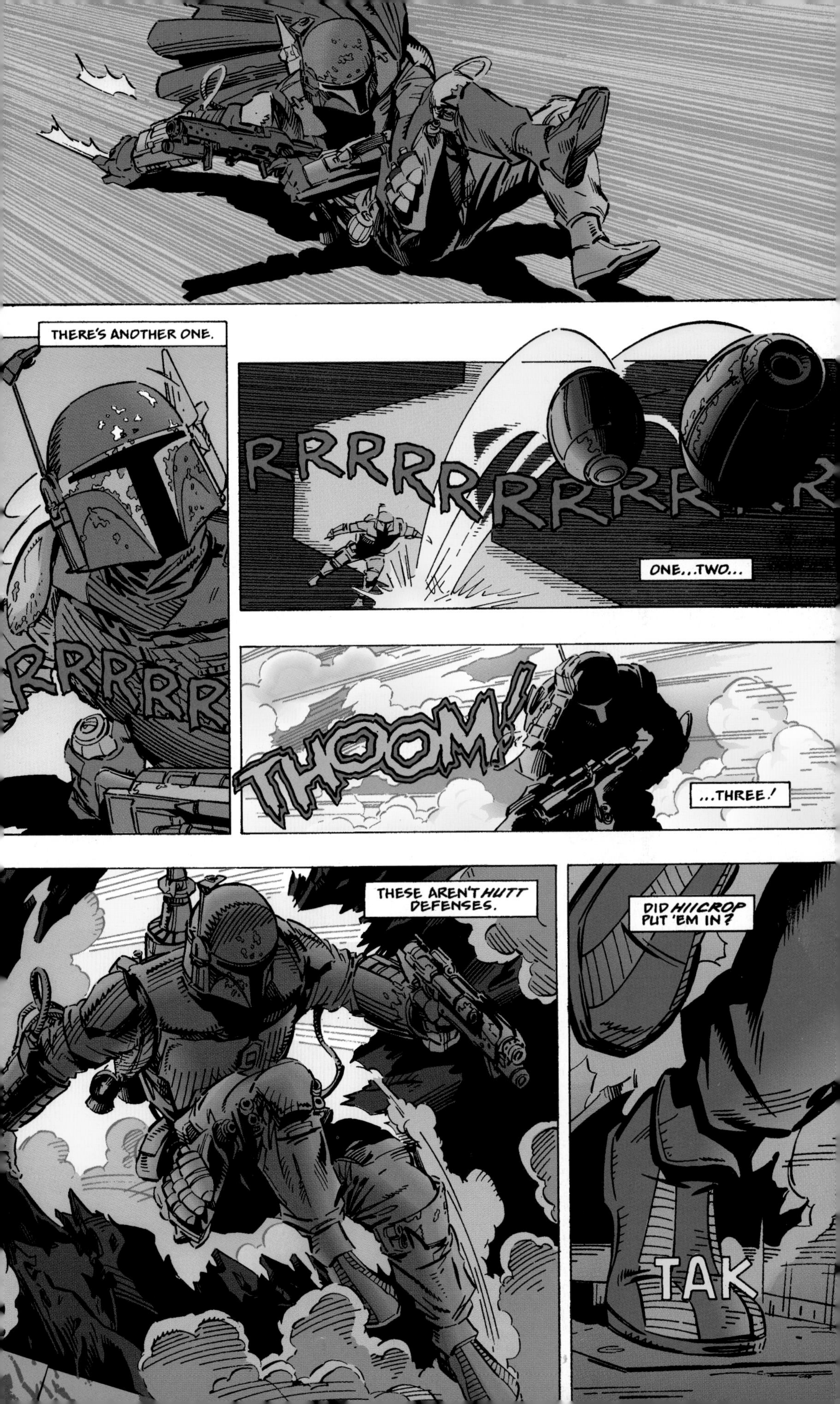
THERE'S ANOTHER ONE.
RRRRRRRRRRRRRR
RRRRRR
ONE...TWO...
THOOM!!
...THREE!
THESE AREN'T HUTT DEFENSES.
DID HIICROP PUT 'EM IN?
TAK

LASER WEBS?

SOMEONE'S GONE TO A *LOT* OF TROUBLE TO KEEP ME AWAY.

WALLS WERE BAREL' SCRATCHED BY THE GRENADE. THEY'RE TOO *THICK.*

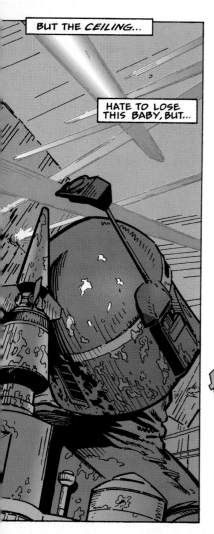

BUT THE *CEILING...*

HATE TO LOSE THIS BABY, BUT...

FWOOSH

WHOOOM

'COURSE, WHEN AM I GONNA USE A MAGNETIC GRAPPLER?"

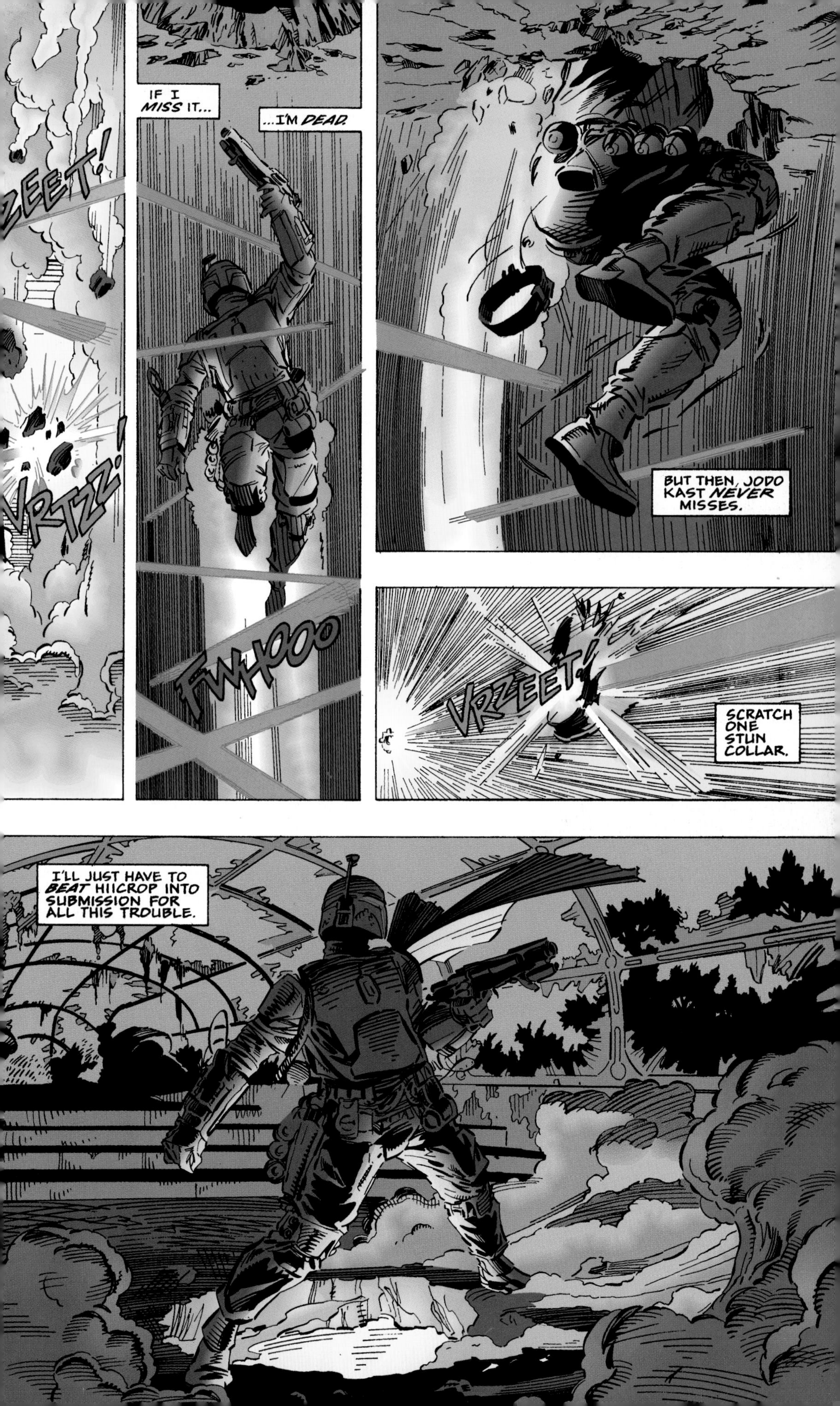

ZEET!
VRTZZ!
IF I MISS IT...
...I'M DEAD.
FWHOOO
BUT THEN, JODO KAST NEVER MISSES.
VRZEET!
SCRATCH ONE STUN COLLAR.
I'LL JUST HAVE TO BEAT HIICROP INTO SUBMISSION FOR ALL THIS TROUBLE.

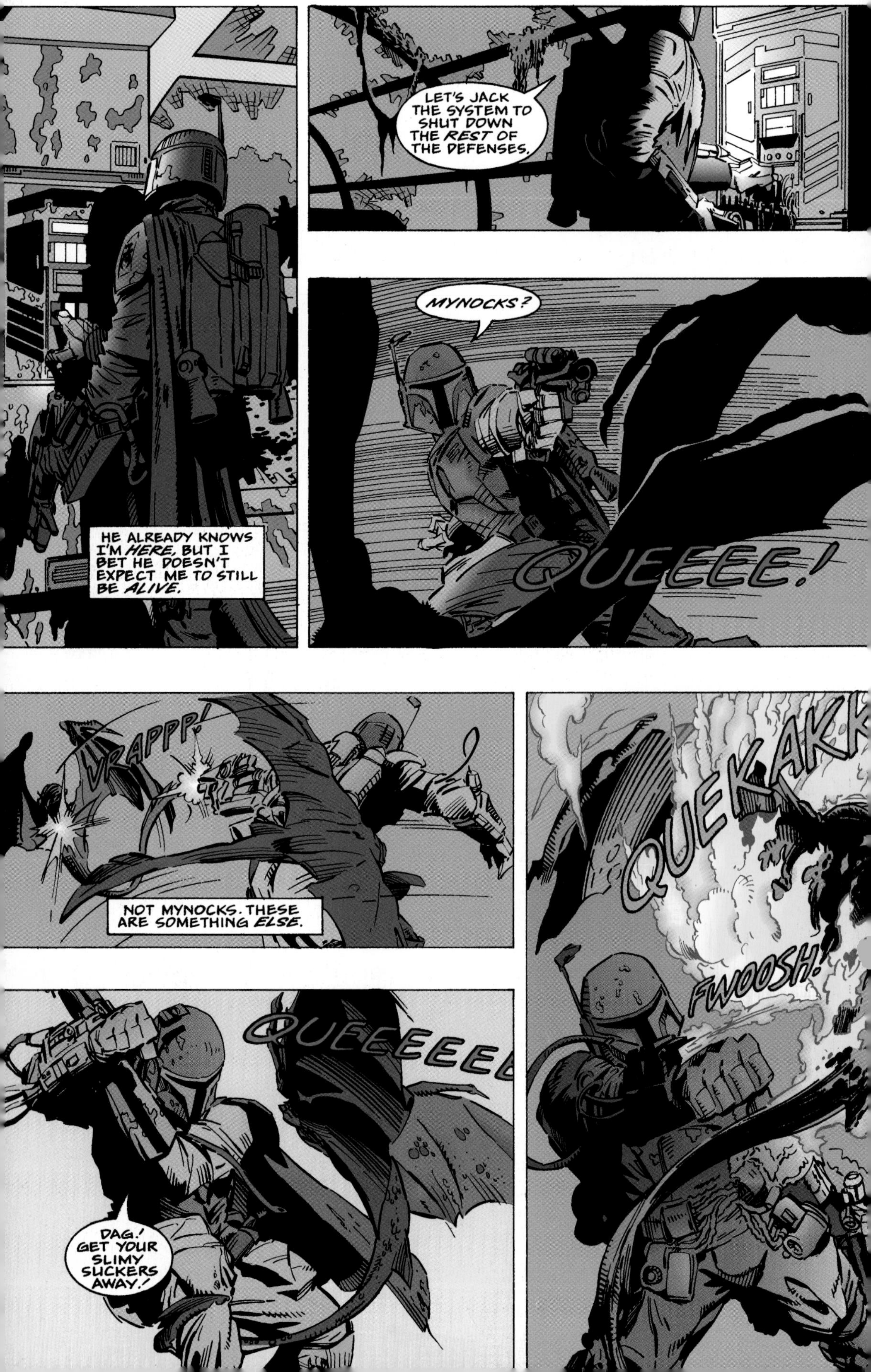
LET'S JACK THE SYSTEM TO SHUT DOWN THE REST OF THE DEFENSES.
HE ALREADY KNOWS I'M HERE, BUT I BET HE DOESN'T EXPECT ME TO STILL BE ALIVE.
MYNOCKS?
QUEEEEE!
VRAPPP!
NOT MYNOCKS. THESE ARE SOMETHING ELSE.
QUEEEEEE
DAG! GET YOUR SLIMY SUCKERS AWAY!
QUEKAKK
FWOOSH!

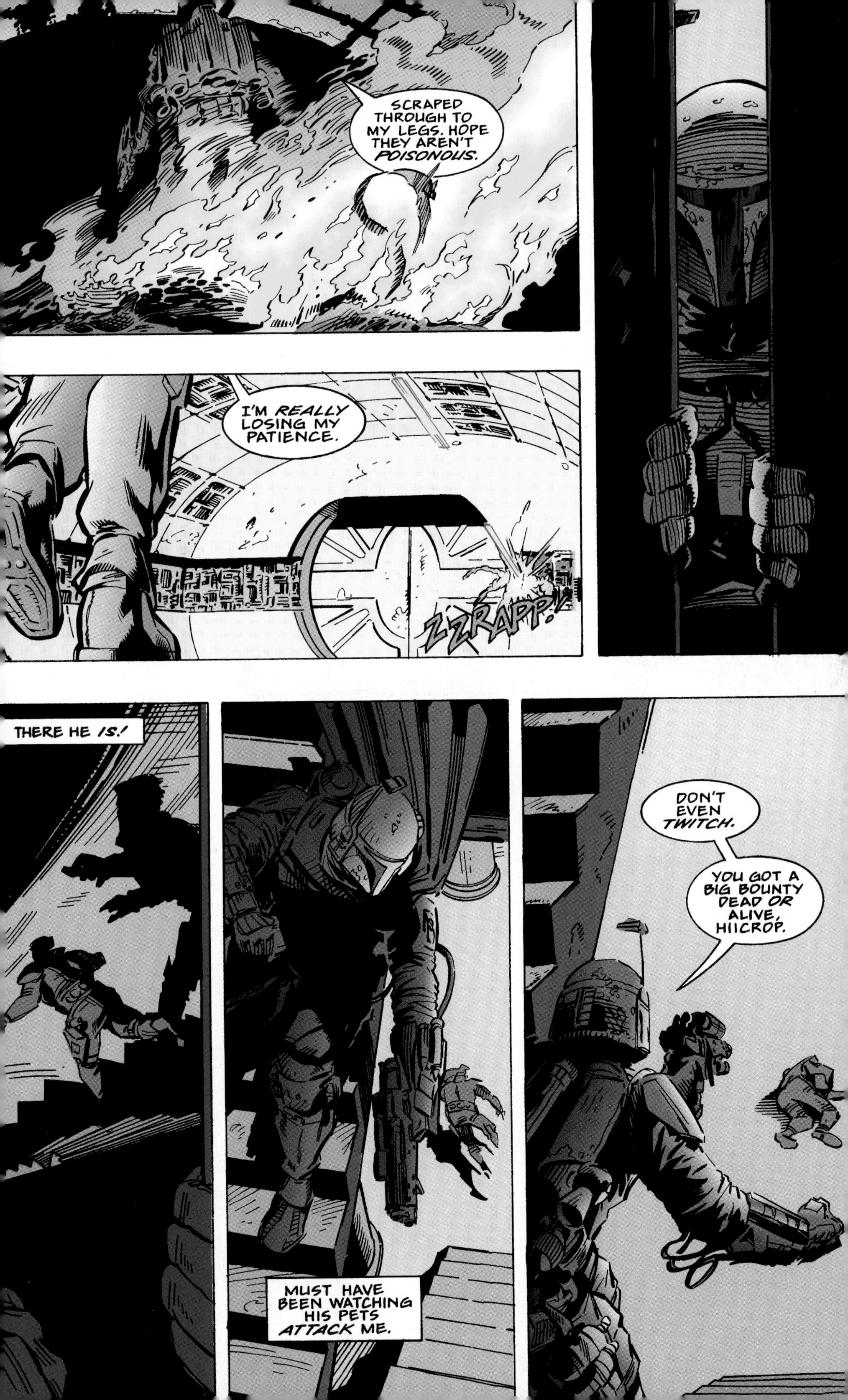
SCRAPED THROUGH TO MY LEGS. HOPE THEY AREN'T POISONOUS.
I'M REALLY LOSING MY PATIENCE.
Z'ZRAPP!
THERE HE IS!
MUST HAVE BEEN WATCHING HIS PETS ATTACK ME.
DON'T EVEN TWITCH.
YOU GOT A BIG BOUNTY DEAD OR ALIVE, HIICROP.

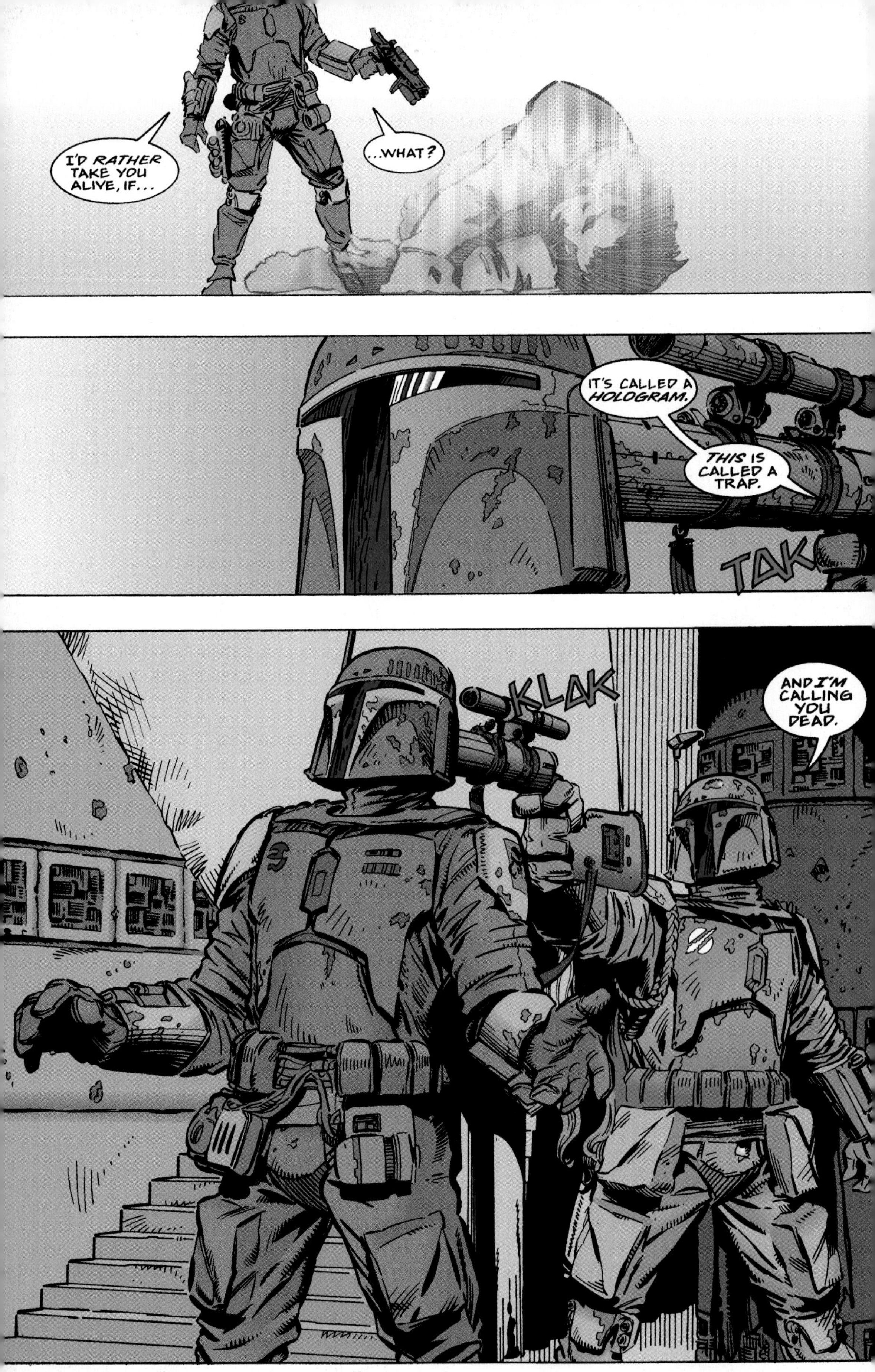
I'D *RATHER* TAKE YOU ALIVE, IF...
...WHAT?
IT'S CALLED A *HOLOGRAM.*
THIS IS CALLED A TRAP.
TAK
KLAK
AND *I'M* CALLING YOU DEAD.

'CEPT FOR ROUNDIN' UP THOSE *QUAMILLA* THINGS. THAT WAS MORE OF A CHALLENGE THAN *SOME* OF MY HUNTS.

COURSE *JODO KAST* HAD TO GO AND *FRY* THEM. AND THEY WERE SUCH *LOVABLE* LEECHES.

HAVE TO ADMIT THE GUY'S BETTER THAN I *THOUGHT* WHEN I SAW HIM BACK ON FLUWHAKA.

TRYIN' TO BE THE BIG-SHOT HUNTER. POSIN' AS THE *BEST* IN THE BUSINESS.

"SITTIN' AROUND ON *NAL HUTTA* FOR THE LAST FEW DAYS HASN'T BEEN THRILLING.

BUT HE'S NO *BOBA FETT.*"

FETT! CAN'T WE *TALK* ABOUT THIS?

YOU *CAN'T* KILL ME. IT'S AGAINST THE *CODE.*

I WASN'T THE *FIRST ONE* TO BREAK THE CODE.

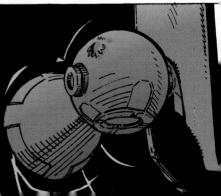

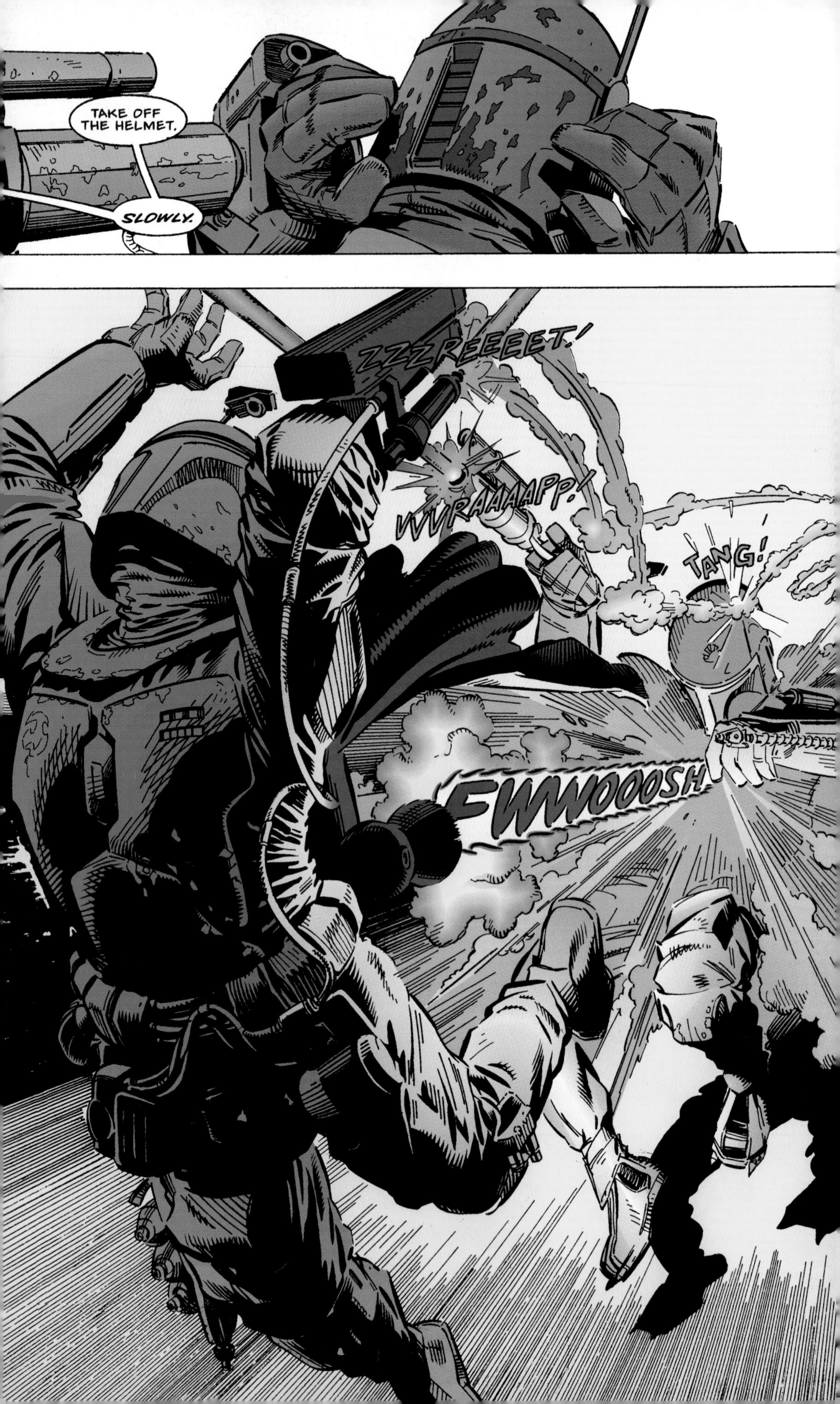
TAKE OFF THE HELMET.
SLOWLY.
ZZZREEEEET!
VVVRAAAAAPP!
TANG!
FWWOOOSH

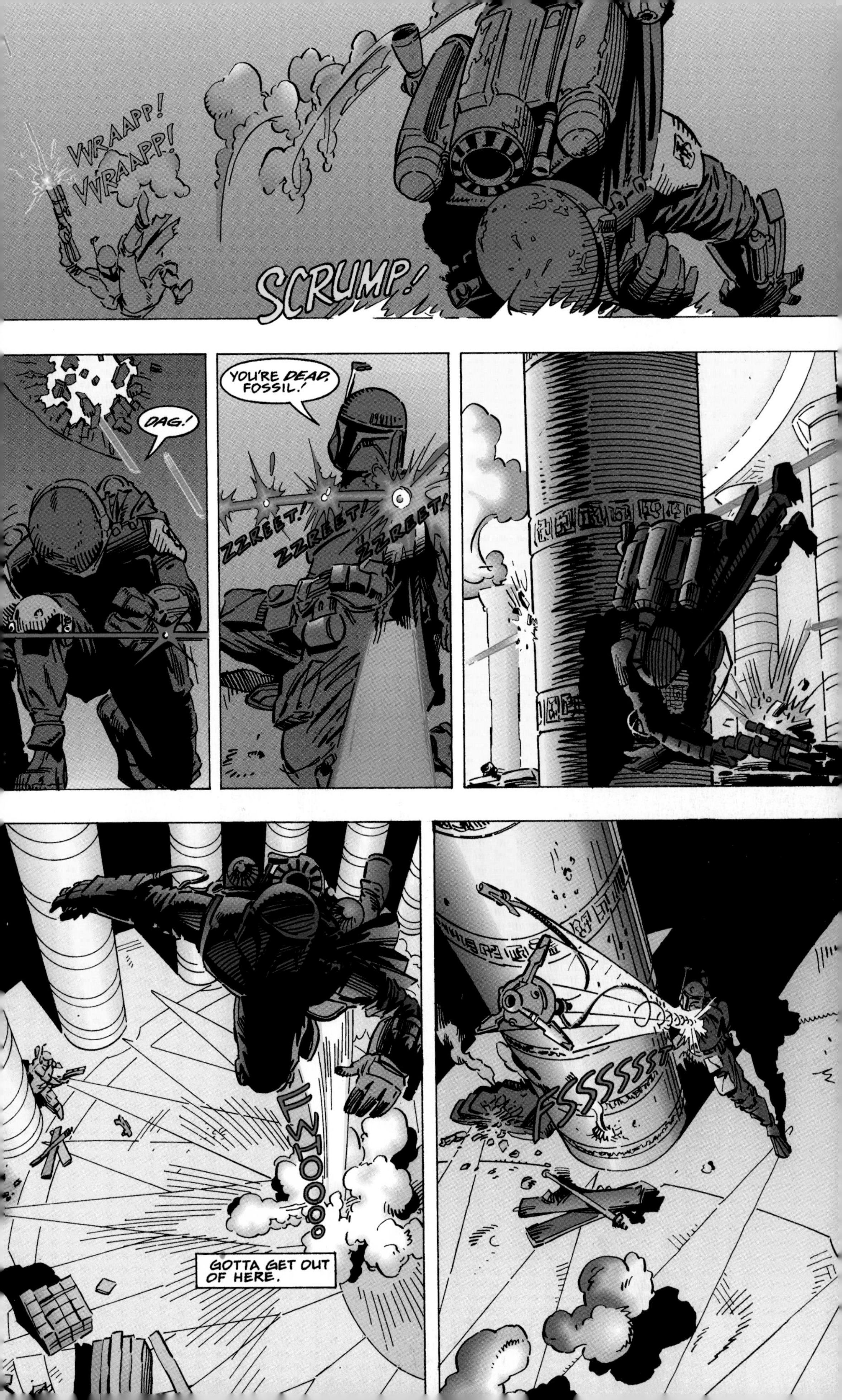
VVRAAPP!
VVRAAPP!
SCRUMP!
DAG!
YOU'RE DEAD, FOSSIL!
ZZREEET!
ZZREEET!
ZZREEET!
WHOOOOO
GOTTA GET OUT OF HERE.
FSSSSSST

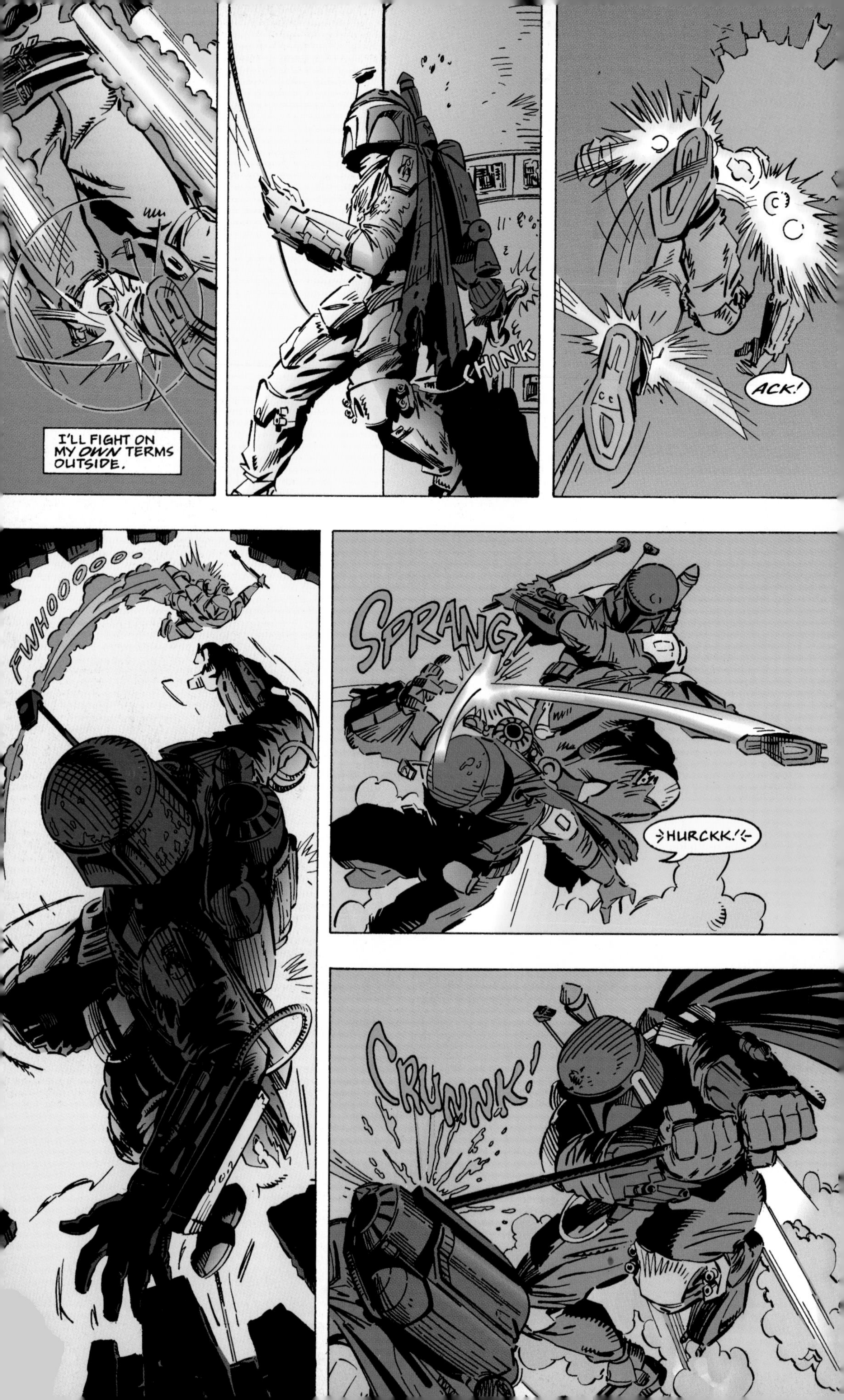
I'LL FIGHT ON MY *OWN* TERMS OUTSIDE.
CHINK
ACK!
FWHOOOOOOO
SPRANG!
HURCKK!
CRUNNK!

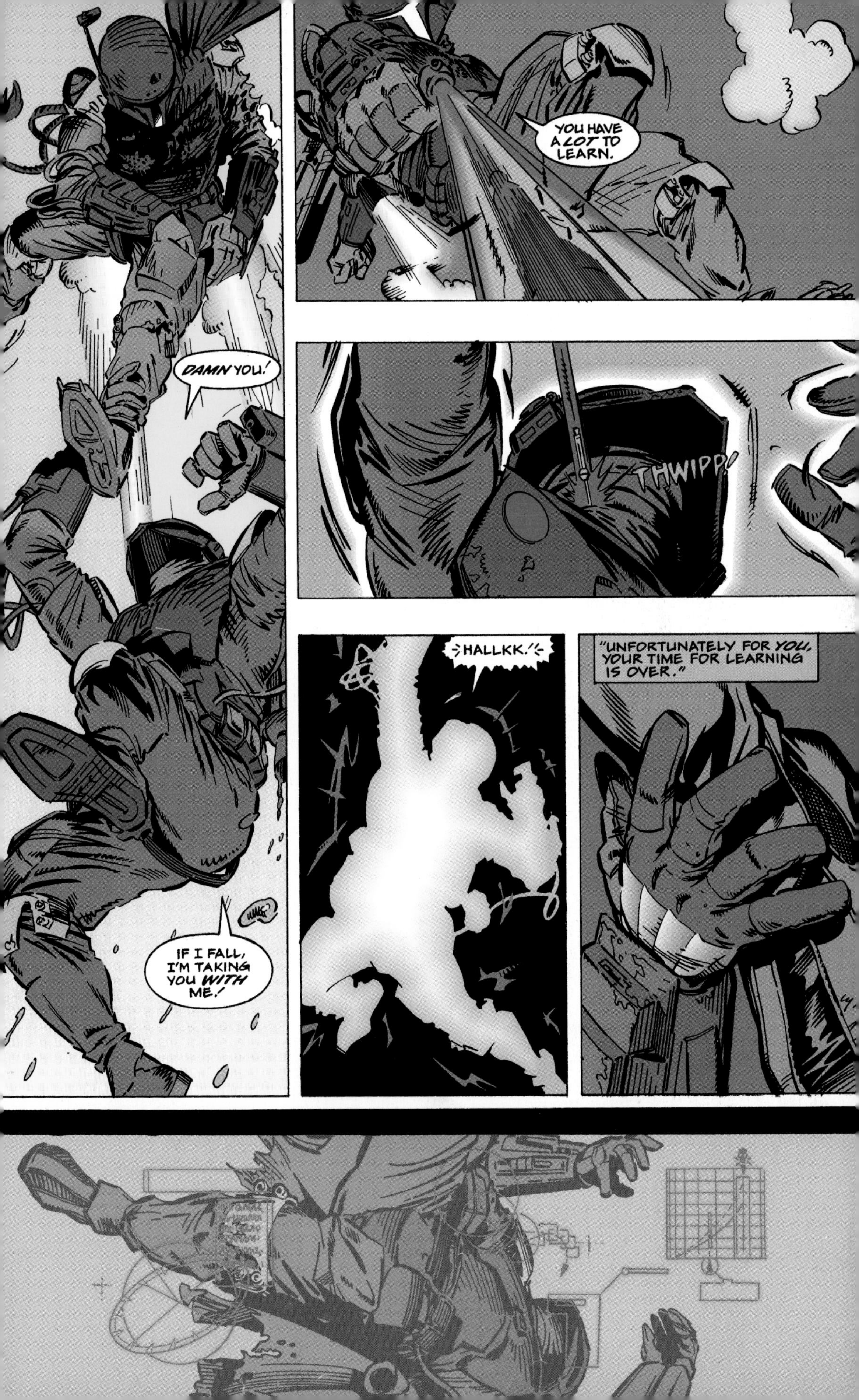
YOU HAVE A LOT TO LEARN.
DAMN YOU!
IF I FALL, I'M TAKING YOU WITH ME!
THWIPP!
HALLKK!
"UNFORTUNATELY FOR YOU, YOUR TIME FOR LEARNING IS OVER."

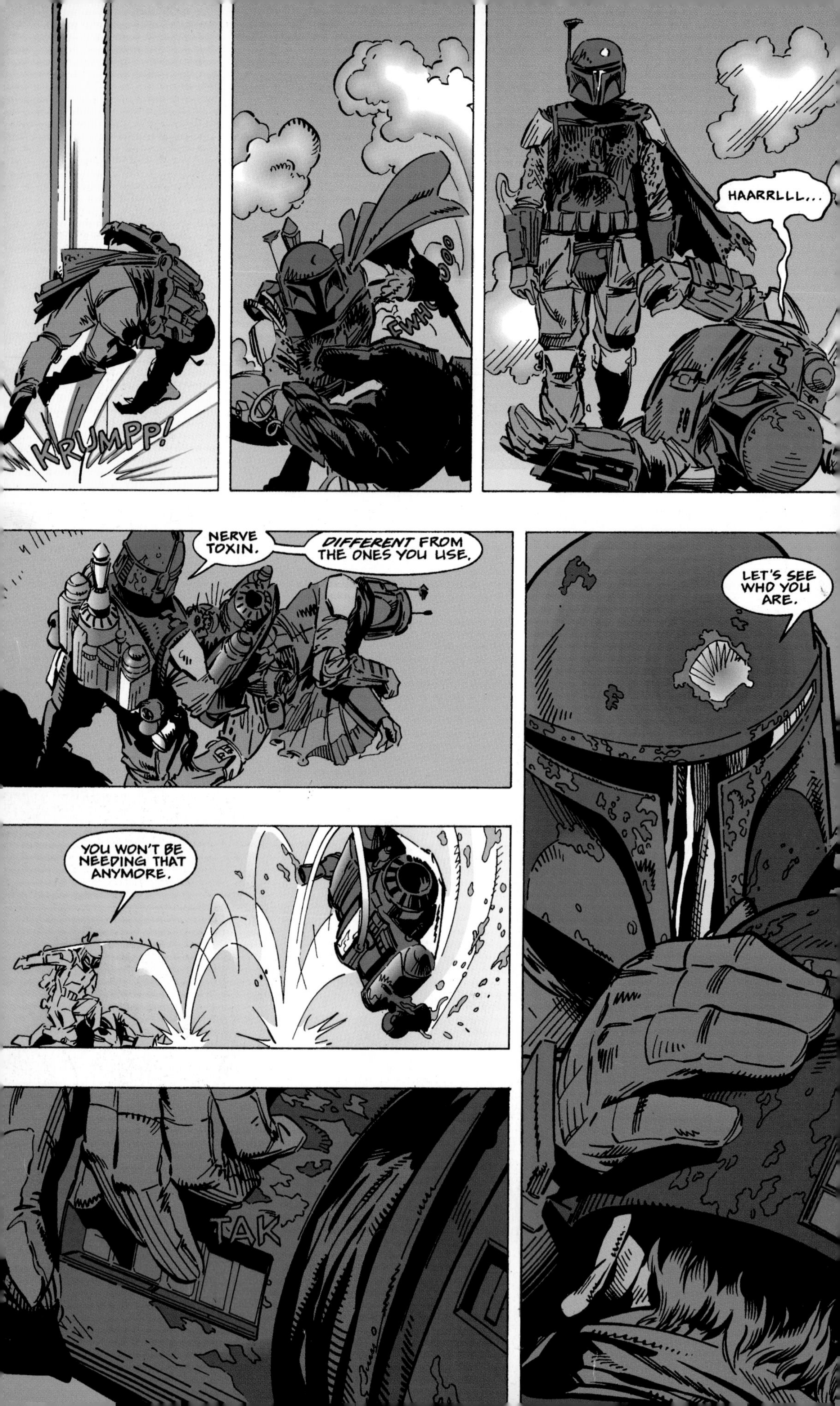
KRUMPP!
FWHOOOOO
HAARRLLL...
NERVE TOXIN.
DIFFERENT FROM THE ONES YOU USE.
YOU WON'T BE NEEDING THAT ANYMORE.
LET'S SEE WHO YOU ARE.
TAK

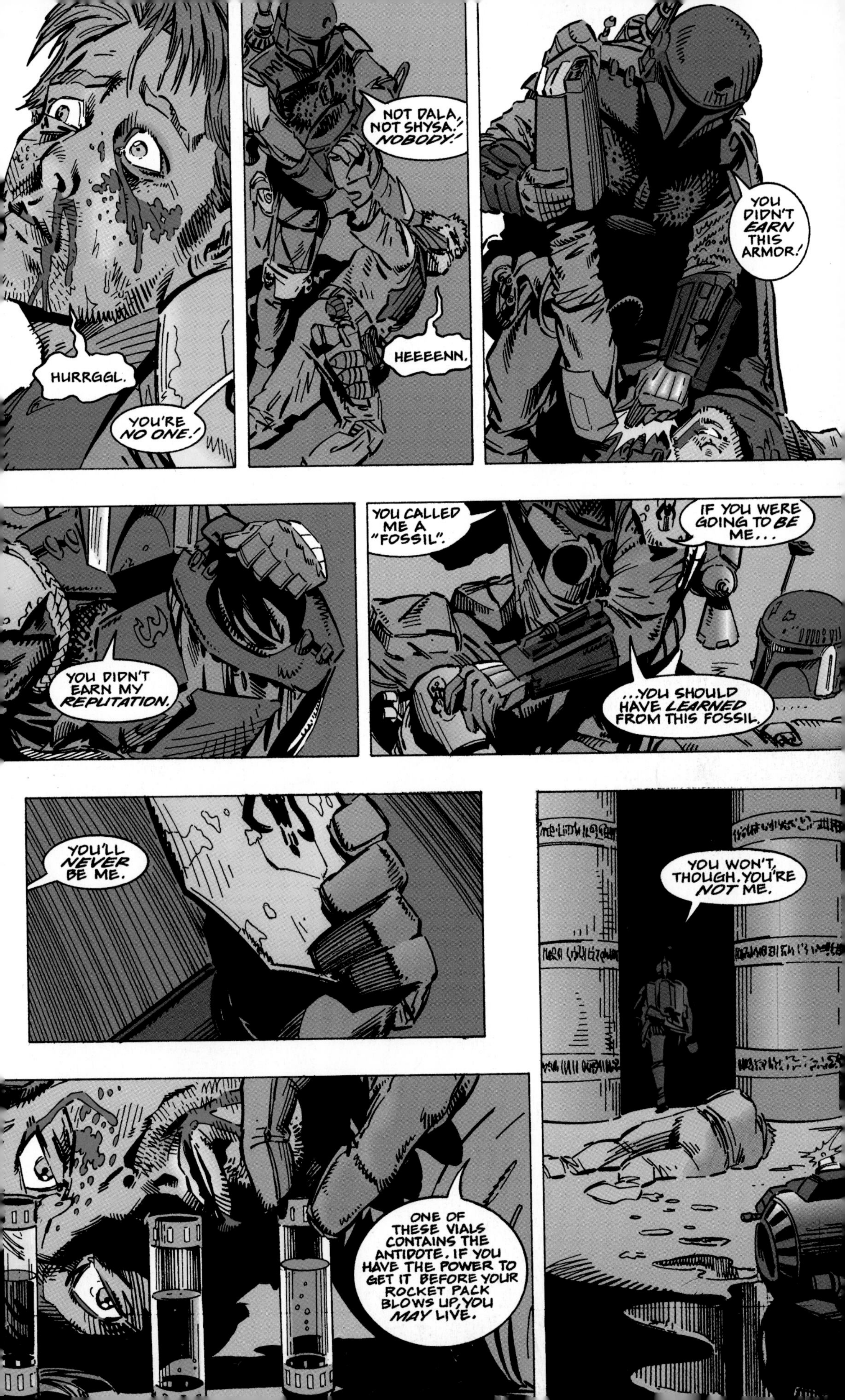
HURRGGL.
YOU'RE NO ONE!
NOT DALA, NOT SHYSA! NOBODY!
HEEEENN.
YOU DIDN'T EARN THIS ARMOR!
YOU DIDN'T EARN MY REPUTATION.
YOU CALLED ME A "FOSSIL".
IF YOU WERE GOING TO BE ME...
...YOU SHOULD HAVE LEARNED FROM THIS FOSSIL.
YOU'LL NEVER BE ME.
YOU WON'T, THOUGH. YOU'RE NOT ME.
ONE OF THESE VIALS CONTAINS THE ANTIDOTE. IF YOU HAVE THE POWER TO GET IT BEFORE YOUR ROCKET PACK BLOWS UP, YOU MAY LIVE.

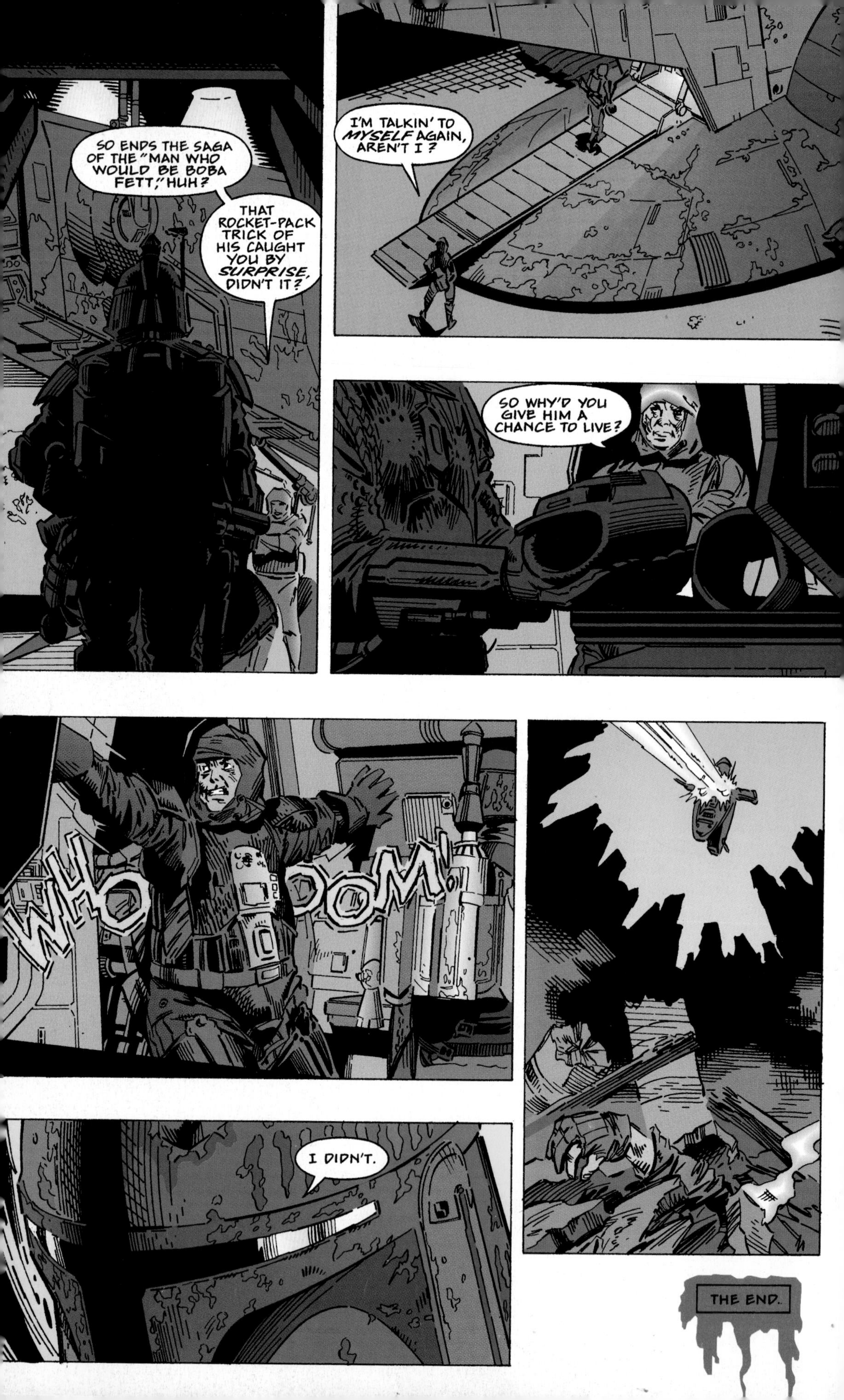
SO ENDS THE SAGA OF THE "MAN WHO WOULD BE BOBA FETT," HUH?
THAT ROCKET-PACK TRICK OF HIS CAUGHT YOU BY SURPRISE, DIDN'T IT?
I'M TALKIN' TO MYSELF AGAIN, AREN'T I?
SO WHY'D YOU GIVE HIM A CHANCE TO LIVE?
WHOOOM!
I DIDN'T.
THE END.

BOUNTY HUNTERS

KENIX KIL

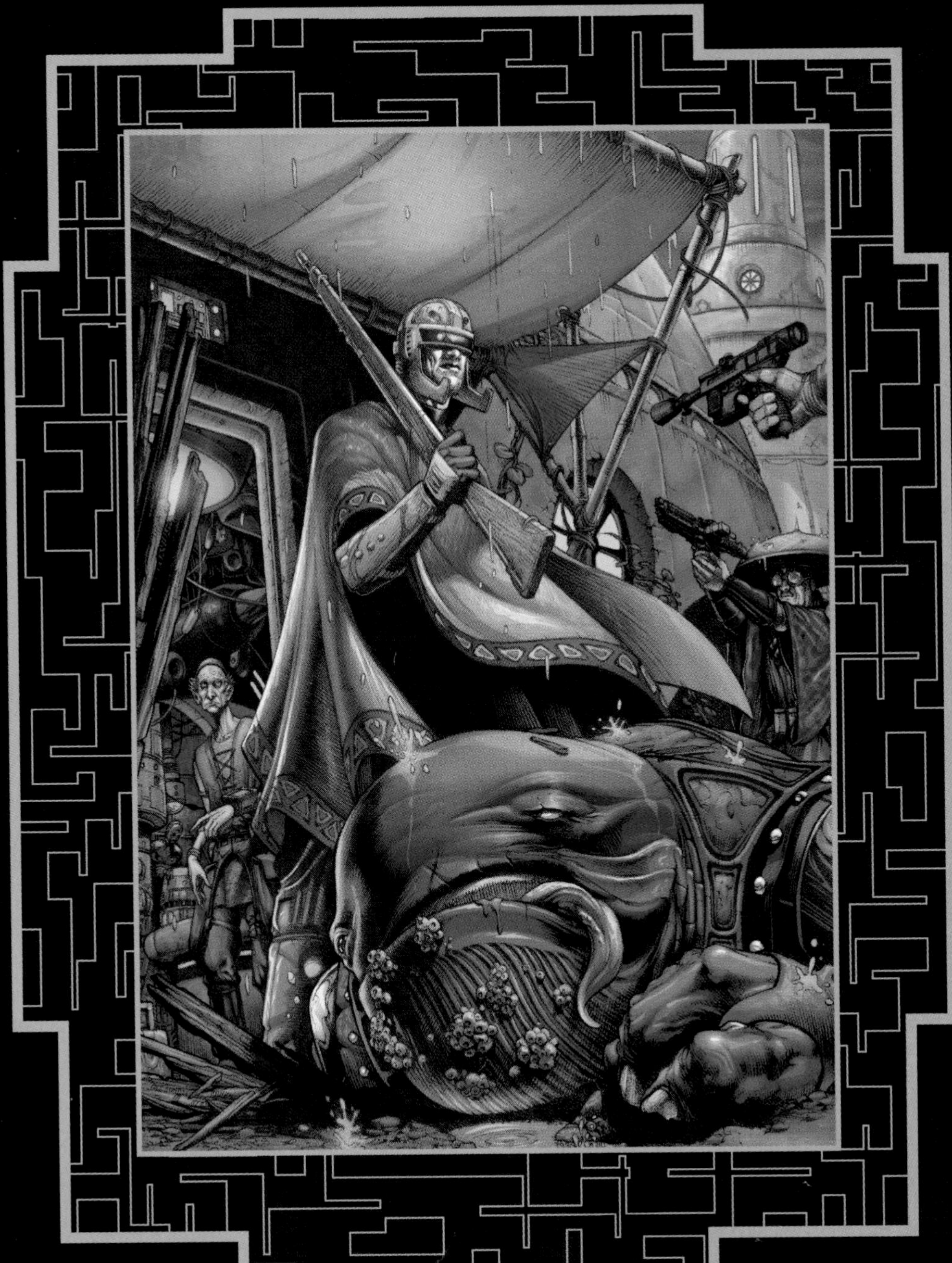

STORY
RANDY STRADLEY

PENCILS
JAVIER SALTARES

INKS
CHRISTOPHER IVY

COLORS
DIGITAL BROOME

LETTERING
AMADOR CISNEROS

TITLE ART
DOUG WHEATLEY
WITH DAVE McCAIG

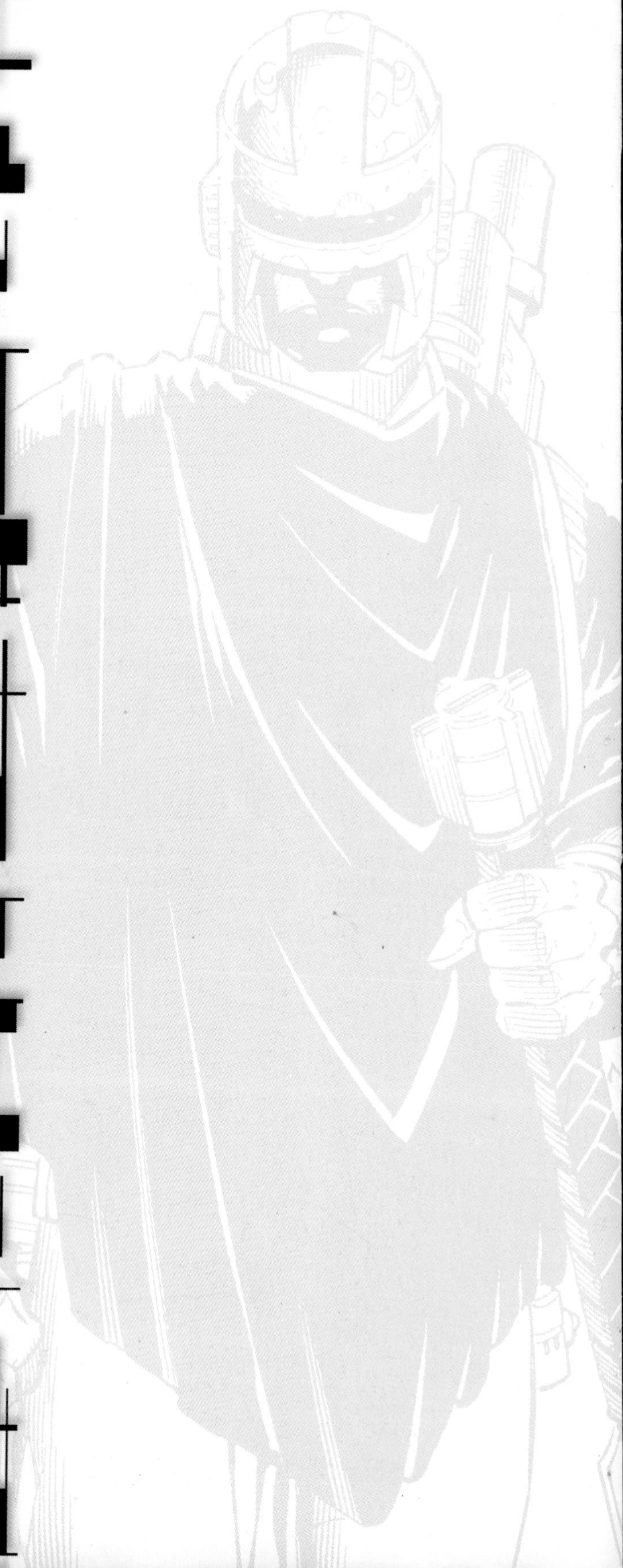

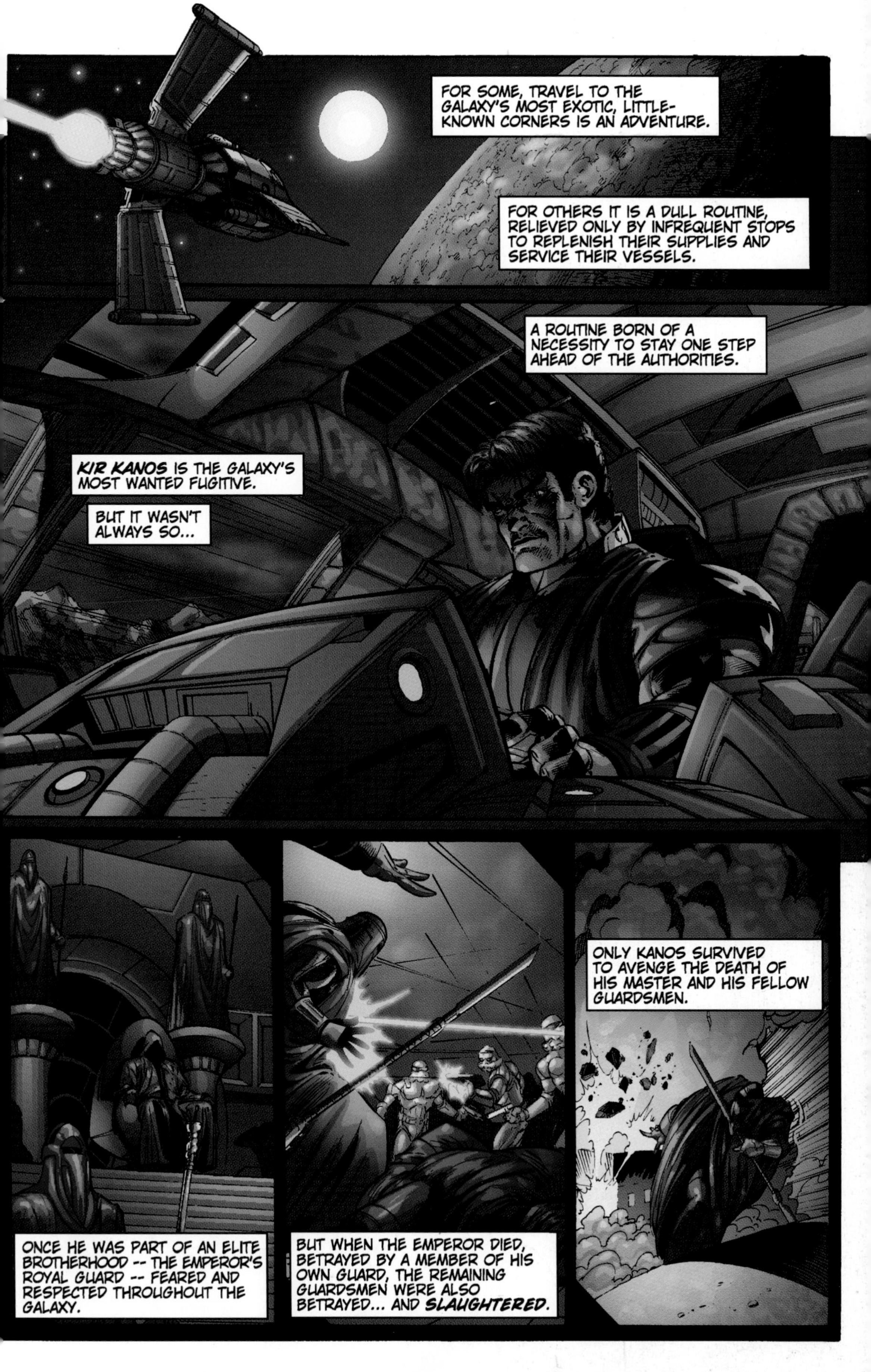

FOR SOME, TRAVEL TO THE GALAXY'S MOST EXOTIC, LITTLE-KNOWN CORNERS IS AN ADVENTURE.
FOR OTHERS IT IS A DULL ROUTINE, RELIEVED ONLY BY INFREQUENT STOPS TO REPLENISH THEIR SUPPLIES AND SERVICE THEIR VESSELS.
A ROUTINE BORN OF A NECESSITY TO STAY ONE STEP AHEAD OF THE AUTHORITIES.
KIR KANOS IS THE GALAXY'S MOST WANTED FUGITIVE.
BUT IT WASN'T ALWAYS SO...
ONCE HE WAS PART OF AN ELITE BROTHERHOOD -- THE EMPEROR'S ROYAL GUARD -- FEARED AND RESPECTED THROUGHOUT THE GALAXY.
BUT WHEN THE EMPEROR DIED, BETRAYED BY A MEMBER OF HIS OWN GUARD, THE REMAINING GUARDSMEN WERE ALSO BETRAYED... AND *SLAUGHTERED*.
ONLY KANOS SURVIVED TO AVENGE THE DEATH OF HIS MASTER AND HIS FELLOW GUARDSMEN.

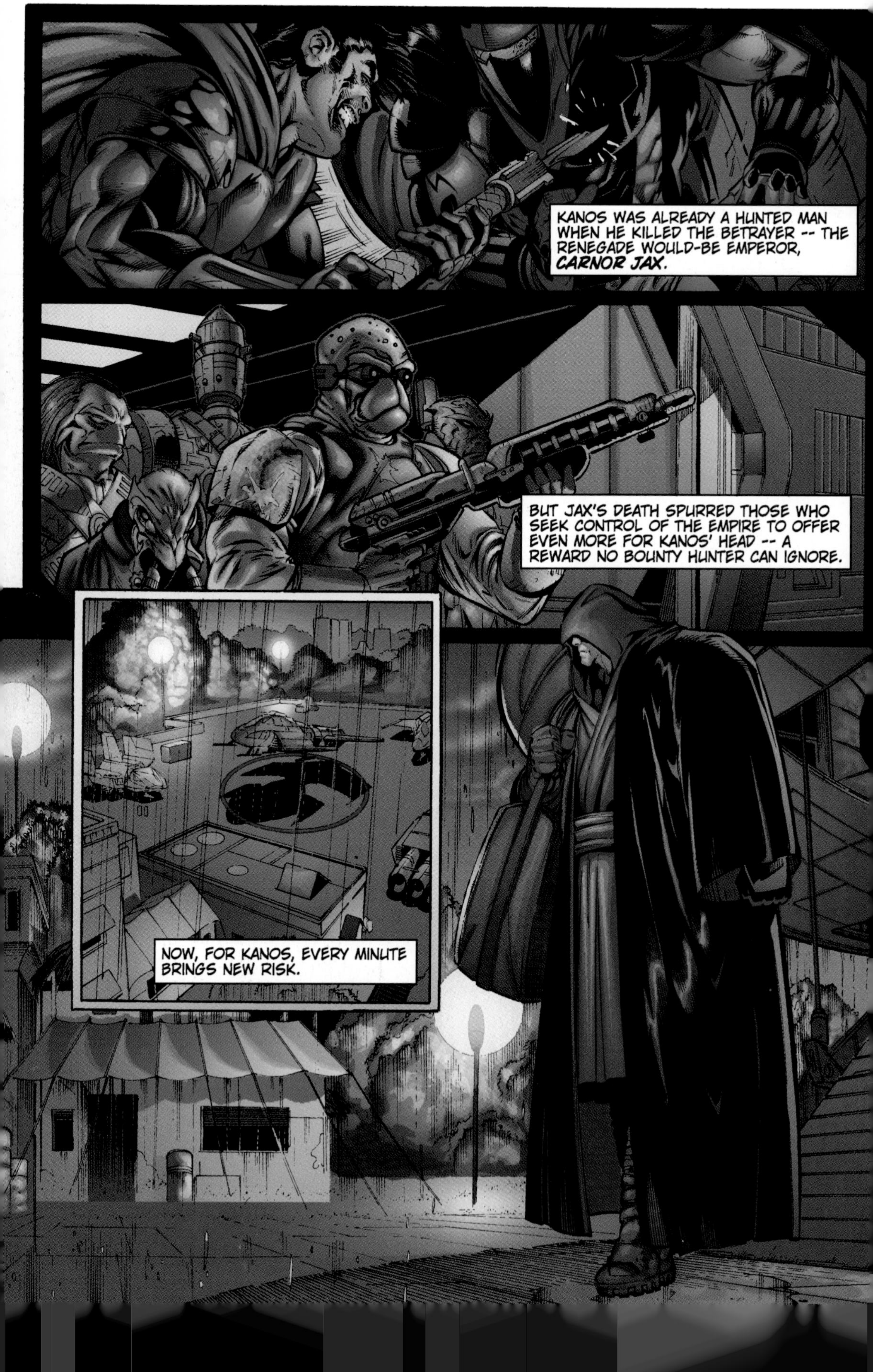
KANOS WAS ALREADY A HUNTED MAN WHEN HE KILLED THE BETRAYER -- THE RENEGADE WOULD-BE EMPEROR, CARNOR JAX.
BUT JAX'S DEATH SPURRED THOSE WHO SEEK CONTROL OF THE EMPIRE TO OFFER EVEN MORE FOR KANOS' HEAD -- A REWARD NO BOUNTY HUNTER CAN IGNORE.
NOW, FOR KANOS, EVERY MINUTE BRINGS NEW RISK.

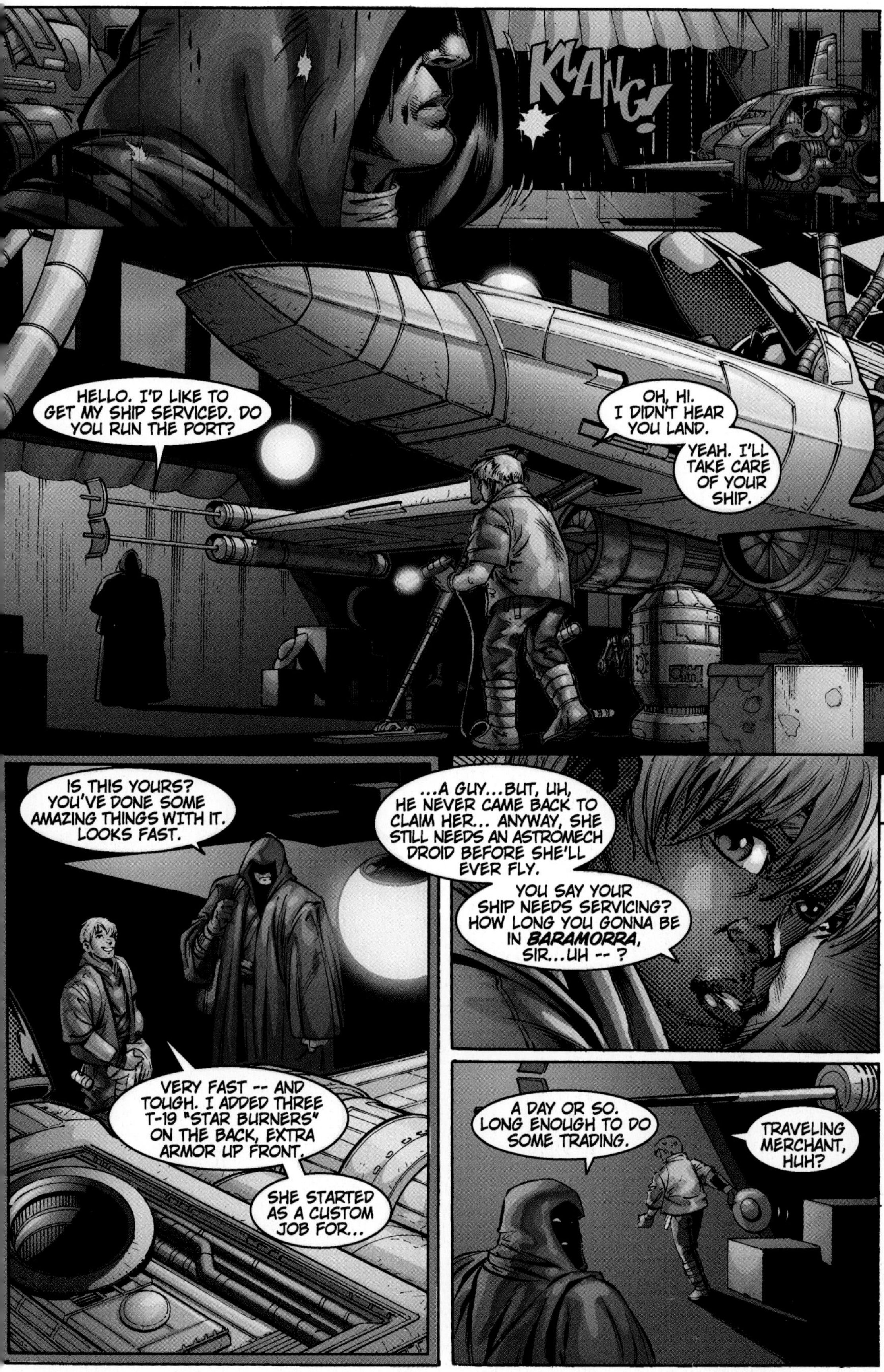
KLANG!
HELLO. I'D LIKE TO GET MY SHIP SERVICED. DO YOU RUN THE PORT?
OH, HI. I DIDN'T HEAR YOU LAND.
YEAH. I'LL TAKE CARE OF YOUR SHIP.
IS THIS YOURS? YOU'VE DONE SOME AMAZING THINGS WITH IT. LOOKS FAST.
VERY FAST -- AND TOUGH. I ADDED THREE T-19 "STAR BURNERS" ON THE BACK, EXTRA ARMOR UP FRONT.
SHE STARTED AS A CUSTOM JOB FOR...
...A GUY...BUT, UH, HE NEVER CAME BACK TO CLAIM HER... ANYWAY, SHE STILL NEEDS AN ASTROMECH DROID BEFORE SHE'LL EVER FLY.
YOU SAY YOUR SHIP NEEDS SERVICING? HOW LONG YOU GONNA BE IN *BARAMORRA*, SIR...UH -- ?
A DAY OR SO. LONG ENOUGH TO DO SOME TRADING.
TRAVELING MERCHANT, HUH?

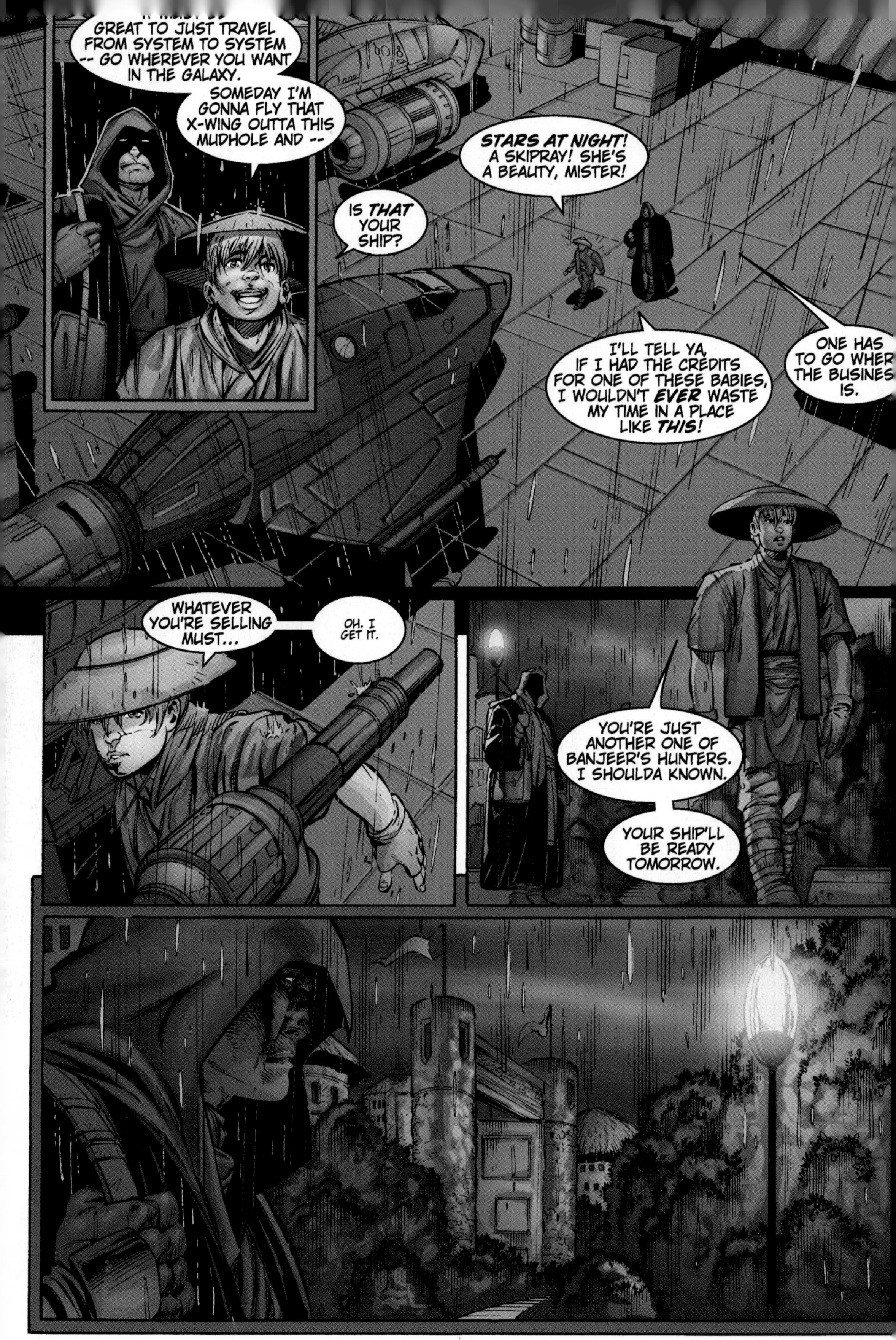
GREAT TO JUST TRAVEL FROM SYSTEM TO SYSTEM -- GO WHEREVER YOU WANT IN THE GALAXY.
SOMEDAY I'M GONNA FLY THAT X-WING OUTTA THIS MUDHOLE AND --
STARS AT NIGHT! A SKIPRAY! SHE'S A BEAUTY, MISTER!
IS THAT YOUR SHIP?
I'LL TELL YA, IF I HAD THE CREDITS FOR ONE OF THESE BABIES, I WOULDN'T EVER WASTE MY TIME IN A PLACE LIKE THIS!
ONE HAS TO GO WHER THE BUSINES IS.
WHATEVER YOU'RE SELLING MUST...
OH. I GET IT.
YOU'RE JUST ANOTHER ONE OF BANJEER'S HUNTERS. I SHOULDA KNOWN.
YOUR SHIP'LL BE READY TOMORROW.

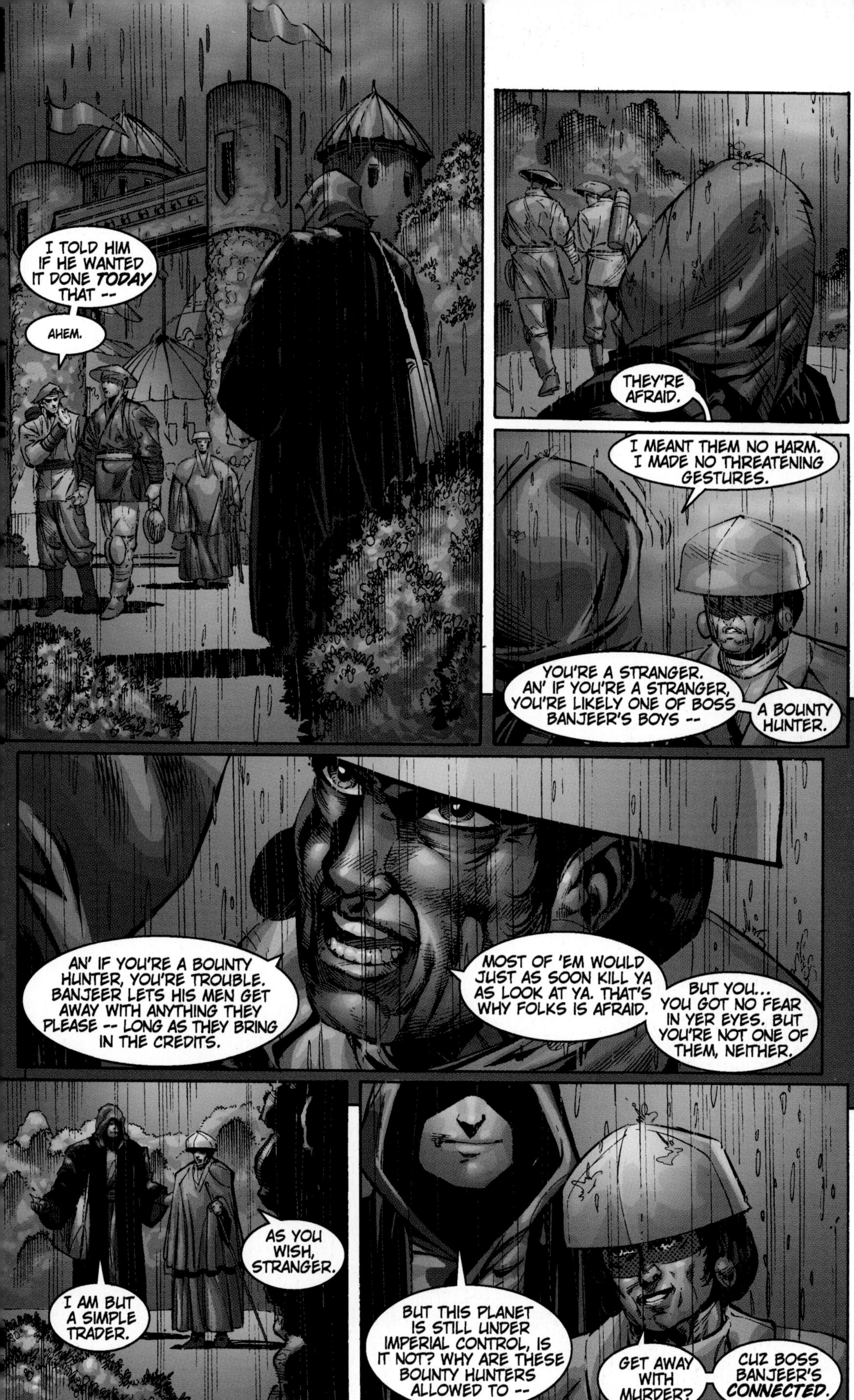
I TOLD HIM IF HE WANTED IT DONE *TODAY* THAT --
AHEM.
THEY'RE AFRAID.
I MEANT THEM NO HARM. I MADE NO THREATENING GESTURES.
YOU'RE A STRANGER. AN' IF YOU'RE A STRANGER, YOU'RE LIKELY ONE OF BOSS BANJEER'S BOYS --
A BOUNTY HUNTER.
AN' IF YOU'RE A BOUNTY HUNTER, YOU'RE TROUBLE. BANJEER LETS HIS MEN GET AWAY WITH ANYTHING THEY PLEASE -- LONG AS THEY BRING IN THE CREDITS.
MOST OF 'EM WOULD JUST AS SOON KILL YA AS LOOK AT YA. THAT'S WHY FOLKS IS AFRAID.
BUT YOU... YOU GOT NO FEAR IN YER EYES. BUT YOU'RE NOT ONE OF THEM, NEITHER.
I AM BUT A SIMPLE TRADER.
AS YOU WISH, STRANGER.
BUT THIS PLANET IS STILL UNDER IMPERIAL CONTROL, IS IT NOT? WHY ARE THESE BOUNTY HUNTERS ALLOWED TO --
GET AWAY WITH MURDER?
CUZ BOSS BANJEER'S *CONNECTED*.

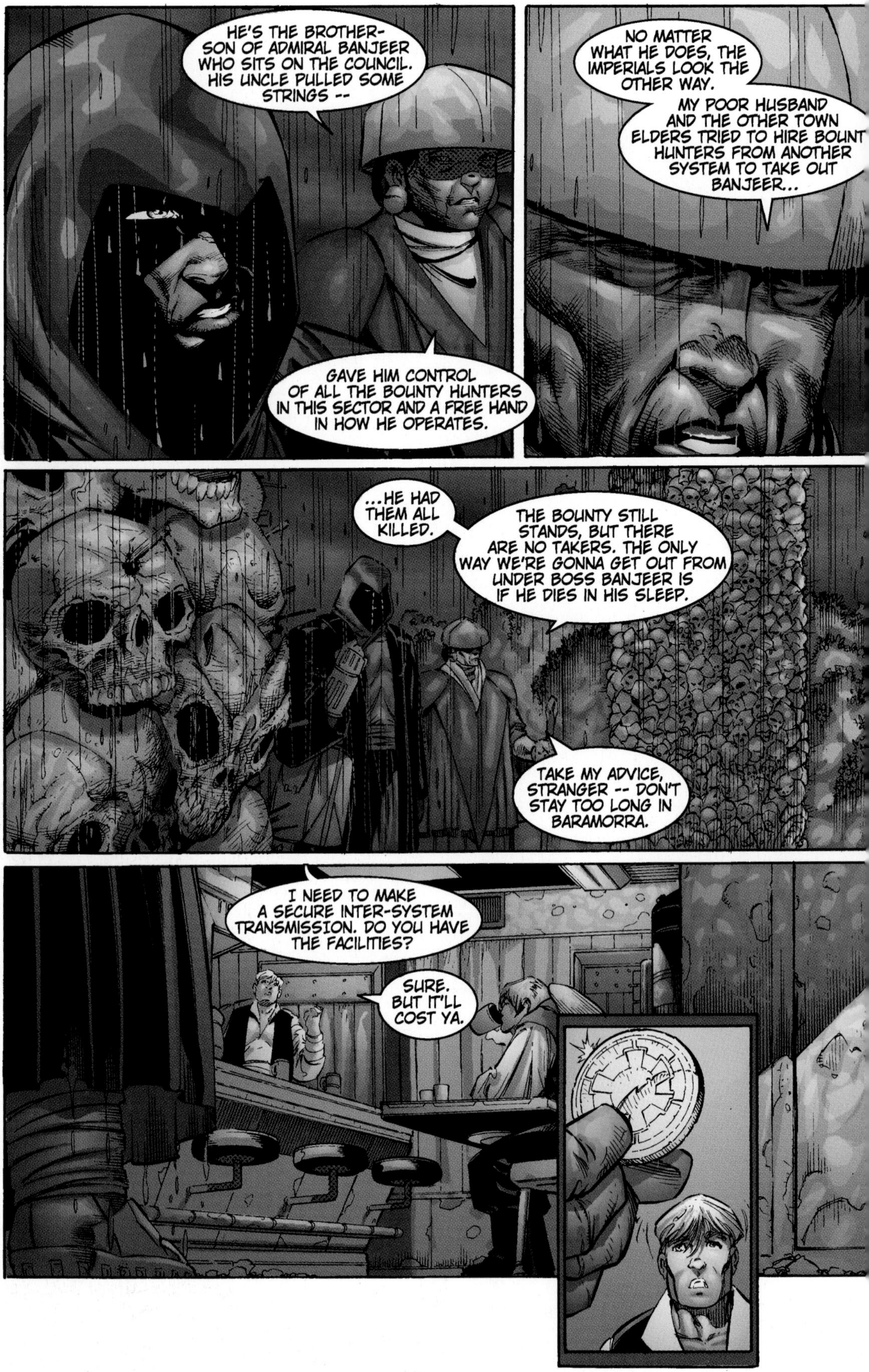

HE'S THE BROTHER-SON OF ADMIRAL BANJEER WHO SITS ON THE COUNCIL. HIS UNCLE PULLED SOME STRINGS --
GAVE HIM CONTROL OF ALL THE BOUNTY HUNTERS IN THIS SECTOR AND A FREE HAND IN HOW HE OPERATES.
NO MATTER WHAT HE DOES, THE IMPERIALS LOOK THE OTHER WAY.
MY POOR HUSBAND AND THE OTHER TOWN ELDERS TRIED TO HIRE BOUNT HUNTERS FROM ANOTHER SYSTEM TO TAKE OUT BANJEER...
...HE HAD THEM ALL KILLED.
THE BOUNTY STILL STANDS, BUT THERE ARE NO TAKERS. THE ONLY WAY WE'RE GONNA GET OUT FROM UNDER BOSS BANJEER IS IF HE DIES IN HIS SLEEP.
TAKE MY ADVICE, STRANGER -- DON'T STAY TOO LONG IN BARAMORRA.
I NEED TO MAKE A SECURE INTER-SYSTEM TRANSMISSION. DO YOU HAVE THE FACILITIES?
SURE. BUT IT'LL COST YA.

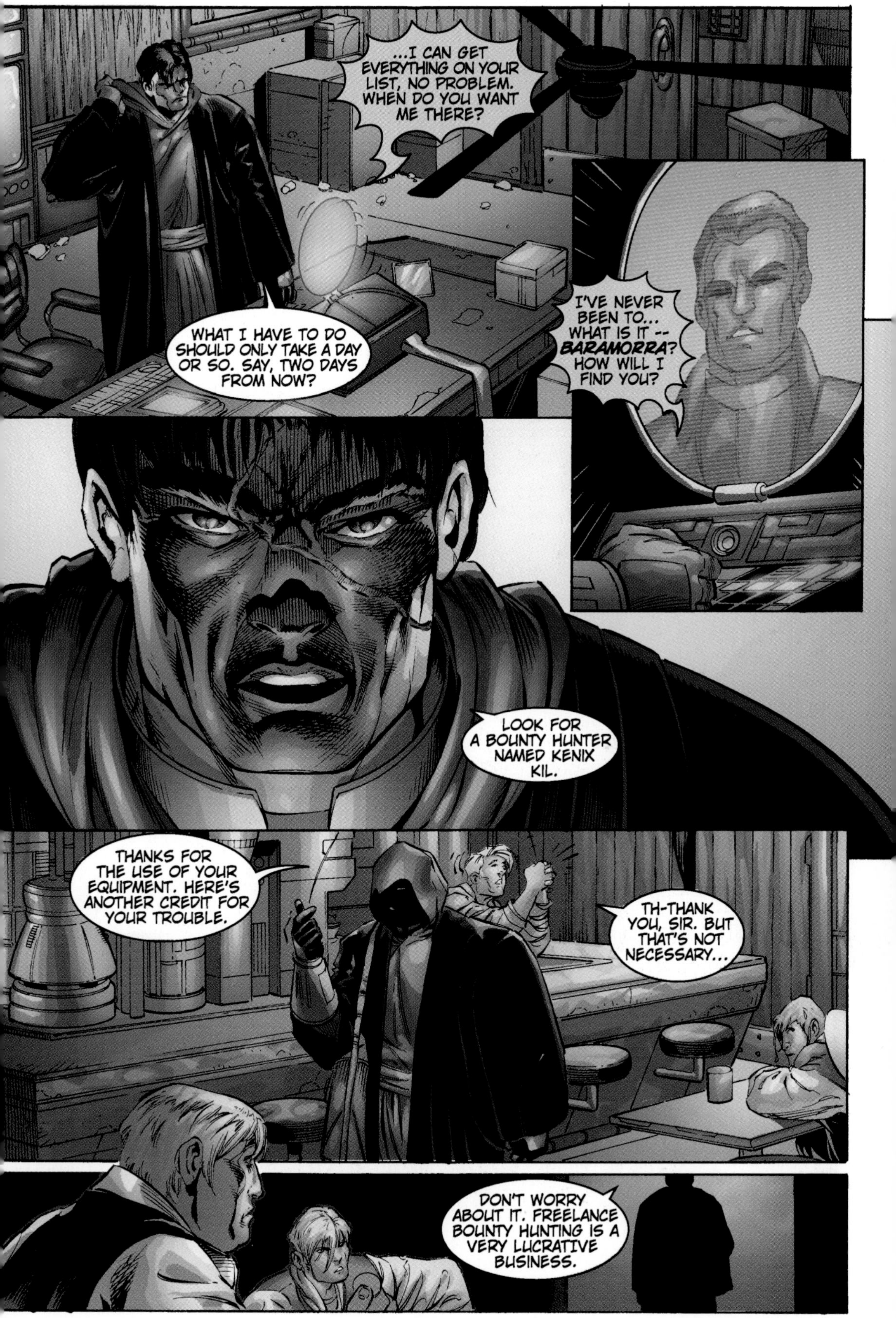
...I CAN GET EVERYTHING ON YOUR LIST, NO PROBLEM. WHEN DO YOU WANT ME THERE?
WHAT I HAVE TO DO SHOULD ONLY TAKE A DAY OR SO. SAY, TWO DAYS FROM NOW?
I'VE NEVER BEEN TO... WHAT IS IT -- *BARAMORRA*? HOW WILL I FIND YOU?
LOOK FOR A BOUNTY HUNTER NAMED KENIX KIL.
THANKS FOR THE USE OF YOUR EQUIPMENT. HERE'S ANOTHER CREDIT FOR YOUR TROUBLE.
TH-THANK YOU, SIR. BUT THAT'S NOT NECESSARY...
DON'T WORRY ABOUT IT. FREELANCE BOUNTY HUNTING IS A VERY LUCRATIVE BUSINESS.

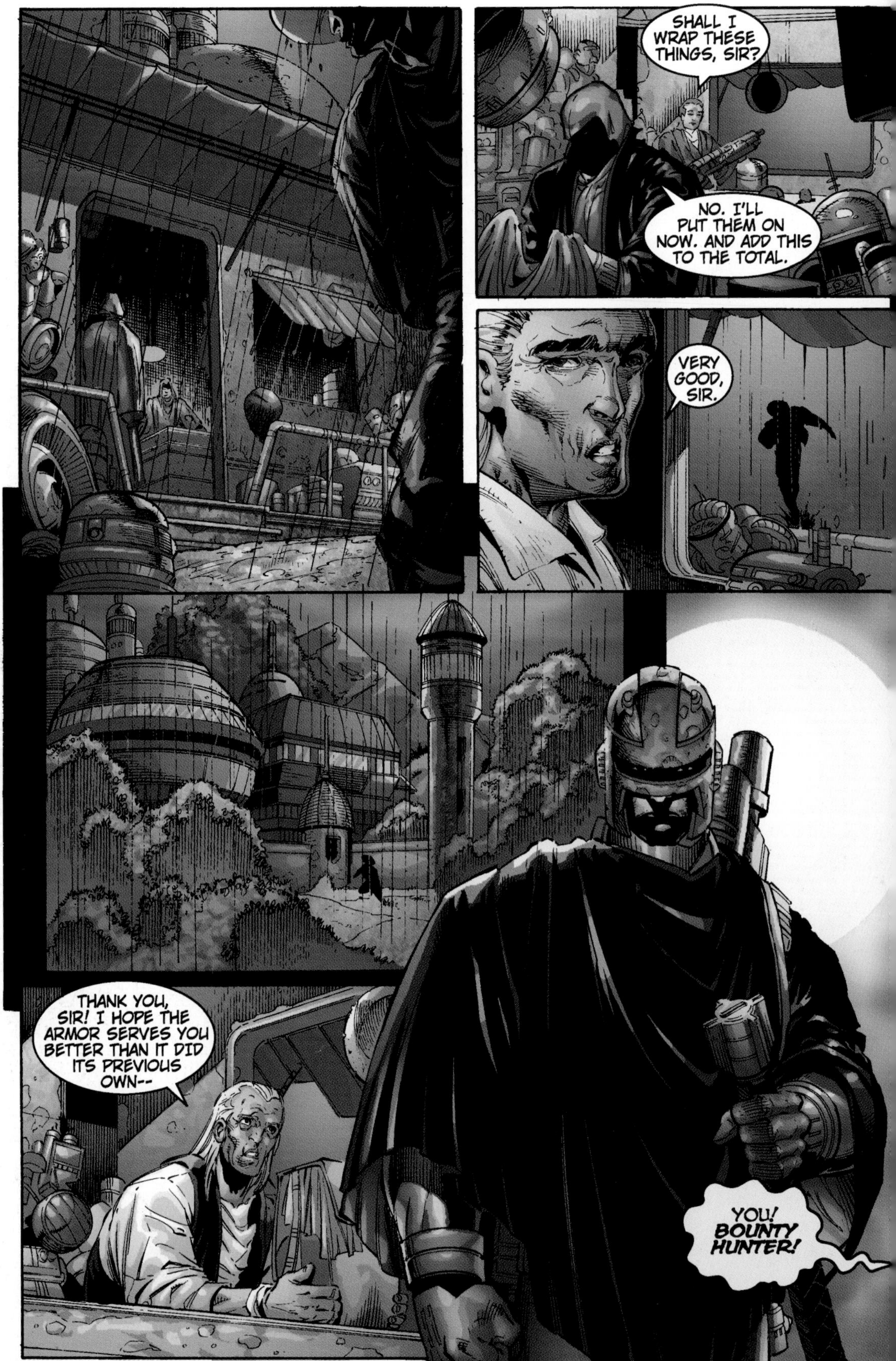
SHALL I WRAP THESE THINGS, SIR?
NO. I'LL PUT THEM ON NOW. AND ADD THIS TO THE TOTAL.
VERY GOOD, SIR.
THANK YOU, SIR! I HOPE THE ARMOR SERVES YOU BETTER THAN IT DID ITS PREVIOUS OWN--
YOU! BOUNTY HUNTER!

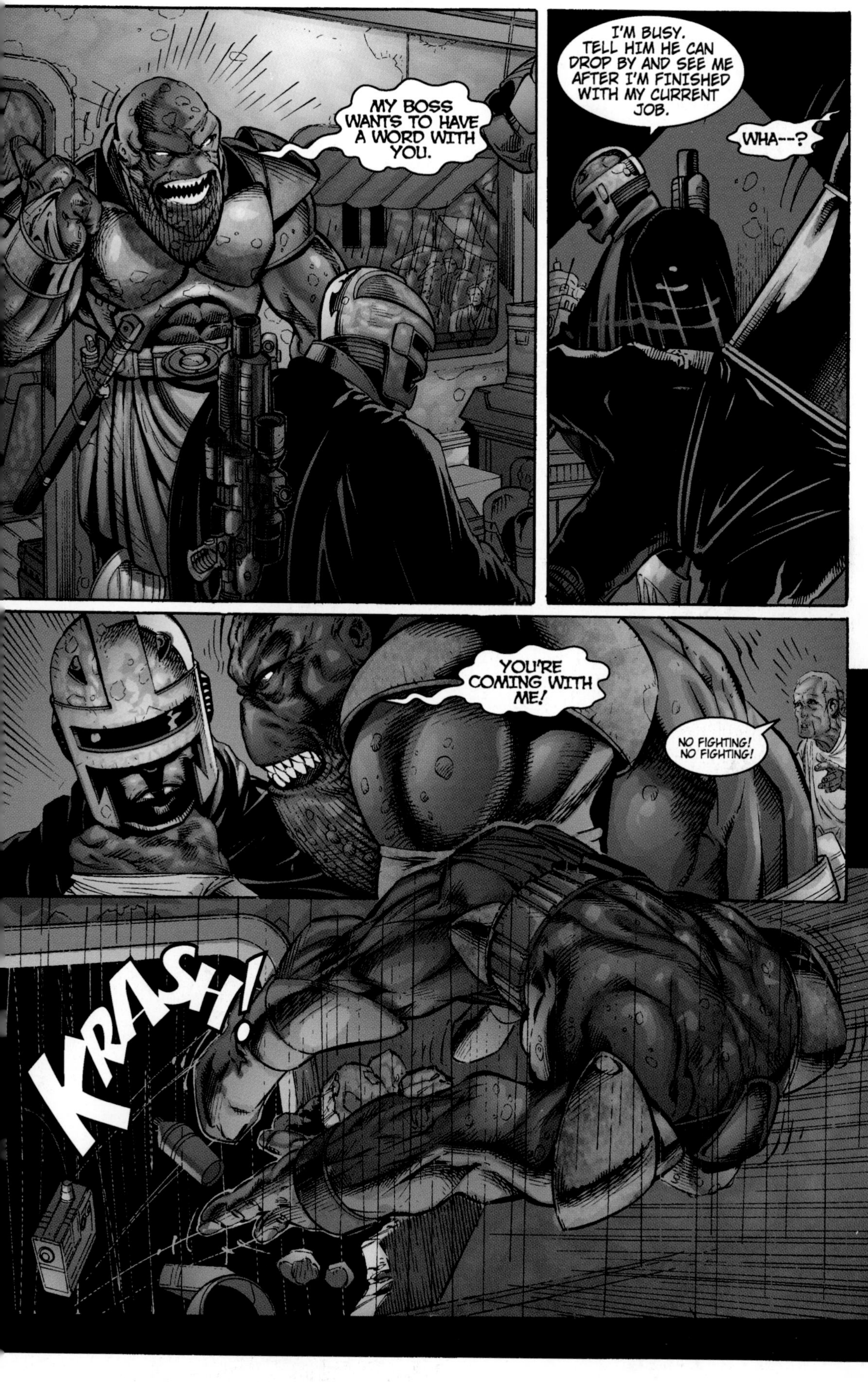
MY BOSS WANTS TO HAVE A WORD WITH YOU.
I'M BUSY. TELL HIM HE CAN DROP BY AND SEE ME AFTER I'M FINISHED WITH MY CURRENT JOB.
WHA--?
YOU'RE COMING WITH ME!
NO FIGHTING! NO FIGHTING!
KRASH!

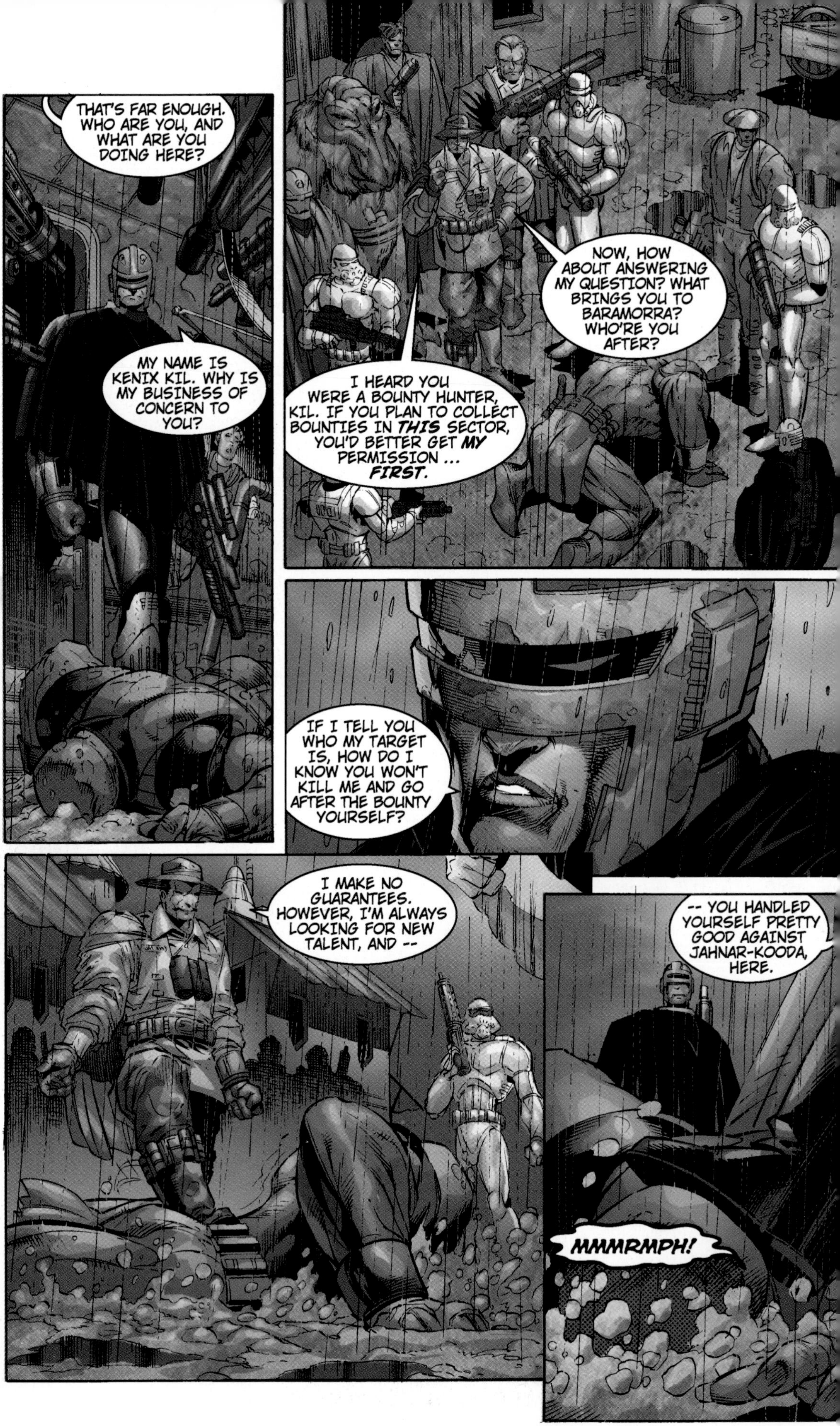
THAT'S FAR ENOUGH. WHO ARE YOU, AND WHAT ARE YOU DOING HERE?
MY NAME IS KENIX KIL. WHY IS MY BUSINESS OF CONCERN TO YOU?
I HEARD YOU WERE A BOUNTY HUNTER, KIL. IF YOU PLAN TO COLLECT BOUNTIES IN THIS SECTOR, YOU'D BETTER GET MY PERMISSION ... FIRST.
NOW, HOW ABOUT ANSWERING MY QUESTION? WHAT BRINGS YOU TO BARAMORRA? WHO'RE YOU AFTER?
IF I TELL YOU WHO MY TARGET IS, HOW DO I KNOW YOU WON'T KILL ME AND GO AFTER THE BOUNTY YOURSELF?
I MAKE NO GUARANTEES. HOWEVER, I'M ALWAYS LOOKING FOR NEW TALENT, AND --
-- YOU HANDLED YOURSELF PRETTY GOOD AGAINST JAHNAR-KOODA, HERE.
MMMRMPH!

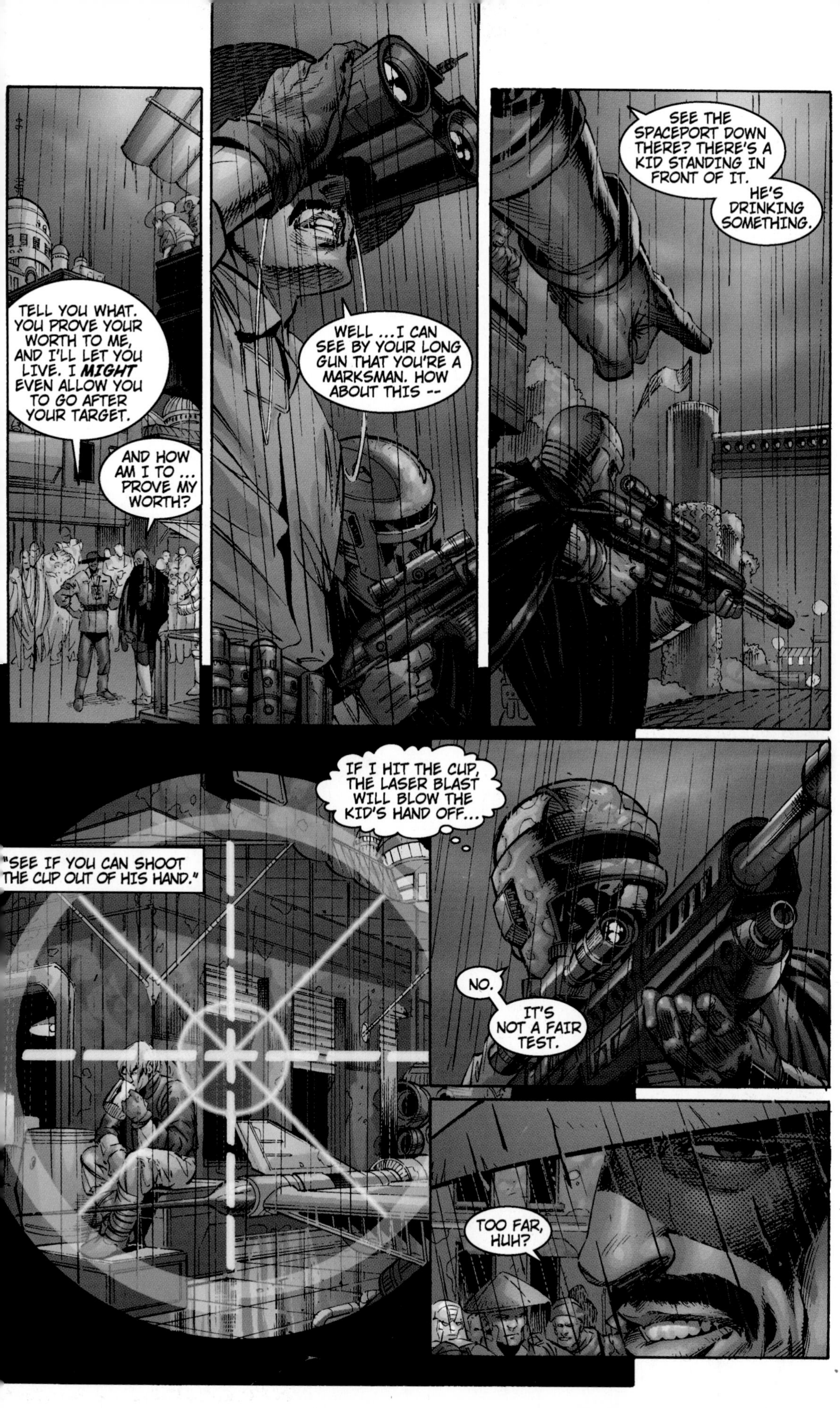
TELL YOU WHAT. YOU PROVE YOUR WORTH TO ME, AND I'LL LET YOU LIVE. I **MIGHT** EVEN ALLOW YOU TO GO AFTER YOUR TARGET.
AND HOW AM I TO ... PROVE MY WORTH?
WELL ...I CAN SEE BY YOUR LONG GUN THAT YOU'RE A MARKSMAN. HOW ABOUT THIS --
SEE THE SPACEPORT DOWN THERE? THERE'S A KID STANDING IN FRONT OF IT.
HE'S DRINKING SOMETHING.
"SEE IF YOU CAN SHOOT THE CUP OUT OF HIS HAND."
IF I HIT THE CUP, THE LASER BLAST WILL BLOW THE KID'S HAND OFF...
NO.
IT'S NOT A FAIR TEST.
TOO FAR, HUH?

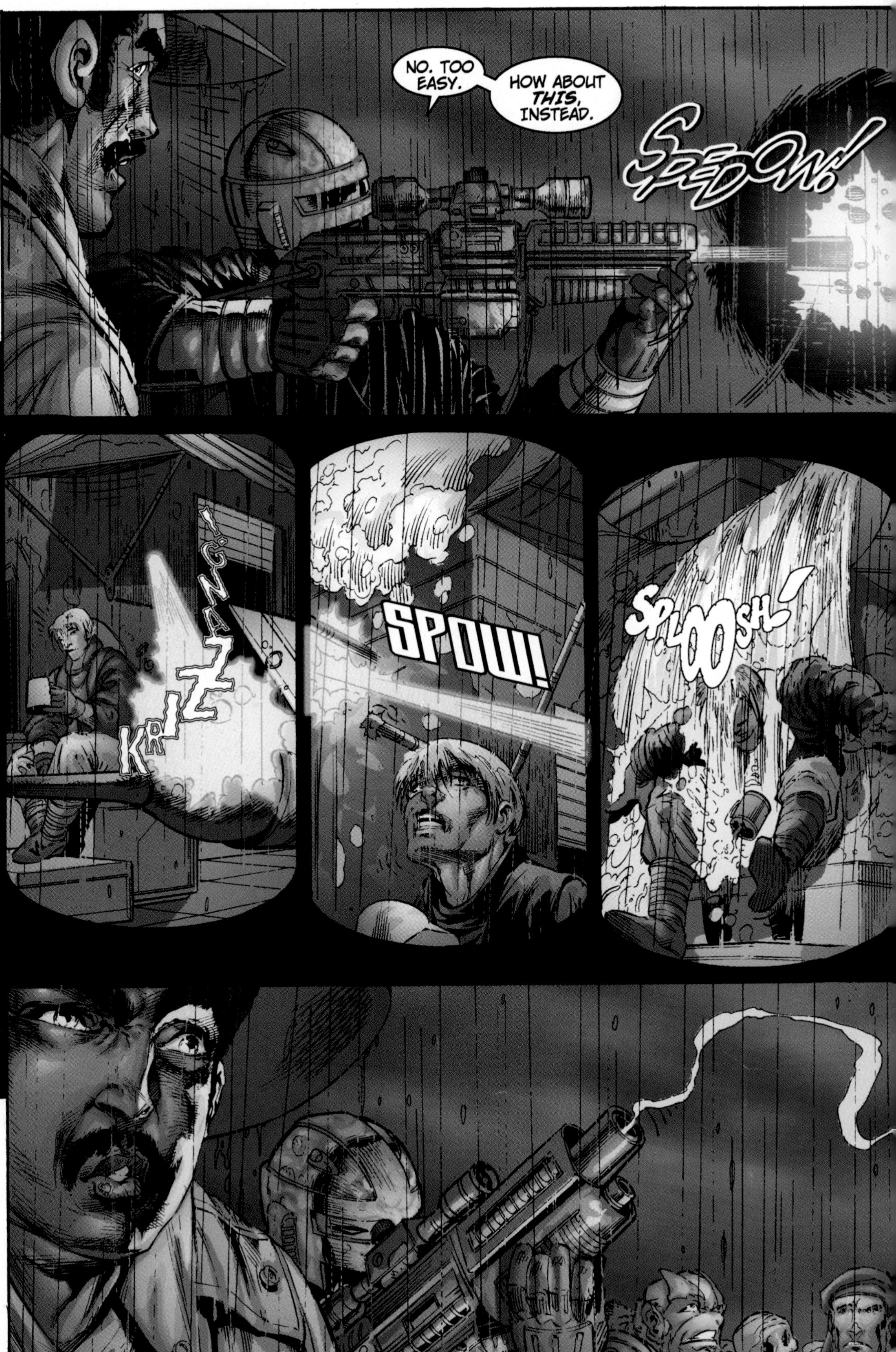
NO. TOO EASY.
HOW ABOUT *THIS*, INSTEAD.
SPEDOW!
SPOW!
SPLOOSH!

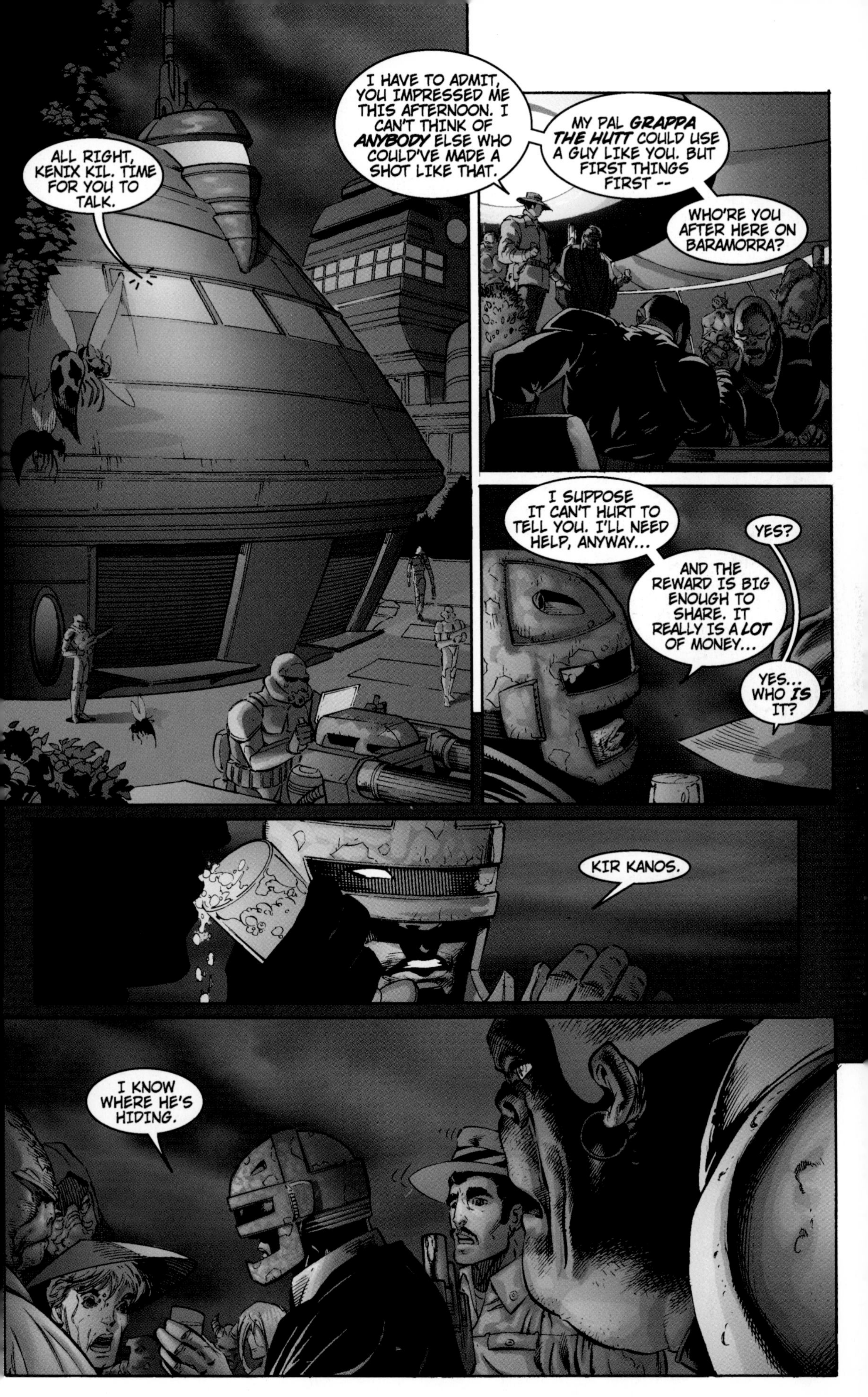
ALL RIGHT, KENIX KIL. TIME FOR YOU TO TALK.
I HAVE TO ADMIT, YOU IMPRESSED ME THIS AFTERNOON. I CAN'T THINK OF ANYBODY ELSE WHO COULD'VE MADE A SHOT LIKE THAT.
MY PAL GRAPPA THE HUTT COULD USE A GUY LIKE YOU. BUT FIRST THINGS FIRST --
WHO'RE YOU AFTER HERE ON BARAMORRA?
I SUPPOSE IT CAN'T HURT TO TELL YOU. I'LL NEED HELP, ANYWAY...
YES?
AND THE REWARD IS BIG ENOUGH TO SHARE. IT REALLY IS A LOT OF MONEY...
YES... WHO IS IT?
KIR KANOS.
I KNOW WHERE HE'S HIDING.

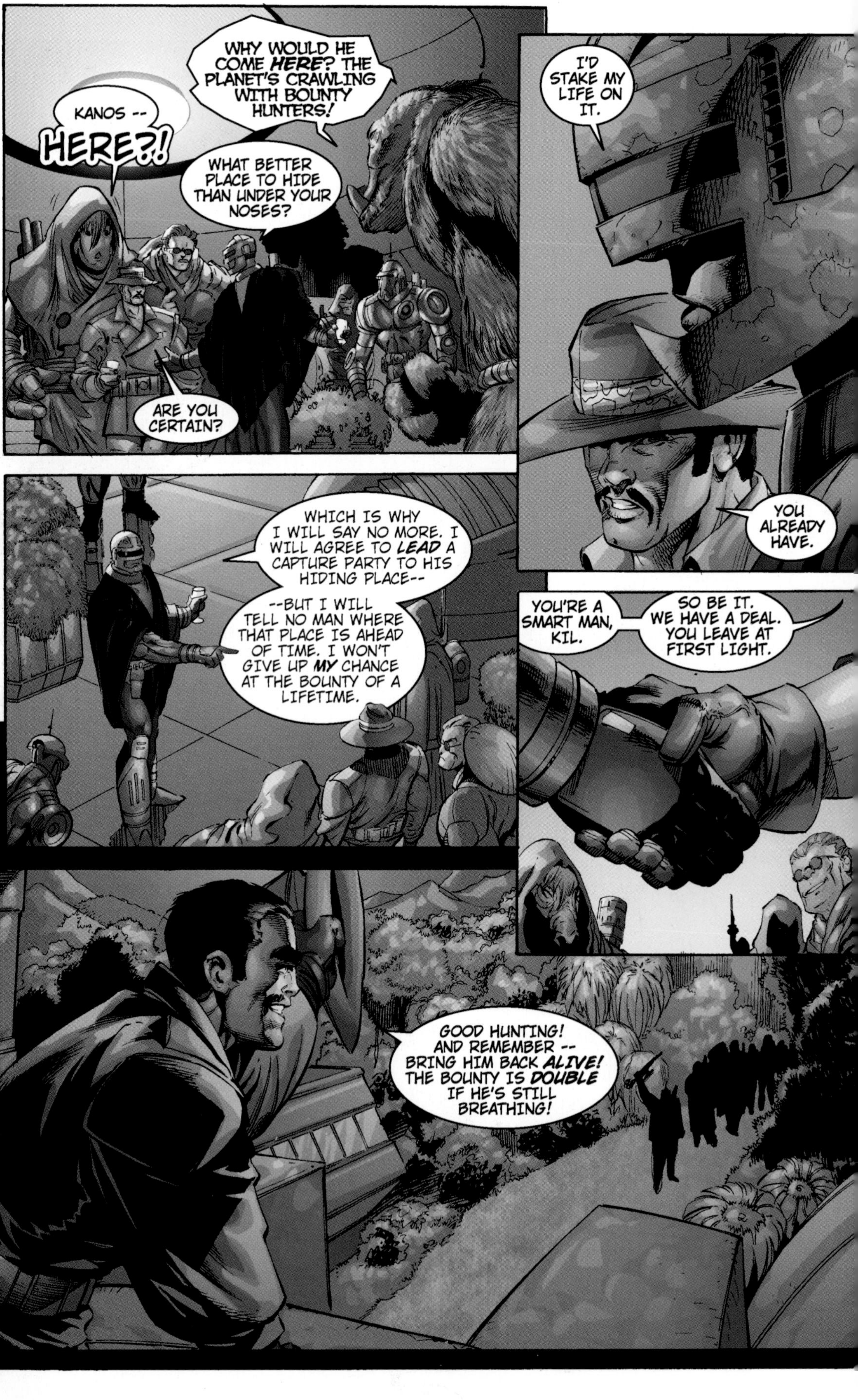
KANOS -- HERE?!
WHY WOULD HE COME HERE? THE PLANET'S CRAWLING WITH BOUNTY HUNTERS!
WHAT BETTER PLACE TO HIDE THAN UNDER YOUR NOSES?
ARE YOU CERTAIN?
I'D STAKE MY LIFE ON IT.
YOU ALREADY HAVE.
WHICH IS WHY I WILL SAY NO MORE. I WILL AGREE TO LEAD A CAPTURE PARTY TO HIS HIDING PLACE--
--BUT I WILL TELL NO MAN WHERE THAT PLACE IS AHEAD OF TIME. I WON'T GIVE UP MY CHANCE AT THE BOUNTY OF A LIFETIME.
YOU'RE A SMART MAN, KIL.
SO BE IT. WE HAVE A DEAL. YOU LEAVE AT FIRST LIGHT.
GOOD HUNTING! AND REMEMBER -- BRING HIM BACK ALIVE! THE BOUNTY IS DOUBLE IF HE'S STILL BREATHING!

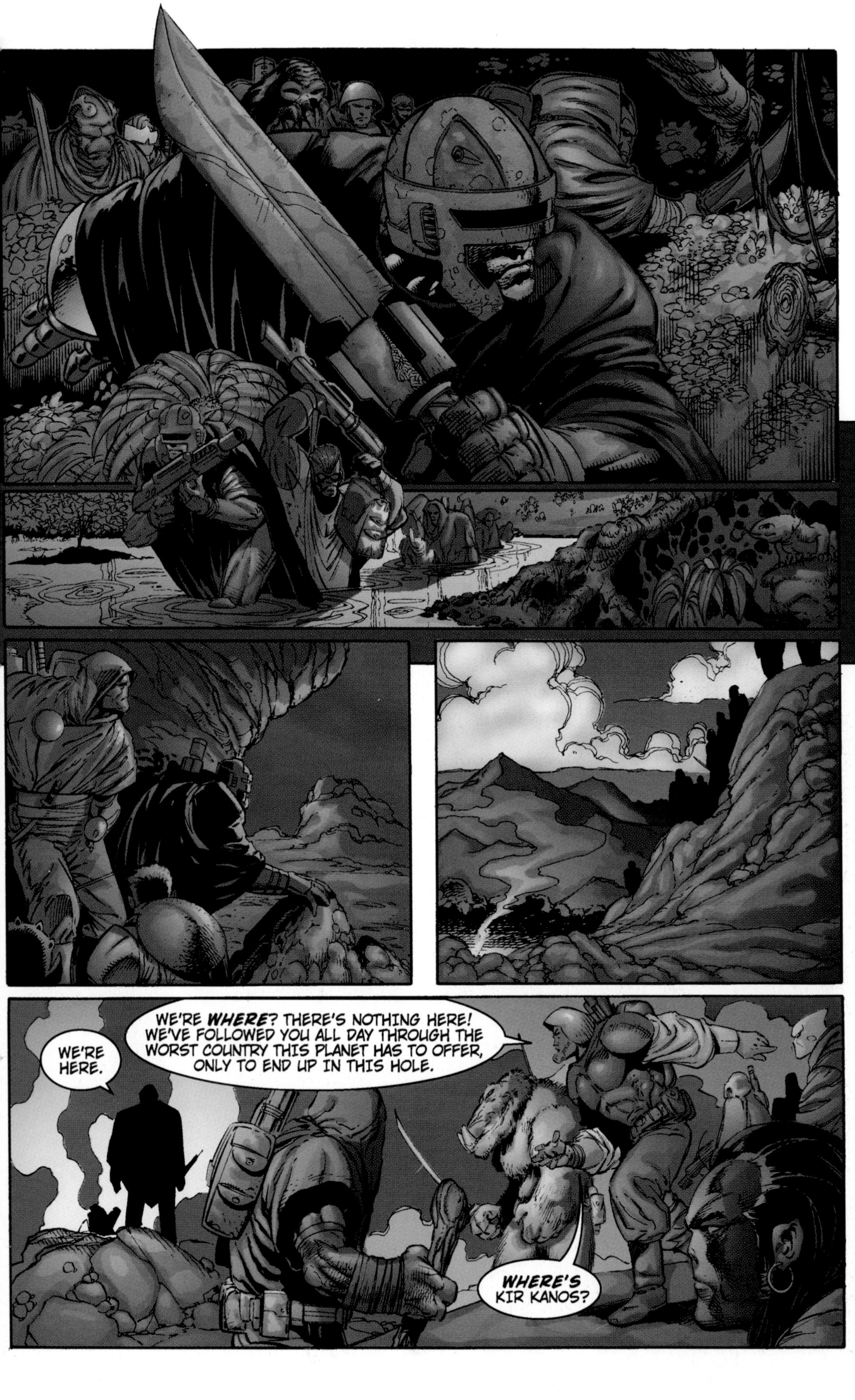
WE'RE HERE.
WE'RE WHERE? THERE'S NOTHING HERE! WE'VE FOLLOWED YOU ALL DAY THROUGH THE WORST COUNTRY THIS PLANET HAS TO OFFER, ONLY TO END UP IN THIS HOLE.
WHERE'S KIR KANOS?

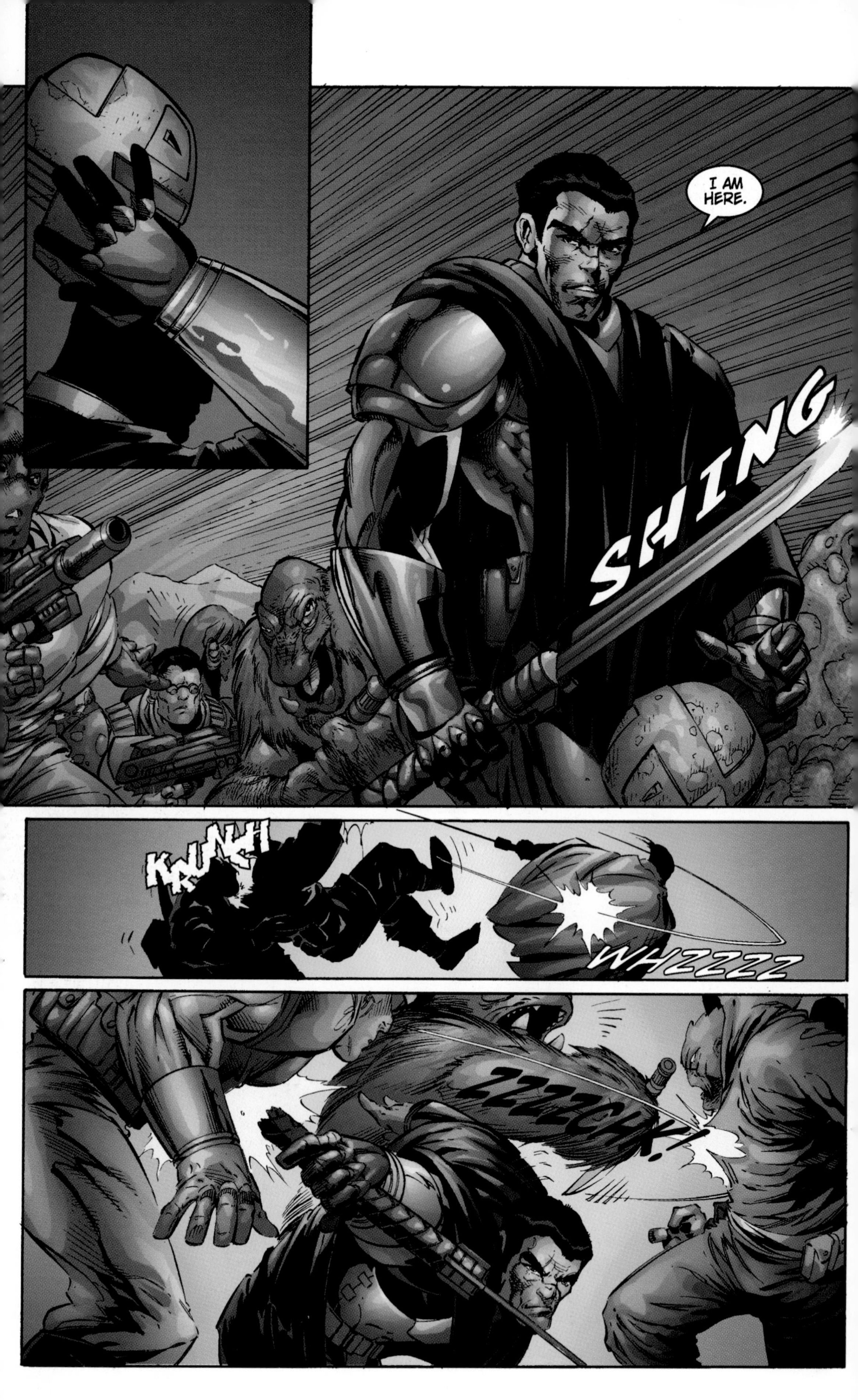

I AM HERE.
SHING
KRUNCH
WHZZZZZ
ZZZZCHK!

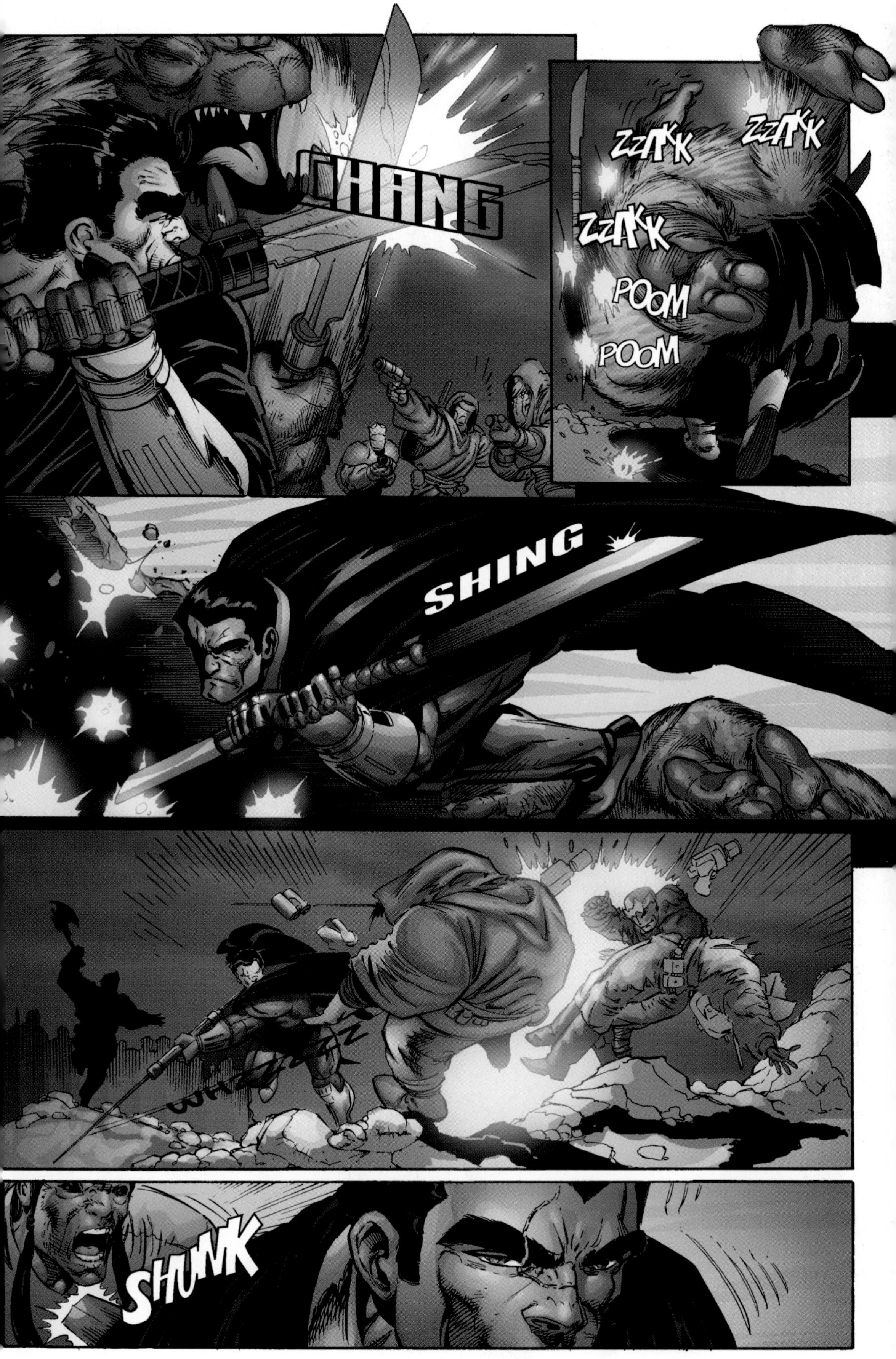
CHANG
ZZAKK
ZZAKK
ZZAKK
POOM
POOM
SHING
SHUNK

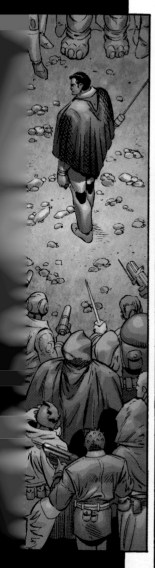

YOU'RE SURROUNDED, KANOS -- AND I CAN'T MISS AT THIS RANGE!

I GUESS THEN THAT YOU'LL BE HAPPY WITH *HALF* OF THE REWARD.

DON'T SHOOT 'IM, FOOL! USE YOUR BLADE!

ATTACK!

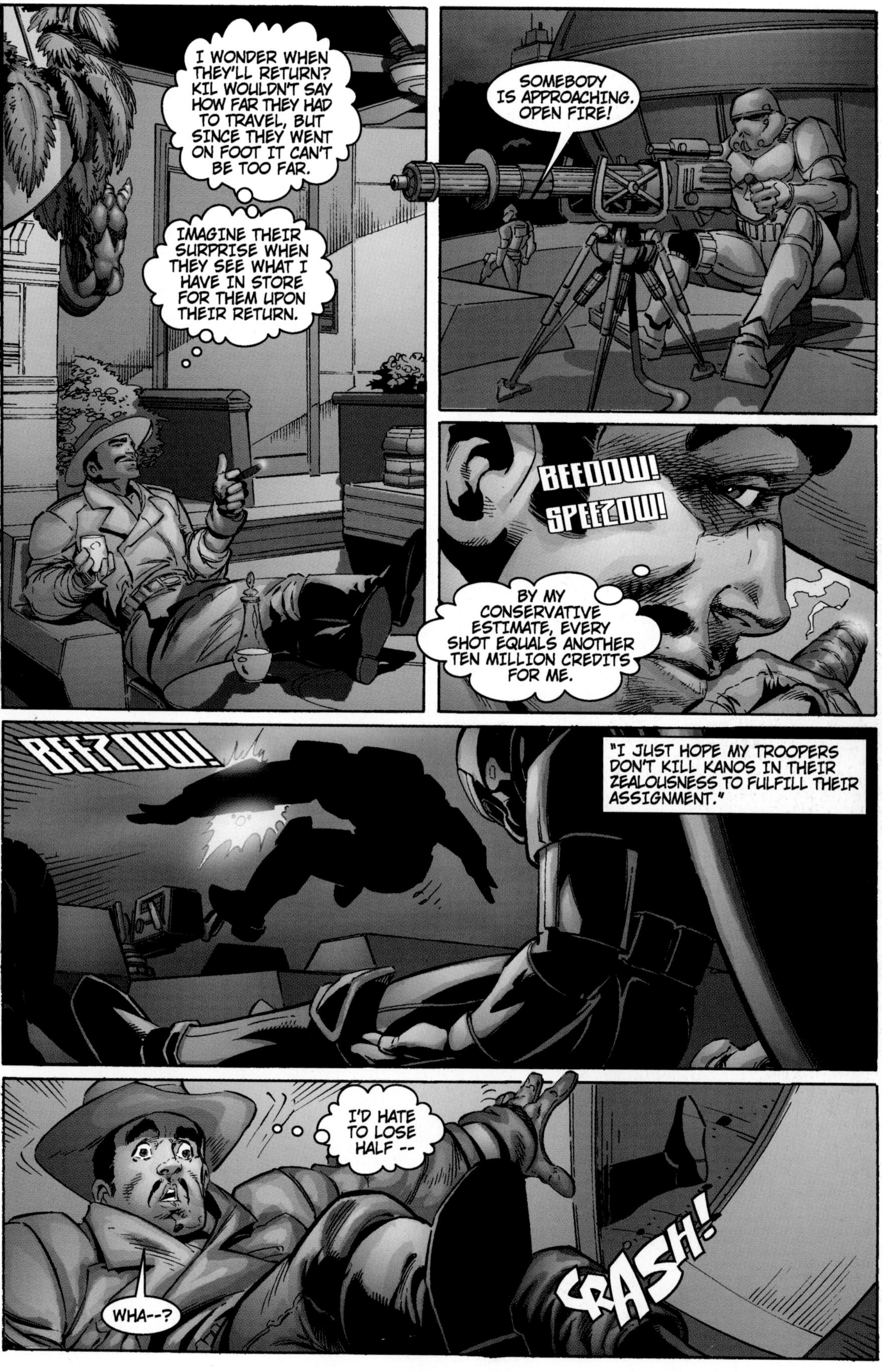
I WONDER WHEN THEY'LL RETURN? KIL WOULDN'T SAY HOW FAR THEY HAD TO TRAVEL, BUT SINCE THEY WENT ON FOOT IT CAN'T BE TOO FAR.
IMAGINE THEIR SURPRISE WHEN THEY SEE WHAT I HAVE IN STORE FOR THEM UPON THEIR RETURN.
SOMEBODY IS APPROACHING. OPEN FIRE!
BEEDOW!
SPEEZOW!
BY MY CONSERVATIVE ESTIMATE, EVERY SHOT EQUALS ANOTHER TEN MILLION CREDITS FOR ME.
BEEZOW!
"I JUST HOPE MY TROOPERS DON'T KILL KANOS IN THEIR ZEALOUSNESS TO FULFILL THEIR ASSIGNMENT."
I'D HATE TO LOSE HALF --
WHA--?
CRASH!

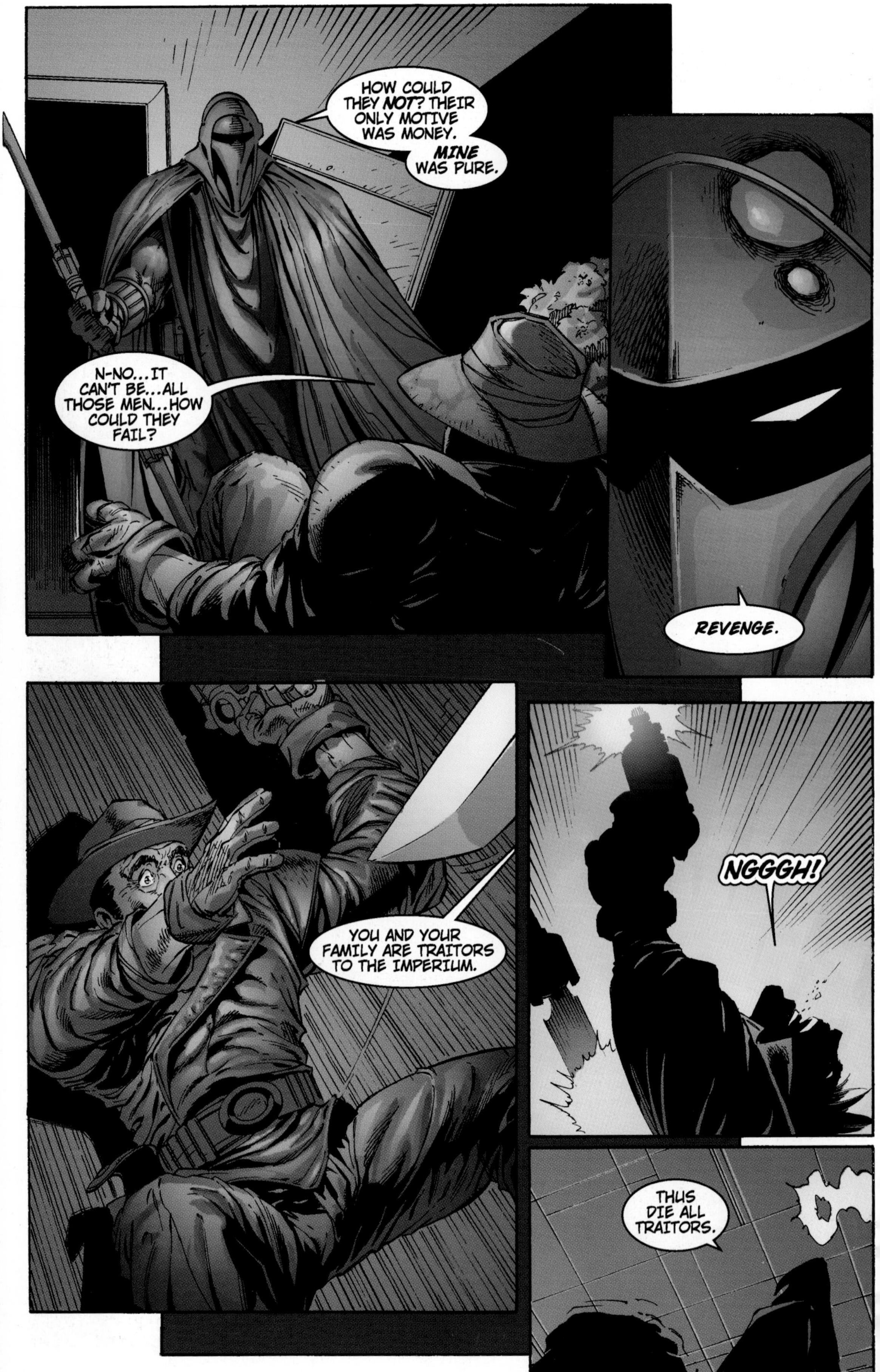
HOW COULD THEY NOT? THEIR ONLY MOTIVE WAS MONEY.
MINE WAS PURE.
N-NO...IT CAN'T BE...ALL THOSE MEN...HOW COULD THEY FAIL?
REVENGE.
YOU AND YOUR FAMILY ARE TRAITORS TO THE IMPERIUM.
NGGGH!
THUS DIE ALL TRAITORS.

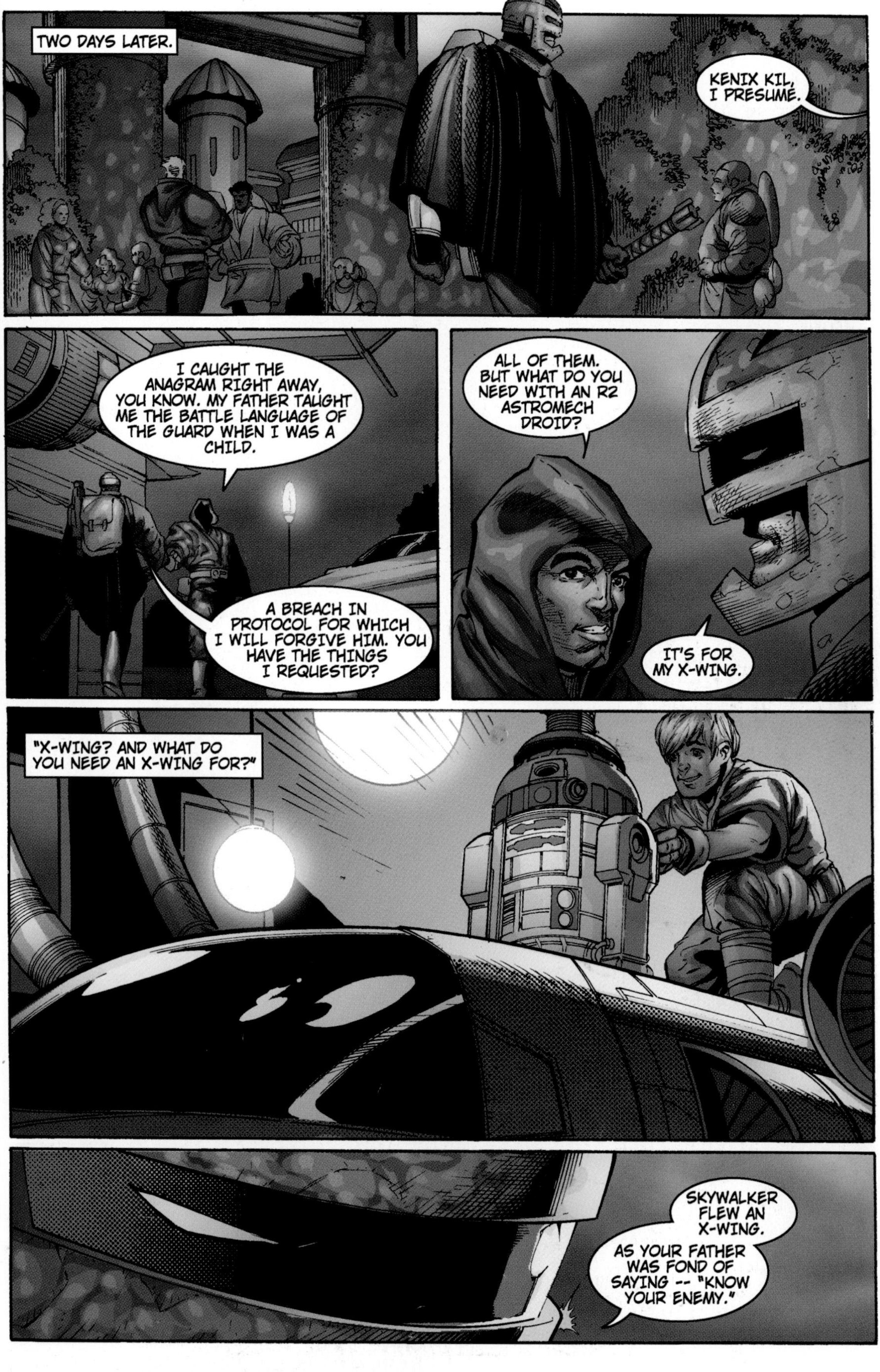
TWO DAYS LATER.
KENIX KIL, I PRESUME.
I CAUGHT THE ANAGRAM RIGHT AWAY, YOU KNOW. MY FATHER TAUGHT ME THE BATTLE LANGUAGE OF THE GUARD WHEN I WAS A CHILD.
A BREACH IN PROTOCOL FOR WHICH I WILL FORGIVE HIM. YOU HAVE THE THINGS I REQUESTED?
ALL OF THEM. BUT WHAT DO YOU NEED WITH AN R2 ASTROMECH DROID?
IT'S FOR MY X-WING.
"X-WING? AND WHAT DO YOU NEED AN X-WING FOR?"
SKYWALKER FLEW AN X-WING.
AS YOUR FATHER WAS FOND OF SAYING -- "KNOW YOUR ENEMY."

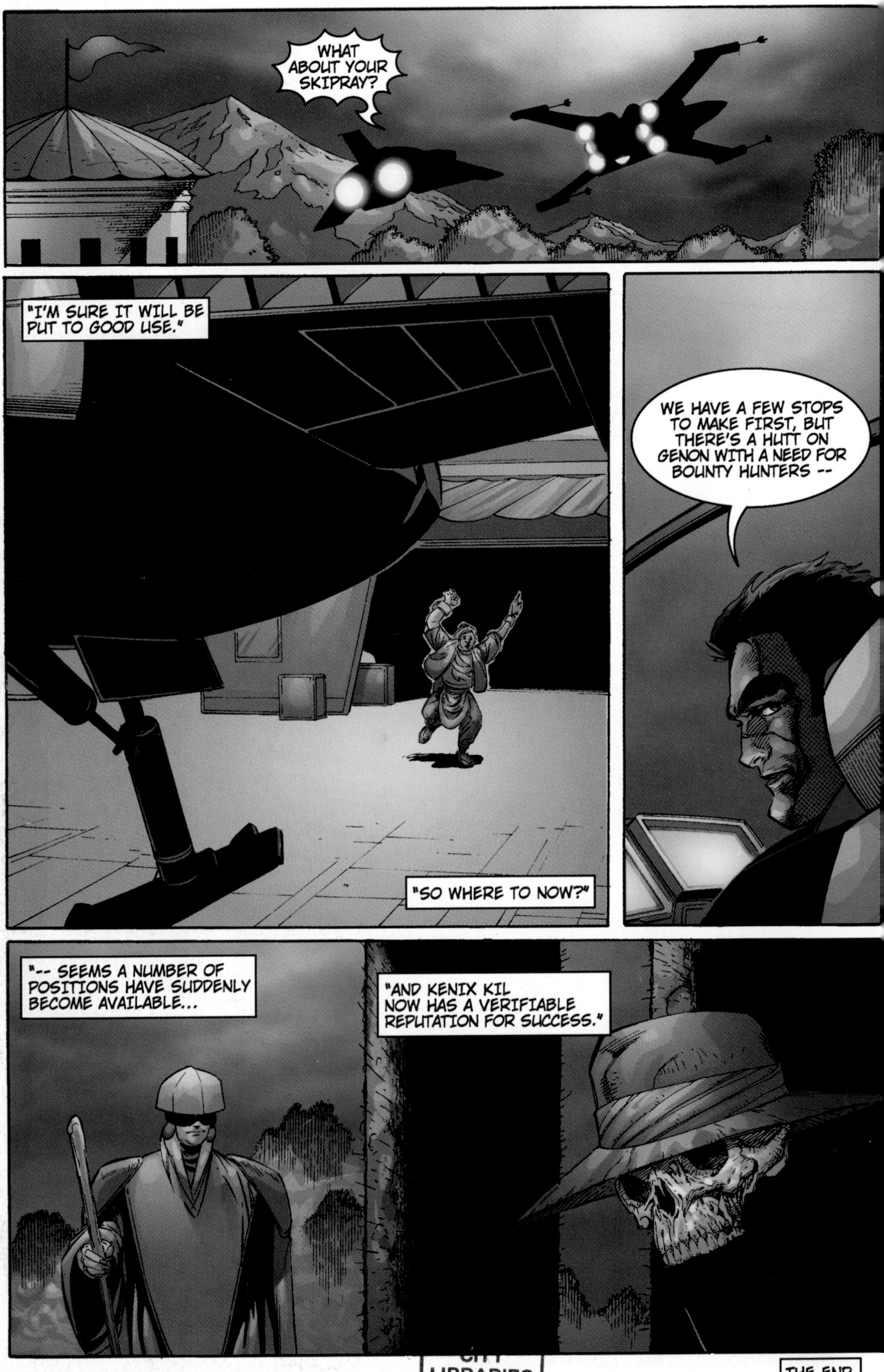
WHAT ABOUT YOUR SKIPRAY?
"I'M SURE IT WILL BE PUT TO GOOD USE."
"SO WHERE TO NOW?"
WE HAVE A FEW STOPS TO MAKE FIRST, BUT THERE'S A HUTT ON GENON WITH A NEED FOR BOUNTY HUNTERS --
"-- SEEMS A NUMBER OF POSITIONS HAVE SUDDENLY BECOME AVAILABLE...
"AND KENIX KIL NOW HAS A VERIFIABLE REPUTATION FOR SUCCESS."

THE END

STAR WARS

WARS

TIMELINE

Date	Title
5,000 BSW4 – 3,986 BSW4	TALES OF THE JEDI
32-2 BSW4	AURRA SING
32-0 BSW4	STAR WARS (Ongoing comics series)
32 BSW4	STAR WARS: EPISODE I THE PHANTOM MENACE
32 BSW4	STAR WARS: EPISODE I ADVENTURES
10-5 W4	DROIDS
10-0 W4	CLASSIC STAR WARS: HAN SOLO AT STARS' END
10-0 W4	BOBA FETT: ENEMY OF THE EMPIRE
SW4	STAR WARS: EPISODE IV A NEW HOPE
0+ ASW4	CLASSIC STAR WARS: THE EARLY ADVENTURES
0+ ASW4	VADER'S QUEST
0+ ASW4	SPLINTER OF THE MIND'S EYE
0+ ASW4	RIVER OF CHAOS
0-3 ASW4	CLASSIC STAR WARS
3 ASW4	STAR WARS: EPISODE V THE EMPIRE STRIKES BACK
3+ ASW4	SHADOWS OF THE EMPIRE
3.5 ASW4	SCOUNDREL'S WAGES
4 ASW4	STAR WARS: EPISODE VI RETURN OF THE JEDI
4 ASW4	SHADOWS OF THE EMPIRE: EVOLUTION
4 ASW4	THE JABBA TAPE
4 ASW4	MARA JADE: BY THE EMPEROR'S HAND
4+ ASW4	CLASSIC STAR WARS: THE VANDELHELM MISSION
4+ ASW4	X-WING ROGUE SQUADRON
5 ASW4	BOBA FETT: TWIN ENGINES OF DESTRUCTION
9+ ASW4	THE THRAWN TRILOGY
10 ASW4	DARK EMPIRE
10+ ASW4	DARK EMPIRE II
10+ ASW4	BOBA FETT: DEATH, LIES, AND TREACHERY
11 ASW4	EMPIRE'S END
11 ASW4	KENIX KIL
11+ ASW4	CRIMSON EMPIRE
11+ ASW4	CRIMSON EMPIRE II
13+ ASW4	JEDI ACADEMY
20+ ASW4	UNION

ABERDEEN CITY

STAR WARS

BOBA FETT: ENEMY OF THE EMPIRE
Wagner • Gibson • Nadeau
112-page color paperback
ISBN: 1-84023-125-4

BOUNTY HUNTERS
Stradley • Truman • Schultz •
Mangels •Nadeau • Rubi • Saltares
112-page color paperback
ISBN: 1-84023-238-2

CRIMSON EMPIRE
Richardson • Stradley
Gulacy • Russell
160-page color paperback
ISBN: 1-84023-006-1

CRIMSON EMPIRE II
Richardson • Stradley •
Gulacy • Emberlin
160-page color paperback
ISBN: 1-84023-126-2

DARK EMPIRE
Veitch • Kennedy
184-page color paperback
ISBN: 1-84023-098-3

DARK EMPIRE II
Veitch • Kennedy
168-page color paperback
ISBN: 1-84023-099-1

**EPISODE I
THE PHANTOM MENACE**
Gilroy • Damaggio • Williamson
112-page color paperback
ISBN: 1-84023-025-8

**EPISODE I
ADVENTURES**
152-page color paperback
ISBN: 1-84023-177-7

JEDI ACADEMY – LEVIATHAN
Anderson • Carrasco • Heike
96-page color paperback
ISBN: 1-84023-138-6

THE LAST COMMAND
Baron • Biukovic • Shanower
144-page color paperback
ISBN: 1-84023-007-X

**MARA JADE:
BY THE EMPEROR'S HAND**
Zahn • Stackpole • Ezquerra
144-page color paperback
ISBN: 1-84023-011-8

PRELUDE TO REBELLION
Strnad • Winn • Jones
144-page color paperback
ISBN: 1-84023-139-4

SHADOWS OF THE EMPIRE
Wagner • Plunkett • Russell
160-page color paperback
ISBN: 1-84023-009-6

**SHADOWS OF THE EMPIRE:
EVOLUTION**
Perry • Randall • Simmons
120-page color paperback
ISBN: 1-84023-135-1

**TALES OF THE JEDI:
DARK LORDS OF THE SITH**
Veitch • Anderson • Gossett
160-page color paperback
ISBN: 1-84023-129-7

**TALES OF THE JEDI:
FALL OF THE SITH**
Anderson • Heike • Carrasco, Jr.
136-page color paperback
ISBN: 1-84023-012-6

**TALES OF THE JEDI: THE
GOLDEN AGE OF THE SITH**
Anderson • Gossett
Carrasco • Heike
144-page color paperback
ISBN: 1-84023-000-2

**TALES OF THE JEDI:
THE SITH WAR**
152-page color paperback
ISBN: 1-84023-130-0

STAR WARS: UNION
Stackpole • Teranishi • Chuckry
96-page color paperback
ISBN: 1-84023-233-1

VADER'S QUEST
Macan • Gibbons • McKie
96-page color paperback
ISBN: 1-84023-149-1

**X-WING ROGUE SQUADRON:
THE WARRIOR PRINCESS**
Stackpole • Tolson
Nadeau • Ensign
96-page color paperback
ISBN: 1-85286-997-6

**X-WING ROGUE SQUADRON:
REQUIEM FOR A ROGUE**
Stackpole • Strnad • Erskine
112-page color paperback
ISBN: 1-84023-026-6

**X-WING ROGUE SQUADRON:
IN THE EMPIRE'S SERVICE**
Stackpole • Nadeau • Ensign
96-page color paperback
ISBN: 1-84023-008-8

**X-WING ROGUE SQUADRON:
BLOOD AND HONOR**
Stackpole • Crespo
Hall • Johnson
96-page color paperback
ISBN: 1-84023-010-X

ALIENS

LABYRINTH
Woodring • Plunkett
136-page color paperback
ISBN: 1-85286-844-9

NIGHTMARE ASYLUM
(formerly Aliens: Book Two)
Verheiden • Beauvais
112-page color paperback
ISBN: 1-85286-765-5

OUTBREAK
(formerly Aliens: Book One)
Verheiden • Nelson
168-page color paperback
ISBN: 1-85286-756-6

ALIENS VS PREDATOR

ALIENS VS PREDATOR
Stradley • Norwood • Warner
176-page color paperback
ISBN: 1-85286-413-3

**THE DEADLIEST
OF THE SPECIES**
Claremont • Guice • Barreto
320-page color paperback
ISBN: 1-85286-953-4

WAR
various
200-page color paperback
ISBN: 1-85286-703-5

ETERNAL
Edginton • Maleev
88-page color paperback
ISBN: 1-84023-111-4

BUFFY THE VAMPIRE SLAYER

THE DUST WALTZ
Brereton • Gomez
80-page color paperback
ISBN: 1-84023-057-6

THE REMAINING SUNLIGHT
Watson • Van Meter
Bennett • Ross
88-page color paperback
ISBN: 1-84023-078-9

THE ORIGIN
Golden • Brereton
Bennett • Ketcham
80-page color paperback
ISBN: 1-84023-105-X

RING OF FIRE
Petrie • Sook
80-page color paperback
ISBN: 1-84023-200-5

UNINVITED GUESTS
Watson • Brereton
Gomez • Florea
96-page color paperback
ISBN: 1-84023-140-8

VARIOUS

**BATMAN / TARZAN
CLAWS OF THE CAT-WOMAN**
Marz • Kordey
96-page color paperback
ISBN: 1-84023-235-8

**PREDATOR VS
JUDGE DREDD**
Wagner • Alcatena
80-page color paperback
ISBN: 1-84023-021-5

**TARZAN VS PREDATOR
AT THE EARTH'S CORE**
Simonson • Weeks
104-page color paperback
ISBN: 1-85286-888-0

All publications are available through most good bookshops or
direct from our mail-order service at Titan Books. For a free
graphic-novels catalogue or to order, telephone 01858 433 169
with your credit-card details or contact Titan Books Mail Order,
Bowden House, 36 Northampton Road, Market Harborough, Leics,
LE16 9HE, quoting reference SWBH/GN.